BETWEEN
TWO
WORLDS

BETWEEN TWO WORLDS

AN INSPIRING STORY OF A KIWI WOMAN
WHO LEFT HER HEART IN UGANDA

EMMA OUTTERIDGE

ALLEN&UNWIN
SYDNEY·MELBOURNE·AUCKLAND·LONDON

First published in 2021

Allen & Unwin
Level 2, 10 College Hill, Freemans Bay
Auckland 1011, New Zealand
Phone: (64 9) 377 3800
Email: auckland@allenandunwin.com
Web: www.allenandunwin.co.nz

83 Alexander Street
Crows Nest NSW 2065, Australia
Phone: (61 2) 8425 0100

A catalogue record for this book is available
from the National Library of New Zealand.

ISBN 978 1 98854 780 0

Text design and maps by Megan van Staden
Set in Bembo 13/17
Printed and bound in Australia by
SOS Print + Media

3 5 7 9 10 8 6 4 2

MIX
Paper from
responsible sources
FSC® C011217

The paper in this book is FSC® certified.
FSC® promotes environmentally responsible,
socially beneficial and economically viable
management of the world's forests.

To Nath, Jack and Charlie
— my greatest loves

To Mama and Daddy-o
for giving me roots and wings

To Dominic and Rose
for all that you do

And to Henry
for igniting the flame

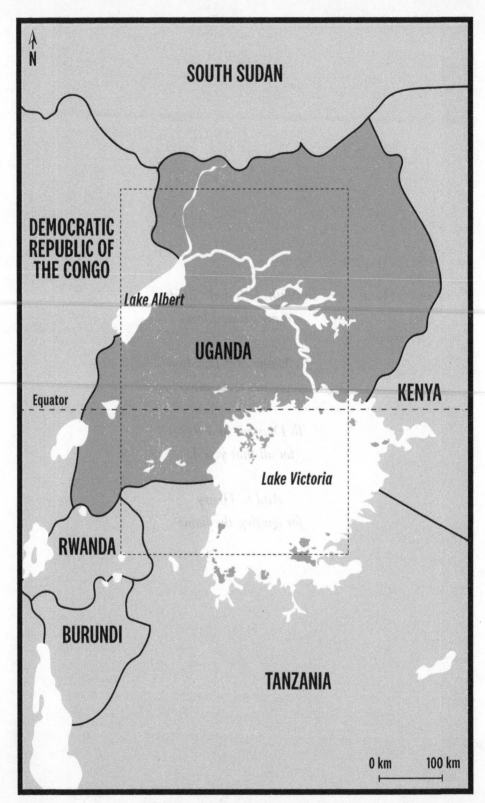

Uganda and surrounding countries.

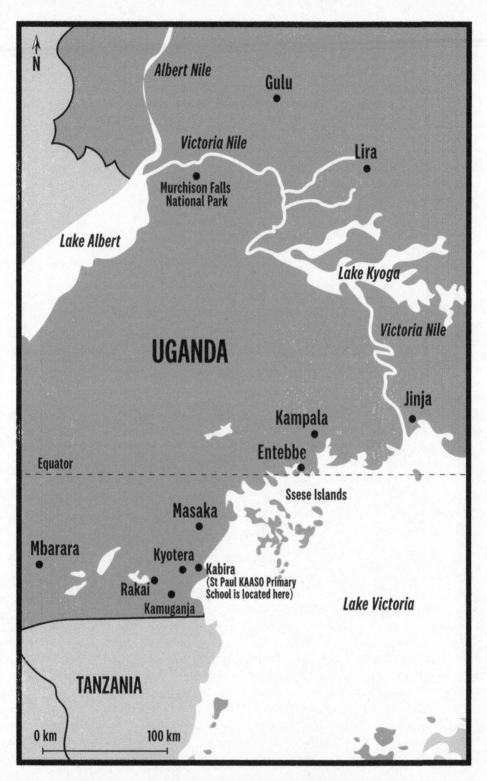

Close-up of the area shown within the dotted lines opposite.
Main cities and key landmarks are identified, along with the
smaller towns and villages that are mentioned in my story.

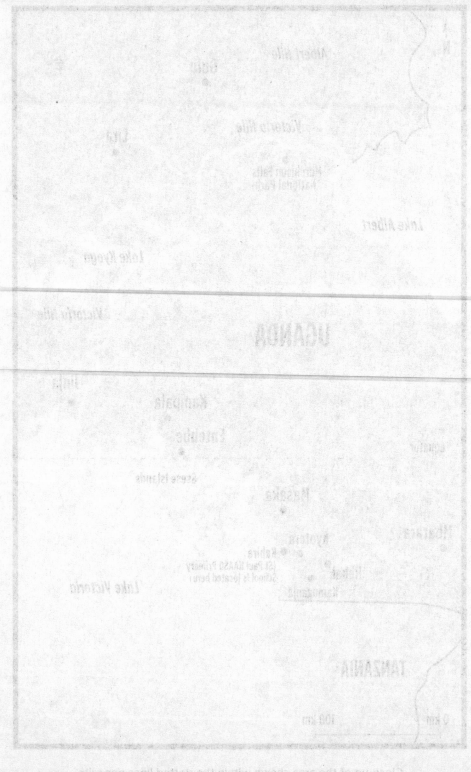

CONTENTS

CONTENTS

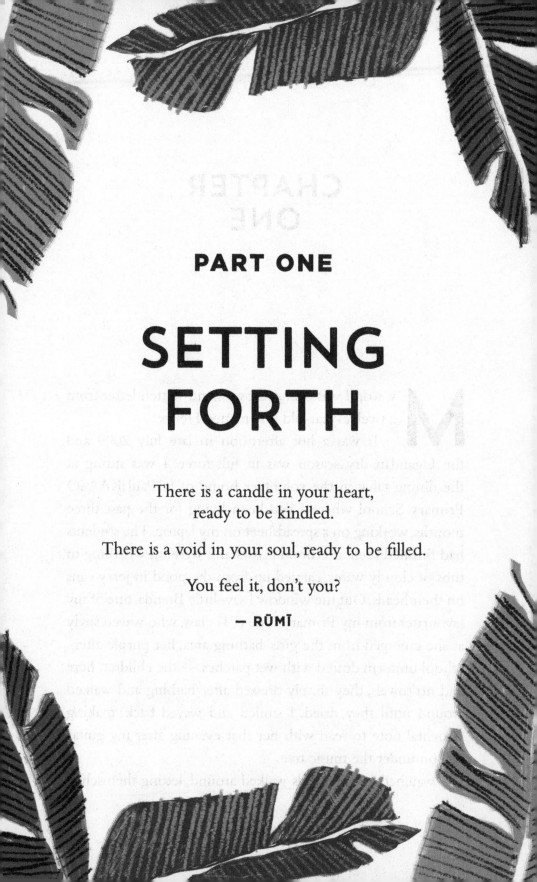

PART ONE

SETTING FORTH

There is a candle in your heart,
ready to be kindled.

There is a void in your soul, ready to be filled.

You feel it, don't you?

— RŪMĪ

CHAPTER ONE

My world was changed by a handwritten letter from a twelve-year-old boy named Henry.

It was a hot afternoon in late July 2009 and the Ugandan dry season was in full force. I was sitting at the dining table in the volunteer house of St Paul KAASO Primary School where I had been living for the past three months, working on a spreadsheet on my laptop. The students had finished their afternoon classes and were busy bathing in tubs of cloudy water, carried up from the pond in jerry cans on their heads. Out the window I saw little Brenda, one of my favourites from my Primary One (P1) class, who waved shyly as she emerged from the girls' bathing area, her purple after-school uniform dotted with wet patches — the children here had no towels; they simply dressed after bathing and walked around until they dried. I smiled and waved back, making a mental note to read with her that evening after my guitar session under the music tree.

I watched as other girls walked around, letting themselves

slowly dry. I recognised students from my various classes, and felt a surge of pride: three weeks earlier, my fellow volunteers and I had launched an email fund-raising campaign and we had been overwhelmed by the response we had received. If this project came off, the money we raised would fund the construction of a 100-bed dormitory to house these girls. I grinned as I turned back to my spreadsheet; it felt good to be working on something I knew would make such a huge difference to the children and to the school as a whole. I found myself humming as I worked through my calculations, adding up the costs of sheets of iron, sacks of concrete and roofing poles.

Then came a knock at the door.

'Madam Emma?'

Henry's voice startled me, and I spun around to see him standing in the doorway, his shoes left respectfully at the entrance, his feet bare on the dusty concrete floor.

'Henry, hi! Sorry, I was in another world. How are you? Come in.' I motioned for him to sit down at the dining table next to me. 'Do you have more books for me to tape?'

Henry took immense pride in his work and liked to ensure that his exercise books were always in good condition. That wasn't easy in a school with no proper desks or lockers — the students sat at narrow wooden tables and their books were stacked on wobbly shelves at the back of the classroom. The spines of the flimsy books often gave way, and Henry would bring his books to me to tape up so that they would last until the end of term. He didn't respond straight away, but instead remained lingering in the doorway.

I was just about to repeat my offer when I realised he had no books with him; instead, in his hands was an envelope.

'Madam Emma,' he began, then stopped. His usual upbeat demeanour was gone and he seemed unsure of himself, strangely nervous.

Henry and I had become fast friends over the past six weeks that I had been helping in his Primary Seven class. He barely reached my shoulder and his tiny frame made him look younger than his twelve years, but there was a certain wisdom behind those glittering eyes that made me want to know more about this boy with the cheeky grin, who viewed the world with such hopeful wonder. He sat in the front row of the classroom and his insatiable hunger for knowledge meant he was always the first to raise his hand and speak, eager to learn more. He was incredibly helpful and would jump up to wipe down the blackboard for me when class was over, then insist on carrying my load of marking back to the volunteer house. It was entirely unnecessary but he loved it and I enjoyed his company, so never refused.

'Yes, Henry,' I said gently. 'What is it? You can tell me anything.'

I had seen him stumped by certain concepts and had watched as he grappled with difficult questions, but I had never seen him lost for words. I began to wonder what that envelope he gripped so tightly might contain.

'Madam Emma, I have . . . this . . . It is a letter,' he said, holding it to his chest. 'For you. I want to give it to you.'

'Oh, Henry. Thank you,' I said, standing and going over to him. 'Shall I read it now?' I asked, slowly taking it from his grasp.

His eyes widened and a look I couldn't decipher crossed his face. Was that fear? Nervousness? I didn't have a chance to decide before he blurted out, 'I'll come back tomorrow to know your answer. Thank you, Madam Emma!' Then he turned abruptly and disappeared out the door.

Now I was thoroughly curious. How could the contents of this letter be so terrifying? The letter was sealed in an envelope that had been handmade from the folded pages of Henry's schoolbooks and carefully glued to form a rectangular enclosure. I slid my fingers down the join and pried the pages open, pulling out the single sheet of paper that was to change my life.

I remained standing in the doorway as I read Henry's neatly formed words. He began by thanking me for all my assistance teaching his English class and helping to repair his torn schoolbooks, then went on to make a request:

> *I would like to be sponsored in my secondary education because I am an orphan. My father died when I was still a baby. It was a pity. I will be happy if my request is considered by you and I promise I will perform better and better.*
>
> *May the good Lord bless and keep you alive!*
>
> *Yours affectionately, Henry*

I stared at the words on the page, saddened to learn that Henry had lost his father at such a young age; I'd had no idea. This school was full of orphans — in Uganda an orphan is classified as anyone who has lost their father, the breadwinner of the family — but still, to hear that my little friend had grown up fatherless was upsetting. I marvelled at how positive he remained in spite of his situation, not sitting around feeling sorry for himself but getting on with life and trying to make the best of what little he had.

However, as I reread Henry's words, a sickening feeling began to creep into my stomach: he was asking me for help. And it was no small ask. Secondary school in Uganda was around $1000 a year and it was six years. That wasn't a lot considering that it covered the students' tuition, boarding, food, uniforms, and basically everything they needed for a full year, but it *was* a lot when you were 26 years old and unemployed, living in a village in Uganda for six months with no employment lined up after your departure. I had heard enough stories about people starting sponsorships and not following through to know the damage that this caused. If I said yes, I would be making a six-year commitment with no option to go back on my word.

My emotions somersaulted from guilt to sadness to confusion to frustration, eventually turning to irrational anger, no doubt fired by the defensiveness I felt rising inside me. What right did Henry have to come in here and demand to be sponsored? There were 600 other children in this school and none of them were lining up with their hands out. Why single me out and make me feel guilty? Did he have any idea how big an ask this was? Was I just a walking ATM who could pay for anything? Didn't he know how much it had cost me to come here, that almost all my savings had gone on simply getting here? And wasn't I already doing enough with the dormitory fund-raiser? The school had identified construction as more important than sponsorship because it benefited the greater good — 100 girls would have a new home thanks to us. This was just one boy.

But as quickly as these ugly thoughts appeared, they were

soon crushed by a voice in my head asking: Have you *really* done enough? The extent of need here was vast and my contribution so far had been just a drop in the ocean. Now I had the chance to make a big difference to a small boy. Henry was my friend, and all he wanted was an education so that he could help his family and give back to his community — a phenomenal attitude for a boy so young — and he had come to me knowing there was a chance I might help. How could I refuse that? Yes, I was currently an unemployed volunteer, but I came from a world in which I knew I would be able to find work relatively easily after my departure. If I saved hard and sacrificed a few comforts in my day-to-day life, I could probably find a way to sponsor Henry.

Deep down, though, I knew why I was reluctant to agree to Henry's request and I was ashamed to admit it. I was scared. Scared to accept such a huge responsibility, scared of biting off more than I could chew, scared to make this long-term promise when my own future felt uncertain. For years after watching *The Motorcycle Diaries*, the words of Che Guevara had been scrawled across my diary — 'Let the world change you and you can change the world' — and while I knew that my time in Uganda would undoubtedly alter the way I saw the world, it still felt like a one-off trip, a rite of passage, something I needed to do to feel that I had earned my fortunate place in the world. I knew that, in all likelihood, after six months I would head on my way, feeling fulfilled that I'd 'done my bit'. I'd probably return to my previous job in the sailing world and end up marrying one of the sailors I met in my travels, and would later look back on my time in the village as an extraordinary landlocked memory — and an excuse to tell my future children how lucky they were to have food on the table so hurry up and eat your greens! I hadn't anticipated it becoming a life-long journey.

I thought back to four years earlier when my Gramps had challenged me to stop just talking about 'saving the world' and actually go and do something about it. I had hesitated then and I was hesitating now, immobilised by that same fear. To agree to sponsor Henry would be to bind myself to Uganda for another six years, and I didn't feel ready for that. Obviously I wouldn't have to live here during that time, but there would be a connection, a link that would keep me tied to KAASO long after my six months were up. It went beyond teaching a few English classes and holding afternoon sessions under the music tree, beyond building a dormitory that was a finite project and therefore something I could walk away from. To sponsor Henry would be to say that this trip was not just a one-off visit but a long-term commitment.

It was too much.

I stared down at my laptop, the curser blinking impatiently. Itemised lists of construction items and dollar figures blurred on the screen. *I'm doing good things*, I told myself. *I'm trying my best, giving all I've got.* I was proud of what we were achieving and felt like I was making a positive impact, volunteering in a way I believed was actually helpful. Before arriving in Uganda I had obsessed over Graham Hancock's *Lords of Poverty*, which attacked the patronising Western perception that impoverished people in developing nations were 'helpless' and dismissed the widespread notion that we, 'the rich and powerful', could 'save them from themselves'. I was all too aware of the white saviour complex, and I knew that as a white girl volunteering in Africa I was at risk of falling into the trap of so many well-intentioned volunteers who inadvertently ended up doing more harm than good. However, Hancock's book was clear on how best to be of use — and how *not* to be — and I took his manifesto to heart:

> *Live like the local people, learn their language, eat their*
> *food. Take time to think, to listen, to absorb. Change*
> *needs to come from within not be imposed externally.*
> *Ensure sustainability and make sure any undertaking*
> *is something that benefits the people — not just*
> *something you want to do. And, most importantly: Is it*
> *necessary? Is it needed? Is it helpful?*

The girls' dormitory was necessary, needed and helpful. In three months' time I could leave Uganda feeling a sense of accomplishment. With my head held high, I could walk out of the KAASO school gates and turn right onto the red dirt road that led to the tar-seal and the road to Masaka. I could pass through the town of Masaka and continue north to Kampala where Entebbe airport and its air-conditioned planes were waiting to whisk me back to the world I knew, the world where I belonged.

There's only so much one person can do, I told myself.

The next morning, when Henry arrived on my doorstep, the roosters were crowing and the air was filled with the excited laughter of children flowing in through the school gates, falling over themselves as they ran across the dusty earth, eager to get to class. It was a day like any other for the rest of the world, but for me and Henry it was a dark day.

'Henry, I'm sorry but I can't sponsor you,' I said. I spoke quickly, pushing the words off my tongue, wanting them to be gone, to stop the aching guilt that gripped my insides. 'I wish I could, but it's just too much right now. You are such a talented boy and I know you will go far but I can't make promises I don't know if I can keep. I'm so, so sorry.'

A flicker of disappointment flashed across his eyes and his face fell, but only for a moment before his bright smile returned. 'Don't worry, Madam Emma, I will be somehow fine! Thank you for considering my request. Keep up that good work!' And just like that, he was gone.

I watched him as he ran into the flow of students, swallowed by a river of blue uniforms. I felt sick with regret and my heart screamed at me to run after him, but my feet were rooted to the ground. As I stood, paralysed in the doorway, I felt all the successes of the past weeks fade away, instead replaced by a crushing sense of failure. It was as if a mirror had been thrust in front of my face, exposing me as the volunteer stereotype I despised — the clueless, 'token experience' kind that came and ticked the 'Volunteer in Africa' box but was unwilling to make any kind of long-term commitment after their volunteer stint was over.

One boy had asked me for help, and I had refused.

The last of the children rushed in through the gates, and the school bell — a brick thrown against a metal ring — sounded, signalling a new day at KAASO. As 623 children found their places in the classrooms, one figure remained standing in the door of the volunteer house, unsure of where to go, what to do, or who she had become.

Had I become the very thing I so badly wanted to avoid?

CHAPTER
TWO

My parents, Jo and Ross Blackman, had always placed huge importance on giving my brother and me 'roots and wings'. We grew up in the small, isolated island nation of New Zealand, so it was important to them that we had an awareness of who we were and where we were from, but they also encouraged us to look beyond our own horizons at the wider world. Mama would quote Robert Frost's poem 'The Road Not Taken', and I always had an image stuck in my mind of his two roads diverging in the woods. I wanted to make sure I chose the one less travelled, the one that would certainly lead to the more interesting, more unusual destination.

The choice wasn't difficult considering that my childhood was far from normal — I would have had a hard time finding the 'normal' road if I'd tried. I was born on a 32-foot yacht in New Caledonia, a French territory nestled in the South Pacific, south-west of Fiji, around 850 nautical miles north-west of New Zealand. In 1981 my parents had sold everything they owned, bought *Joshua*, a Cavalier 32 yacht, and set sail from Auckland bound for Rarotonga in the Cook Islands. Casting off their lines in the midday sun, they headed out of the harbour in search of adventure with no set plans but a vague hope of eventually reaching Hawaii, almost 4000 nautical miles away.

What was most impressive was that while Dad was a capable sailor, Mama had only recently started sailing and had never even been on an overnight passage before. It would have been courageous enough for her to simply agree to go along on this journey into the unknown, but Dad, busy with his many other jobs on the boat and having huge faith in Mama, had also asked her to be the navigator, at a time long before GPS and satellite positioning were around. Navigation in the 1980s meant compasses, sextants and long hours of mathematical calculations.

Mama had learned her skill over one month of night-school classes at their local yacht club in Auckland. While her classmates, a bunch of salty old seafarers, were learning navigation simply out of interest, honing their skills for the odd overnight coastal race, Mama was learning out of necessity, cramming in as much as she could to ensure that she understood enough to guide their boat safely to shore.

Fortunately, she picked it up quickly, and although she was seasick during the two-week passage to Rarotonga she still managed her daily calculations on board *Joshua* — which was a good thing: out in the Pacific Ocean, land is a distant dream, contingent on finding the pinprick of an island in the vast ocean. To be off in your calculations by a single degree could mean missing land completely. They did finally reach land in Rarotonga, but by then Mama had lost so much weight she had to use a piece of rope to keep her trousers up.

My parents quickly settled into the cruising life, and after that first initial bout of seasickness, Mama found her sea legs and was never ill again. They island-hopped through the Cook Islands and French Polynesia, listening to reports of the Falklands War and concluding that if the world dissolved into World War III they would simply keep on sailing. They fell easily into the rhythm of life at sea, tuning into the ocean swells, its currents and changing moods, observing the weather, which was an ever-present force in their world, and discovering the sea and bird life that swam and swooped around them. Ashore on some distant island or atoll, they would make an effort to get to know the local people, their culture, language and customs, and often found themselves invited to dinner by the local chief.

The community of cruising sailors was a friendly one, and people would gladly give their last spare parts to help a fellow sailor in need. While cruising through one remote island group, my parents ran out of money when they discovered that there were no banks for hundreds of miles and they had no way to buy supplies. Some Spanish cruisers they had only just met insisted on giving them $100 — a lot of money in 1981 — and happily waited five months to be repaid when they crossed paths again in Fiji.

Mama loved to cook and was always asking the locals ashore which berries to gather and where to find the best breadfruit, mangoes, pineapples and bananas. She would hang the fruit to dry in the sun to help preserve it until the next island. They lived largely on fish, which Dad caught on trolling lines out the back of the boat as they sailed between islands. Dad joined local fishing expeditions and enjoyed learning their new techniques, in turn teaching them about making sails and fixing their broken radios and cassette players.

In the end, my parents never made it to Hawaii. They fell so in love with the relaxed lifestyle of the remote islands of French Polynesia that they stayed on for Christmas, unfazed that it was the middle of the cyclone season. They sailed as far north-east as the Marquesas Islands before turning west and heading towards New Caledonia. Eventually settling in Nouméa, the capital, Dad helped establish a yacht-charter and sail-making company with a previous colleague from his time as a sail-maker in Auckland. My parents lived aboard *Joshua* at anchor, and each morning Dad windsurfed between reef sharks to work while Mama worked in a local cafe by day and, back on the boat in the evenings, enjoyed cooking up delicacies from the plentiful produce she found ashore.

I entered the world in June 1983, a little brown berry with no hair that woke up smiling each morning. Far from the world of other people's opinions on how to raise a child, my parents created a simple life for me. My favourite entertainment was the trickling hose at the charter-yacht marina, which I licked like an ice cream. Bath time meant filling the cockpit of *Joshua* in a rain squall and splashing among the soapsuds. Each night my parents would turn on the engine to charge the boat's batteries and I would nod off to the dull thud of the 12-horsepower diesel engine, which had me fast asleep within a dozen rotations.

When I was six weeks old, my parents decided to circumnavigate New Caledonia and write a cruising guide of the islands. We would be spending several months anchored off remote villages with limited access to supplies, so before setting sail Mama took me to my paediatrician, Doctor

Champagne, to see whether there was anything she should be worried about.

Doctor Champagne simply picked me up by one leg, shook me firmly, and laughed. 'You see? *Le bébé*, very flexible!'

'Ah right, okay . . . And if my breast milk . . . ? There will be plenty, you think? *Le lait* — it keeps producing?'

The doctor smiled, leaned back in his chair and, in my imagination, probably lit a cigarette. '*Pas de problème, ma cherie.*'

And so the three of us set sail into the unknown. We anchored in secluded coves and discovered hidden gems that had been untouched for years, getting as far north as the remote Belep Archipelago, which at that time was still located in uncharted waters, helpfully labelled '*dangereux*' on the only chart there was of the area.

Every time we went ashore, my parents would wrap me up and lie me in an inflatable baby bath, which was then inserted into a waterproof sailing bag and zipped up. The idea was that if our little dinghy capsized in the waves as we made our way ashore through the surf breaks, I would simply float until rescued. My parents would arrive at the beach, pull up the dinghy, haul out the sailing bag, unzip it before a crowd of curious onlookers and *Voilá! Le petit bébé avec les yeux bleus.* At that point someone would usually grab me and disappear into the lush, tropical vegetation to show me to their chief. Most had never seen a white baby before, never mind one with *les yeux bleus*. Blue eyes were beyond a rarity. Eventually my parents learned that if they slowly followed the commotion inland, they would track me down, reclaim me and be generously plied with food and coconuts in welcome.

Four months later, the cruising guide complete, it was time

to set sail for home. Granny Essie, Mama's mother, fearing that it wasn't safe for a tiny baby to cross an ocean, had sent over plane tickets for Mama and me to fly straight back to New Zealand. Mama, however, refused to take them, knowing that without us, Dad would do the trip alone. Although she knew he was capable of doing so, she didn't like the thought of him navigating solo through the less-than-hospitable waters of the south-west Pacific off the north coast of New Zealand. And besides, she had come this far — two years and several thousand nautical miles — and she was not about to bow out of the final leg of the journey.

The weather was fine as we left Nouméa and the first few days were smooth sailing. But the closer we got to home, the more difficult the conditions became as the gentle trade winds turned to gusty southerlies coming up from New Zealand. While Mama no longer had to battle with seasickness, she now had to juggle her navigation and sailing duties with breastfeeding a five-month-old baby.

'Jo! I need you to come and help me reef the main. The wind's picked up and we've got too much sail up.'

'Just a minute, I'm feeding Ems! I'll come up when I can.'

'Forget the baby, I need you now!'

'I don't care about the sails, I'm feeding our baby!'

I can only imagine how tense it must have been. Mama later told me that halfway through the passage she was silently wishing she had taken Granny's offer to fly, but she was committed now. We cleared customs at Ōpua in New Zealand's Bay of Islands in November 1983, rowed ashore and took our first shaky steps on solid ground. We checked into a motel, and after a long, hot bath I was put to sleep in a real bed. I slept soundly while my parents ordered fish and chips and beer and celebrated our arrival home. We sold the boat, rented a house and remained in the Bay of Islands for the next four years.

Just over a year after we arrived in New Zealand, my brother Nick was born and, now a family of four, we moved across the bay to Paihia. It was not the first move in my young life and certainly would not be the last; I celebrated a birthday in a different house or boat every year until I was twelve.

In Paihia it was a time of transition as my parents adjusted to life back in New Zealand with their new family, and brainstormed ideas for what the future would hold. In the meantime, to put food on the table, Dad worked making sails in a friend's sail loft during the day and played the guitar and sang a couple of nights a week in a local hotel bar while Mama looked after us. We didn't have a lot of money but we had a lot of love. Our house was full of music and laughter, and my parents taught us that it was better to do things than to have things, always focusing on giving us experiences rather than material objects.

In the end they decided to establish a marine business in the Bay of Islands. Dad excelled at selling boats and boat parts to the enthusiastic boaties of the area, and the business went well. We built a house in the bush just outside Paihia, and my brother and I spent countless hours constructing huts from native fern fronds and planting traps for each other in our seemingly endless backyard of wild, untamed New Zealand native bush.

It was during this time that Dad got a call from Tom Schnackenberg, an old friend and business partner from Dad's sail-making days, asking him to join the New Zealand team for the 1988 America's Cup. The oldest and most-sought-after trophy in sailing, the America's Cup began in 1851 with a race around the Isle of Wight in England. Won by the schooner *America*, the trophy was taken to the United States where it remained for 132 years until the Australians won it in 1983 and, as was their right, took the Cup home to Australia. It was quickly won back by the Americans, who had held it ever since. Teams from around the world were eager to break the Americans' winning streak, and New Zealand was no exception.

Dad was being asked to move to San Diego, California, to manage the New Zealand Challenge sail loft, and would be responsible for producing the enormous spinnakers and sails that powered the race yacht. It was the opportunity of a lifetime, and one that was to change the course of our family history forever. My parents sold their business, packed our bags and off we went. Thus I found myself, a wide-eyed five-year-old, alongside my over-excited three-year-old brother, boarding my first international flight, hands tightly clenched around my parents' as we set off for a new life in California.

The 1988 America's Cup was a controversial campaign full of design loopholes and lengthy protests. Our team, New Zealand Challenge, didn't have a chance as the American catamaran, *Stars & Stripes*, ran circles around the 'Big Boat', *KZ1*, our huge monohull that couldn't keep up with the faster, lighter catamaran. We lost two races to none, which was a huge disappointment to my father; but for my five-year-old self it was a magical time of discovery. It opened my eyes to the big wide world out there, and I fell in love with the excitement of being in a new place, hearing different accents and languages and seeing new ways of life.

We left San Diego and went back to New Zealand, this time moving to Auckland, but when the chance came to return to San Diego for 18 months for the 1992 America's Cup, it was a unanimous family decision to go back.

The America's Cup community had become like a family to us, and we were excited to be reunited with old friends from the 1988 campaign and be introduced to new ones. The New Zealand team all lived in an apartment complex together, each night communally eating meals provided by the team chef. Nick and I went to school with the other 'Cup kids', and we all took sailing lessons together at a local club. We made friends with families on other teams from all over the world, all thrown together in our new home-away-from-home.

In Dad's third campaign in 1995, Team New Zealand was finally victorious in winning the America's Cup, bringing the Cup — and the event — home to New Zealand. With that, my family moved back to Auckland where I was able to complete high school in the same place, at the same school, with the same friends. I enjoyed having some semblance of a routine through my high-school years, but upon graduating from my final year I was ready for a new adventure.

I moved out of home to set up a new life in Wellington, New Zealand's capital, a vibrant city that throbbed with culture and innovation. I instantly fell in love with my new city; I was an operatically trained singer and had studied classical piano for years, and soon got involved in the local theatre scene, performing in Wellington's Opera House and attending as many theatre performances as my student budget could stretch to.

The winds roared through the city, funnelling across Cook Strait, the thin stretch of water that separates the North Island from the South, and bringing with them a hurricane of ideas and bone-rattling revelations. Every day I climbed the steep streets up to Victoria University, whose old brick buildings and sweeping views gave it an aura of enlightenment that I hoped I might absorb if I concentrated hard enough. The lecture theatres filled and emptied with waves of knowledge-hungry students who carried their books and aspirations on their backs and in their faces, their eagerness to be part of something great so evident you could almost taste it.

A cast of newfound friends emerged from creases of the country I'd never even heard of. We spent hour upon hour engaged in impassioned debates about politics, philosophy, religion, human rights, literature and global development. Everything felt important, every issue urgent as we grappled with Asia's emerging role in the world, the disenchantment with religion in the West, the free-spirited wanderings of the Beat poets, and other such university-inspired debates. It is said that Wellington has more bars, restaurants and cafes per capita than New York, and we took full advantage of these, fuelling our debates with strong coffee and cheap wine.

Thrown headlong into a world of questioning, of searching, I felt like the cover had been ripped off the world to expose a seething pool of injustice and disparity, the extent of which had previously been hidden from my view. I began to realise just how privileged my life had been and I developed a longing to do something meaningful, to make a difference, something that would justify my fortunate place on this Earth. But I felt overwhelmed by where to begin on this ambitious quest, and unsure exactly what my journey would entail.

One night I was out with my new friend Sumi at Espressoholic, a cafe where an eclectic mix of artists, musicians and students gathered for late-night caffeine-fuelled debates. We were engaged in one of our usual animated conversations about how to reconcile the disparities we saw in this unfolding world. I was eyeing the bottom of my empty cup, trying to decide whether I'd ever sleep if I ordered a third coffee, when Sumi stopped mid-sentence. I followed her gaze to see what had interrupted her stream of consciousness. The walls of Espressoholic overflowed with graffiti art and posters advertising fringe-theatre performances, alternative-art exhibitions and street markets, layer upon layer of paper curling from the walls. It was a dizzying array of information but there, in the midst of it all, were three hand-scrawled words on a piece of crumpled paper.

'Open Your Eyes'.

Three simple words to change the way we would view life. *Open your eyes.*

Sumi looked at me and smiled. 'So simple, but so true. That's really all there is to it.' Those three words summed up everything we had been searching for and trying to understand. Who knows who had pinned it there, or what it was for, but we adopted it as our motto, our philosophy on life, and in the weeks and months that followed we often referred to that evening at Espressoholic. To us it seemed as if that note had been pinned there especially for us, giving us a way to begin our navigation, a coordinate from which to plot our journey. Live with open eyes — *truly* open eyes — and the world would unfold.

While up until now most of my life had revolved around the ocean, the next path that unfolded took me inland. There was a job fair at my university, and employers from ski fields across the United States and Canada came to recruit students from Down Under to work on the slopes during our long summer holidays, the northern hemisphere's winter. After fifteen-minute interviews in the university quad, both Sumi and I, along with another friend, Megs, were offered jobs by the team from Aspen, Colorado.

I would be working at the Aspen Mountain Club, waiting on the rich and famous who graced the club's exclusive membership list. Each morning I would catch the first gondola up before the mountain opened, and would be required to work through until the mountain closed, on my feet for around ten hours a day. It wasn't exactly glamorous work but that didn't bother me — the job came with a free ski pass for the season. I was a 21-year-old who had spent every family holiday on a boat, so I felt it was high time I learned how to ski. And what better place to do so than at one of the world's most-famed powder slopes in Colorado's Rocky Mountains? I accepted the job immediately, never imagining that it would be in this unlikely context that my eyes would be irreversibly opened and Africa would first make its mark on my consciousness.

Aspen itself was every bit as glitzy and glamorous as I had been told: women in one-piece leopard-print ski suits strolled the heated footpaths, enjoying cocktails for après-ski, their hair and make-up miraculously perfect after a day up the mountain. Walking the streets of Aspen was like walking through the pages of *Vanity Fair* magazine. But there was a huge divide between those who *went* to Aspen — the one-piece ski-suit crowd — and those who *worked* in Aspen — a bunch of rowdy Kiwis, Aussies, South Africans and South Americans, plus the Mexican labourers who were usually relegated to the laundries and kitchens below ground. Aspen seemed unashamed of its economic and class disparities, however, and catered to both sides, with exclusive cocktail bars for the 'it' crowd and $10-all-you-can-drink dive bars for the rest of us. My job was made entertaining by a team of lively workmates from around the globe, and we would regularly volunteer to be cut early from our shifts to enjoy the rest of the afternoon skiing the pristine, tree-speckled slopes of Aspen Mountain.

One afternoon, Megs and I had come down from our last run of the day and had a few hours to kill before a workmate's farewell party that evening. There was a beautiful old brick cinema in town that happened to be playing *Hotel Rwanda*, a true story set during the Rwandan genocide. I had barely heard of Rwanda, never mind the genocide, but the film sounded interesting and it was more appealing than catching the bus back to sit in our cramped room at the staff accommodation. Taking our seats in the theatre, Megs and I chatted about our day up the mountain while we waited for the film to start. I had no idea that the next two hours were about to alter the course of my life.

The film began and I watched, stunned, as another world unfolded before my eyes. The violence and inhumanity were sickening as Rwanda disintegrated further and further into chaos. There was the terror, the machetes, the orphaned children, the complete and utter destruction of a people. It was devastating. The scene that disturbed me most was not one of hacking pangas, however. It was the image of a bus pulling up in front of a hotel on a mission to carry people away to safety, away from the bloodbath that was engulfing the country. But as a crowd of people burst through the hotel gates, flooding in from the streets to seek refuge from the murderous roadblocks that were spreading like poison ivy, a distinction soon became clear: this bus was not for *all* people. It was just for the foreigners who had the misfortune to be in Rwanda in April 1994. I watched in disbelief as United Nations peacekeepers turned away Rwandan children, prying them from the clutches of white nuns who pushed them forward, insisting that the children be allowed on the bus too.

The UN peacekeepers explained that the orders were for no Rwandans on the bus, only foreign nationals. They spoke as if this was an acceptable reason for refusing the children. Tears of frustration spilled down my cheeks, and I watched with embarrassed guilt as white faces pressed against the windows of the bus as it drove out the hotel gates, whisking them away to safety. They left behind a crowd of Rwandans standing in the rain outside the hotel, left without help, left to die.

I bit down nausea as I tried to comprehend *how*. How could people be saved by the colour of their skin? How could people turn their backs on children who had done nothing wrong? What kind of a world did we live in that could allow such a thing to happen? But as I continued to watch in disgust, a small voice at the back of my mind asked me what *I* would have done. Would I have stayed to be slaughtered? Or would I have got on that bus with the rest of them? I squeezed my eyes shut and tried not to think of the answer.

The film ended and, unable to speak, Megs and I stumbled out into the snow and sank to the ground. We sat side by side on the curb, but I was barely aware of her presence. The world fell silent and it seemed that time stood still as the snowflakes floated softly from above, mixing with the hot tears that spilled from my eyes. Sure, this was a Hollywood depiction of events so perhaps some liberties had been taken, but the basic facts remained concrete: hundreds of thousands of innocent people had been killed, and this had happened in 1994. During my lifetime. How could I have been so ignorant? I had always prided myself on being an outward-looking 'citizen of the world' and yet, while I had been preparing for another move to San Diego, across the globe such atrocities were being committed against children my own age and I had been unaware. The O.J. Simpson murder case was going on at the same time and I had heard all about that. Princess Diana and Prince Charles' marital problems were splashed across the tabloids; I knew the intimate details of those. But somehow 800,000 Rwandan Tutsis brutally murdered over the course of 100 bloody days had slipped beneath my radar.

I could feel nothing but the frozen earth beneath me and the throbbing ache in my heart. I ached that I lived in a world where such a thing could happen, I ached that the international community stood by and watched, and I ached for the staggering, incomprehensible waste. Megs and I finally walked in silence past the festive bar where the party was being held, unable to bring ourselves to enter. We sat wordlessly on the bus back to our staff accommodation, and when I fell into bed, sleep did not come. I lay awake, wide-eyed, my mind racing. In the darkness I knew Megs was awake too, but we said nothing. There were no words. I had seen something that I could not un-see, had been shown a world that would not leave me. Something inside me had changed and could never be the same again.

I felt ashamed to realise that I was hardly the worldly girl I had believed myself to be. That night I vowed that I would never again be so oblivious to the suffering of others, never again take for granted the privileges afforded to me simply by an accident of birth. I had done nothing to deserve being born into a loving Kiwi family who were able to feed and clothe me. And it was through no wrongdoing of their own that others had been born in a place where radical extremists had appealed to the population through hate-inducing radio stations, urging people to take to their neighbours with machetes.

An accident of birth.

Lying in the dark, I made a decision. Simply opening my eyes was not enough. I needed to go and *do* something. The lucky accident that had allowed me to get a good education, enabling me to pursue my dreams and succeed in life, also meant that I had an obligation to do something with it. As Bill Gates has said, *With great wealth comes great responsibility.* While my wealth was hardly great, I was in a position where I could — and should — help others. It was time to stop just talking about the injustices of the world I so despised, and start actually doing something about them.

CHAPTER THREE

B ack in Wellington, my bookshelf was soon filled with African political histories and memoirs. *Hotel Rwanda* had brought Africa rocketing into my consciousness, and all of a sudden I couldn't get enough of everything African. I enrolled in a class on post-colonial literature and studied Nigerian author Chinua Achebe's *Things Fall Apart*, hanging on every word. As we traced the history of colonialism and the debris left in its wake, I felt ashamed of the colour of my skin, and of the thoughtlessness with which my forebears had trampled across tribes and cultures.

Every book I read now had to be about Africa, and for my birthday that year Mama bought me a copy of *Emma's War* by Deborah Scroggins. It was the story of a British aid worker who moved to Sudan, determined to make a difference in a country wracked by the longest-running civil war in Africa. Although her actions were controversial at best — not the least of which was her marriage to a rebel warlord — and her story ends in tragedy, my young, idealistic self felt secretly inspired by this fearless woman who shared my name.

Looking back, it seems that 'Africa' became more of an idea than a place to me, a symbol of my desire to 'do good' in the world. Although I knew that Africa was not a single place but a vast continent of 54 diverse countries, I became fixated on the idea of going to 'Africa', to volunteer, to help, to 'save the world'. It was a naïve dream but it held me captive; Africa was a beacon that shone on my horizon, daring me to draw near with the allure of adventure. My dad had always said to my brother and me: 'Kids, your twenties are your crazy years. Go and do as many wild and crazy things as possible, because there may come a time in life further down the track when your priorities change . . . So do it all now, while you can.' I saw volunteering in Africa not only as taking the wild and crazy path, but also as a representation of my commitment to doing something meaningful in the world.

I became fixated on the notion that one's lot in life is simply an accident of birth. It bothered me that, although no one had a say as to where or to whom they were born, so many people who landed in privilege wore their good fortune like a badge of honour, something they had 'earned' — oblivious to the fact that a twist of fate could just as easily have delivered them to a mud hut as one of the thirteen children of a subsistence farmer. The older I got and the further I travelled, the more I understood just how fortunate I was and I began to feel guilty for my lucky accident, and uncomfortable with the fact that my life had been too easy. I wanted to challenge myself, to struggle, to give back to a world that had always treated me kindly.

It was 2005, and as 'Make Poverty History' campaigns rolled out around the world, my impatience for change grew. The campaign protested the world's failure to act on the United Nations' proposed Millennium Development Goals and the widening gap between rich and poor. Students spoke out against the unjust global trade system and developing nations' crippling debt levels, so often caused by ineffective aid. I wore my white band, argued fervently at pot-luck dinner parties and continued to read all I could.

In the month before my final university exams I was on a study break back home, and Gramps, my paternal grandad, had come to stay. One night over dinner, glass of wine in hand, I began to engage the table in a debate about politics. I was young and idealistic and full of my newfound knowledge of the world — and unashamedly outspoken with it. My left-wing, liberal self collided with my conservative war-generation Gramps, and Mama was soon stepping in to suggest that perhaps we shouldn't talk about religion or politics. I obeyed for a time, but was soon steering the conversation back to my latest gripes — the disparity between rich and poor and the fact that the world turns a blind eye while people are suffering. I continued to attack our society and the way we all lived in oblivion, until Gramps interrupted.

'Well, Miss Emma, that's all very well,' he said, forming his words slowly and purposefully. 'But if you feel so strongly, then why don't you go and *do* something about it?'

I was taken aback. I took a quick gulp of wine and stared at him dumbly.

Why didn't I? Hadn't I vowed that it was time for action?

I feebly mumbled some excuse about still being at university and having to finish my studies, and finished lamely by saying 'Well, maybe I will ...'

In bed that night, my mind was exploding as thoughts

pinballed through my brain, colliding with confusion, excitement, anticipation and, most urgently, fear. I desperately wanted to go and volunteer in Africa, but deep down I was terrified of the path I was setting myself on, unsure of where it would lead. I tried to sleep but felt myself bobbing restlessly, adrift down a river. The current picked up and suddenly I was falling, falling into the *Heart of Darkness* of my nightmares. My eyes snapped open. I turned on the light, grabbed my diary and began to write:

> *I'm scared. I feel like I've set myself loose down a steep*
> *path with nothing to hold onto. Something has been*
> *awoken within me and I am unable to extinguish it. I*
> *feel an incredible sense of duty — rather, a longing —*
> *to do something for people that, through no fault of*
> *their own, are suffering. I have opened my eyes and*
> *now I cannot close them. I know that I must act. It's*
> *just that it scares me.*

For all that I liked to believe I was changing the world and pushing boundaries, it took my cautious, content-with-the-simple-life Gramps to point out that words alone would not change the world, that real courage meant to *act*. The questions presented themselves squarely: Could I follow through on my words? Was I brave enough to act? Scrawled in the back of my diary was a poem about faith that I had come across in my final year of high school. The poem was about having the courage to step off into the unknown, and now the words played over in my mind. My heart was racing as I searched deep within myself — did I have the faith to take that step?

I would get there eventually, but the road I took was certainly not a direct one. After finishing my double degree in English Literature and Marketing, I spent my first year out of university undertaking my 'social experiment' — a year in the corporate world. I had spent four years studying hypothetical solutions to business problems, and was curious to see what all the fuss was about, so I donned a suit, hobbled in my high heels, and took a job in sales and marketing. I quickly became snowed under by deadlines and sales targets, and felt myself losing sight of my youthful ideals, moving further and further from what mattered to me. I was self-conscious about the fact that I had still not done what I had set out to do, and so I filled my evenings reading and talking about Africa — still without taking action.

I deviated further from the path when a phone call came with an offer I could not refuse. In 2003 I had spent my university summer holidays working in the America's Cup Louis Vuitton Media Centre in Auckland. Louis Vuitton had been involved in the America's Cup since 1983, organising the challenger series: a set of round robins, semi-finals and finals for the various challengers vying for supremacy on the water. Whichever team came out on top won both the Louis Vuitton Cup and the right to line up against the defender in the America's Cup match.

In spite of the contrast between my glamorous sailing world and my socially conscious student life, I had been thrilled to work on the sailing event that had always been such a huge part of my life. As the 'New Zealand International Press Liaison', I happily donned my Louis Vuitton boat shoes and began fielding the enquiries of media from around the world. Now, four years later, my former boss from Louis Vuitton, Christine Bélanger, was calling asking me to join her team in the coastal Mediterranean town of Valencia for the upcoming 2007 America's Cup. I'd had enough of the corporate world — but this wasn't Louis Vuitton the handbags, it was the Louis Vuitton Cup, and the allure of the sailing life I had grown up with was strong. It felt like too incredible an opportunity to turn down, and I knew that if I said no I might not get another chance. Putting my volunteer aspirations on hold once more, I accepted the offer.

I had no idea that the America's Cup world, which at the time felt like a deviation from my path, was actually to become a vital part of the journey itself. Inspired by the stories I felt compelled to tell, some of the world-class sailors I would be working with over the coming years would be moved to support the people in Uganda of whom I spoke so passionately. I would become, unknowingly, a bridge between these two so seemingly disparate worlds — the luxurious world of international sailing events and a rural Ugandan village community.

But Uganda was the last thing on my mind when I arrived in Valencia, bewildered and exhausted after a 49-hour trip. I was full of anticipation as Christine explained that I would be looking after Louis Vuitton's VIP Events and Hospitality programme, hosting guests both on and off the water. Along with high-profile media and celebrities, Louis Vuitton's top clients would also be invited to Valencia to watch the races on board our 121-foot superyacht. It would be my job to accompany them on the water to ensure that the guests understood the races, that the catering was perfect, and that everything ran smoothly to give the full luxury VIP experience. Returning to shore after racing, we would welcome guests into our custom-built VIP lounge, where champagne and canapés would be served on our private terrace looking out over the race village.

Work started with a vengeance and I found myself quickly engulfed by the frenetic pace of the events world. While I loved my job, and the excitement of it all, I couldn't help but feel guilty as I boarded the superyacht each day alongside guests sipping Moët & Chandon, watching multi-million-dollar yachts battle it out for sport's oldest trophy. I was torn; this was a world I loved so much and the spectacle was incredible, but the excess of it all was overwhelming. Working insane hours without a minute to breathe, there was no time to dwell on issues of morality, however. My days began not long after sunrise and I would often get back to my apartment in the early hours of the morning after hosting our guests at yet another late-night Spanish dinner party.

Africa still hung on my horizon, but it was well and truly relegated to the back burner as I struggled with the exhaustion and stress of my daily life in Valencia. On a rare two-day break I travelled to Tarifa in the south of Spain with my boyfriend at the time. It was there that I caught my first glimpse of the African continent. It took my breath away. The mountains of Morocco rose hazily in the evening light, and the glittering minarets seemed to be winking at me across the horizon as the sun slipped away. The Mediterranean divided us, but that was *Africa*, right there. It seemed so close. I felt like I was living in the shadow of Africa — the *idea* of Africa and what that represented to me — and yet, as much as I still dreamed of volunteering in Africa, I was too drained to summon the energy to think about it properly. All my world-changing zeal was gone. I knew I couldn't continue living at this pace much longer. I was running on empty and my soul was crying out for repose, but the regatta was almost over; I just had to hang in there for a little longer. Our short break ended and we drove back north, leaving Africa behind; a hazy memory fading in our wake.

On the final day of the America's Cup, everything came undone. In the last race of the match Team New Zealand lost by one second, my job ended, my visa expired, I had to move out of my apartment and I broke up with my boyfriend. I felt I had lost everything.

After several weeks of travelling aimlessly around Europe, nursing my broken heart and fragile soul, salvation came when I was offered a job working on flotilla boats in the Greek Islands. I wasn't sure exactly what I would be doing, but I knew that, whatever it was, it would be far from the demands of high-maintenance VIPs and the excesses of the world of luxury yacht racing. It was yet another step away from what I really wanted to do, but at that point I was so broken that I didn't care.

The day before flying to Greece I decided I wanted to learn the guitar. I missed my days of performing on stage; in spite of my love of music it had been months since I had sung or played — a piano is hardly practical when you're backpacking around the world. So I bought a cheap nylon-stringed guitar and arrived at the marina in Corfu with my guitar on my back. I watched the faces of my crew turn to dismay as I explained that no, I didn't actually *play* the guitar, but I was going to *learn*. Our boat was not so big. Sitting up the bow each day as we sailed from one island to the next, I would strum my guitar, training my fingers to form different chords, unaware how useful this skill would come to be two years later in a village in Uganda. My guitar would be the key to my early relationship with the children, going beyond the barriers of language and culture, and helping me to find my purpose during my early days in the village when my fear of doing the wrong thing held me back.

My life in Greece was everything I'd hoped for and I quickly lost myself in the pleasure of boats, friends and sunshine. I lived on board a 30-foot yacht with a skipper and an engineer and, as hostie, it was my job to jump aboard each of our twelve client boats at the end of the day to have a chat, hear about their day's sailing, explain what there was to do on this island, point out where to find the best moussaka — and yes, a G&T would be lovely, thanks. Our company had fourteen other lead crews in the Ionian Sea where we were based, all of us in our early twenties and footloose and fancy-free, enjoying being paid to live on yachts in the Greek Islands. 'Another day, another bay' was our motto.

As one season turned into another, I felt the life flooding back into me. Strumming my guitar as we sailed from one bay to the next, I couldn't have been happier. My days were full of music, friendship, sailing and exploring. Life was simple. But as I regained my spirit, I could feel an old familiar restlessness stirring within me, returning from where it had been buried since finishing university. I looked at the books that lined the little shelf in my boat, my portable library: *The Poisonwood Bible*, *What is the What*, *Blood Diamonds*, *The Zanzibar Chest*. They were all pointing in one direction. Despite the sailing, the dancing, the partying, the romances and the adventures, my soul was longing for something more and I knew it was time to address the ache within me. At last, I felt ready to give shape to my undefined, hazy notion of 'Africa'.

I grabbed my phone. Cherie Broome, an old flatmate from my corporate year in Auckland, had joined me working in Greece and we had become close friends. She shared my desire to volunteer in Africa; we had spent hours talking about it. Without giving myself a chance to change my mind, I quickly dialled her number, connecting to her phone on a boat 50 nautical miles away.

'Hey Cherie, do you have a minute? I need to talk to you,' I said, feeling a sudden sense of urgency.

'Ems! Hi! How are you? Is everything okay?' Cherie was one of the kindest people I knew, always looking out for those around her. While our friendship had been forged over many a G&T, there was a depth to it that went beyond most of the best-friends-for-now relationships being formed around us. We believed in the same things and shared so many philosophies on life. I knew she would understand where I was coming from, so I just launched right in.

'I want to go to Africa,' I blurted out. 'It's been on my mind for so long now. I've been thinking and talking about it for way too long and I don't know why I didn't just go earlier but I was ... I felt ...' I trailed off. Three years earlier Gramps had suggested that I stop just *talking* about the injustices in the world that I so passionately condemned and instead *do* something about them. And what had I done? I had taken a job in the corporate world in Auckland, moved to Spain to work for Louis Vuitton, and then run away to the Greek Islands. I felt embarrassed by the deviations from my path I had taken and by the fear that had held me back from following through on what I believed in. Africa had been the elephant in the room for too long; now it was time to act. 'Look, I don't want to be someone who just talks about things and never does them. I love it here, but I know that my life won't be complete until I go and volunteer in Africa. Most people probably think I'm crazy but I know you feel the same way.' I took a deep breath. 'Will you come with me?'

Back in Auckland, Cherie had been working for a company that organised exchange programmes and they had been starting up a volunteering division when she left. She had been deeply affected by the projects she had visited in Cambodia, and knew that volunteering was definitely a path she wanted to pursue. 'Well, you know I've been thinking about volunteering in a lot of different places,' she said. 'I'm pretty sure I could start with Africa!'

'Okay, great!' I said. 'So, we're going to Africa!'

'Yes!' she said. 'Let's do it.'

'You *are* serious, aren't you?'

'Of course!' she laughed. 'Why, aren't *you*?'

'I have never been more serious about anything in my life,' I said.

And that was that. We were going to Africa.

It seems strange, looking back now, that it took me so long to get to that point. The transition from *talking* to *doing* took almost four years, and, while I could argue that it was due to life's distractions, I know it was really because I simply wasn't ready. I was surprised to find that in spite of being constantly encouraged by my parents to take the road less travelled, it was still so hard to do. But at last I felt ready — ready for Africa to stop being just an idea floating on my horizon, for it to come to life as a real place. I had finally come to have faith that when I stepped off the edge of my known realm, I would be taught to fly.

From then on, Cherie and I were on a mission. It was hugely important to us to find the right organisation to volunteer through, as there were so many 'pay $3000 for your volunteer experience' organisations out there and we both hated that idea. Those organisations claimed to equip volunteers with 'all the tools' needed to 'set them on their way', providing 'in-country support and back-up in the field'. Surely if I was in a village somewhere in Africa and things went wrong, the people *there* would be the most helpful, considering that it was their country, their systems and their time zone? We didn't want to be paying exorbitant fees to some marketing team in London or New York that had never even been to the country we were in; we wanted a small, grassroots organisation that put emphasis on the project rather than on the Western-based office. This was not only a moral stance; it was also a financial one — we didn't have a lot of money, and we wanted to make sure that whatever funds we were able to scrape together would directly benefit the project rather than buying the Starbucks latte of a Western employee.

This was two and a half years before the *Three Cups of Deceit* scandal broke out, but even then we were wary of seemingly 'good' organisations that, after we delved deeper, turned out to be not all they promised. When *Three Cups of Tea* first hit the book shelves, I was among the thousands of readers who were hugely inspired by Greg Mortenson and his journey. I presumed him to be one of the truly good people doing work for real change. So it came as a rude shock to learn that Mortenson's story was not necessarily all it claimed to be. I didn't want to believe the rumours and probably would not have read *Three Cups of Deceit* had it not been written by Jon Krakauer, an author and journalist I respected greatly. Krakauer's book and the subsequent flood of news reports that came out all just reiterated, yet again, the importance of finding a legitimate organisation to volunteer through.

Eventually, we stumbled across Kids Worldwide. It was an organisation committed to a different kind of volunteering — one where the fees went directly to the projects that needed help, and volunteers paid for their food and accommodation at the local rate. Unlike other organisations we had found, Kids Worldwide was not hand-holding in its approach, and encouraged volunteers to take responsibility for their own experience. The organisation itself was run entirely by volunteers; no one 'working' for it was paid, and instead the staff offered their time freely because this was something they believed in. It was exactly what we had been looking for.

Cherie and I pored over the different Kids Worldwide projects on offer around the world, quickly narrowing our search to East Africa, where most of my reading had been focused. We found ourselves drawn towards the rural projects; we didn't want to be in the city, we wanted to be fully immersed in village life where the culture and traditions would be strongest. We submitted our applications and were thrilled when we were accepted at KAASO, receiving a warm welcome from Casey, the Volunteer Coordinator, who had spent three months at KAASO in 2007. She wrote that the friends and family of KAASO were most grateful to us for applying and looked forward to receiving us. She sent through the KAASO volunteer manual, which I printed and carried around as my bible from then on.

'St Paul KAASO (Kabira Adult Attention and School for Orphans) is a boarding school in the Rakai District of Uganda,' the manual explained, 'located near the shores of Lake Victoria and the border of Tanzania. This district was hit hardest by the HIV/AIDS crisis, affecting every family in the region surrounding KAASO. Attesting to this is the number of children attending the school in the rural village of Kabira, over 600 and growing. Despite the devastation caused by this disease, you'll find the children with open, giving hearts, ready to express joy and delight in the simplest pleasures. We invite you to become part of this story of hope.'

It was that story of hope that I so badly wanted to be a part of.

As I boarded my final flight to Uganda, clutching the volunteer manual, I tried to look more confident than I felt. It had taken us six months to plan our trip and while I was excited to be on my way at last — Cherie was flying in separately — a week of emotional goodbyes had left me drained. The hardest had been with my parents. They had come of age when Idi Amin was making headlines as the Butcher of Uganda and they were wrestling with those memories. It was estimated that up to half a million citizens had been tortured by Amin's death squads, murdered and mutilated under his rule. Although

Amin was exiled in 1979 and died in Saudi Arabia in 2003, stories of atrocities so vile did not fade quickly. His memory still hung sourly over the country and my parents' minds.

I had tried to shake off their worries, reminding them that they had hardly been examples of conservative living. Sailing across the Pacific Ocean with a tiny baby was something most people would consider to be an insanely risky undertaking. Not to mention the fact that they were about to start their next adventure, sailing from the Mediterranean back to New Zealand on *Sojourn*, their 43-foot cruising yacht. Wasn't *that* dangerous? Apparently not; while Dad had incredible respect for the ocean, he felt he could manage the dangers out at sea by taking calculated risks, carefully monitoring the weather systems and ensuring that the on-board safety equipment was always up to date. Mama trusted him unconditionally. In contrast, my security in Uganda was a danger they couldn't control and that made my parents feel helpless; safety is a relative perception. Fortunately they are adventurers at heart and after a bit of gentle coaxing — and constant reminders that Amin had spent 24 years in exile and was no longer alive — they came around to the idea of me volunteering in Uganda.

But not everyone was so supportive. One night not long before my departure, I was chatting to a girl I'd just met at a barbecue. I was back in Auckland on a short-term contract for Louis Vuitton, working on a new sailing regatta called the Louis Vuitton Pacific Series. I watched the girl's face light up when she heard I was working for Louis Vuitton. However, just as quickly her jaw dropped into her wine glass when I added that I would soon be finishing my job to move to Uganda.

'Wait, isn't that in *Africa*? Are you crazy? You're going to be raped and killed! And doesn't everyone there have, like, AIDS or something? Not to mention all those other terrible diseases . . .' She waved her hand vaguely, implying that I should know what diseases she was talking about. 'Man, I wouldn't be caught dead in — what, Ghana, was it?'

'Uganda,' I replied through clenched teeth. 'East Africa. Ghana is in West Africa.'

'Oh, whatever. All the same to me,' she shrugged, polishing off the last of her wine. 'So you said a school, right? Are you a teacher? Wait, do they even have schools over there? Don't they all live in mud huts and work in the fields or something? Why would they even bother with school? Hell, if I could have got out of school to run around with Tarzan in the jungle, I sure would have!' She grinned, and I wondered whether she actually expected me to agree with her. I bit my tongue so hard that I thought I might have drawn blood. Oblivious, the girl just laughed and breezed off to find more wine.

I stood watching her go, fuming. *What does she know?* I thought angrily. *She's probably never even left New Zealand.* Didn't she know how lucky she was to have gone to school — even if she clearly hadn't learned much? Didn't she know that there were children around the world who would give anything to have the opportunities she had been handed? Didn't she understand that life was an accident of birth? Obviously not. And how dare she presume that everyone who went to Africa would be raped and killed. How ignorant! Where did she get her information from?

In spite of my attempts to calm myself down, a niggling fear crept into the back of my mind. What did I really know about Uganda, anyway? Sure, I'd done my research, but all I'd seen of the country so far, besides the pictures in the volunteer manual, were scenes from *The Last King of Scotland*, and they were certainly not worth bringing to mind right now.

But none of that mattered as our plane made its final descent into Uganda. I was finally doing this; I was committed. Pushing any doubts aside, I turned my gaze to the window. I'd read that Uganda is surprisingly lush, not the dry, acacia-dotted savannahs that most people picture when they think of Africa, and the scene out the window confirmed that. A patchwork of tangled green stretched out below and the waters of Lake Victoria sparkled gloriously. Kabira was only an hour's drive from the shore of the lake and I pictured myself diving into the cool waters. I was later to learn that the lake is actually rife with bilharzia, a disease caused by parasitic worms that enter the bloodstream and attack internal organs, so swimming is not advised. But for now, Lake Victoria looked as if she was welcoming me with open arms, quelling a little of my distress at being in a landlocked country, hundreds of kilometres from the ocean.

I began to make out the shape of the runway, stretching alongside the lake's shore, and a smile took over my face. Everything had finally come together. All the conversations I'd had, the books I'd read, the films I'd seen that had simultaneously inspired and haunted me, they were behind me now. This was *it*. No longer living in the shadow of Africa, I was going to be there, in among it. I was doing the right thing; I felt it in the core of my being. For six months I would be a blank slate, open for the world to paint its picture on me. I was well and truly on the road less travelled, and nothing had ever felt so right.

What I didn't know was that this was actually just the

beginning. It's ironic that at the time I believed that taking this 'final' step of the journey would give me closure and resolution, satisfying the restlessness that had been stirring within me for so long. Instead, my one-off trip to Uganda was to become far more than a mere adventure taken by an idealistic young girl hoping to make her mark on the world. It would be the start of a lifelong journey — one that would be full of struggles, challenges and heartache, but ultimately one that would come to define me.

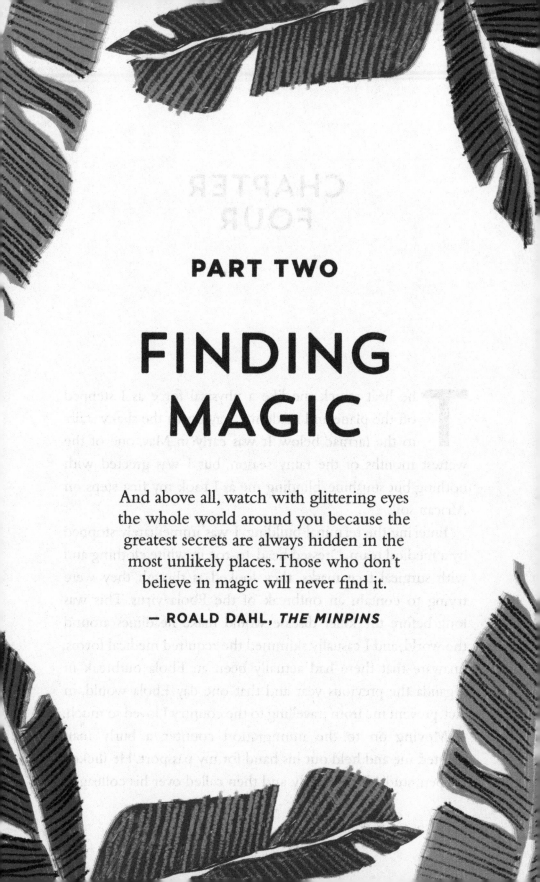

PART TWO

FINDING MAGIC

And above all, watch with glittering eyes
the whole world around you because the
greatest secrets are always hidden in the
most unlikely places. Those who don't
believe in magic will never find it.

— ROALD DAHL, *THE MINPINS*

CHAPTER FOUR

The heat struck me like a physical force as I stepped off the plane and made my way down the shaky stairs to the tarmac below. It was early in May, one of the wettest months of the rainy season, but I was greeted with nothing but sunshine, blinding me as I took my first steps on African soil.

Entering the terminal building, I was immediately stopped by a medical team. Dressed head-to-toe in white clothing and with surgical face masks, they looked as though they were trying to contain an outbreak of the Ebola virus. This was long before the killer disease would make headlines around the world, and I casually skimmed the required medical forms, unaware that there had actually been an Ebola outbreak in Uganda the previous year and that one day Ebola would, in fact, prevent me from travelling to the country I loved so much.

Moving on to the immigration counter, a burly man greeted me and held out his hand for my passport. He flicked it open, studied me closely, and then called over his colleague from the next booth. My heart began to race as I watched them deliberate, scrutinising my passport and eyeing me suspiciously. Beads of sweat were forming as I pictured myself being carted off for questioning, when suddenly the two men threw back their heads and roared with laughter.

'Blackman? You — a black man? Eh, this lady thinks she is a black man!' Relief washed over me. They were simply laughing at my name.

'Yes, Blackman,' I said with a shaky smile. 'Emma Blackman.'

'Eh? But you're no black man! You're a white woman!' That started them off again. They called over the rest of the immigration officers, who crowded around to see this strange white girl who called herself Blackman. Without any further questions, the man peeled a page-sized visa from his sheet and stuck it into my passport, having another chuckle as he filled in my name. 'Okay, Blackman, all done. Welcome to the Pearl of Africa!'

I moved through to the baggage-claim area where I scanned the crowd for Kirsty, who had been seated on the other side of the plane. A friend of Cherie's from Auckland, Kirsty had decided at the last minute to join us for three of our six months in Uganda. Kirsty and I had met for the first time over lunch the previous day, and I had been relieved to find that conversation flowed easily. While she immediately struck me as strong-willed and determined, it was apparent that she also had a great sense of humour. We hit it off straight away. This was fortunate; going to Uganda with a close friend would be testing enough, never mind embarking on a three-month blind date with someone you'd only just met. Kirsty and I had flown out together and Cherie would be arriving later that night.

The two of us shouldered our exploding backpacks, which looked as if we had packed for a ten-year survival trek around the globe, and stumbled into the arrivals hall. My head spun, overwhelmed, as I scanned the teeming crowd of taxi drivers, safari guides, ex-pats and volunteer organisations all waving their arrival signs. There, in the midst of them all, was the most welcome sign imaginable: *Kids Worldwide. St Paul KAASO. Emma Blackman & Kirsty Simons.* The sign was being held by a short, stocky man with a shiny black face and the biggest smile I'd ever seen. His white teeth radiated against the darkness of his skin and he beamed as we approached.

'Dominic?' Kirsty asked.

'Yes! I am Dominic Mukwaya. Welcome! It is really so great to see you at last!' He extended his hand eagerly, and we both shook it in turn. Dominic had an easy-going manner, was quick to laugh and his eyes gleamed as he spoke. His enthusiasm was contagious and I liked him immediately.

We followed him out to the car park where we were met by a swarm of taxi vans, cars and motorbikes careering over the uneven pavement. Soldiers loitered lazily, overseeing the chaos, swinging their guns as casually as if they were umbrellas. We stuck close to Dominic.

'Okay! Here we are,' he announced as we approached a mud-splattered sedan that had clearly been well used by many owners. 'You can put your bags in here,' he said, opening the boot.

Grateful to put down my heavy backpack, I turned sideways, wriggling to loosen the straps. I was leaning over with half my body folded into the boot when I was accosted by something loud and feathery. I screamed and jumped back as a startled chicken came hurtling towards me, flying straight into my face. I flung it away, tripping over Dominic as I leapt backwards. I have always been terrified of birds, and chickens are no exception. Dominic's face crinkled with laughter while I stood open-mouthed with shock. How naïve of me not to have realised that the boot doubled as a chicken coop.

I kept my distance as the offending bird was returned to its place, nestled between two huge bunches of *matooke* — green bananas that looked as if they would never ripen. I was later to learn that in Uganda there are more varieties of banana than there are days of the week and that *matooke* never turn yellow. I was grateful when Dominic shut the boot, muffling the screeches and putting a little distance between the chicken and me. Clutching my guitar, I clambered into the back seat and searched for my seatbelt. There wasn't one. Dominic threw the car into gear and we were off, headed for the bright lights of Kampala.

As we drove into the city I was mesmerised by the lively scenes that played outside my window. For all the uncharted waters I'd sailed and the unknown paths I'd strayed down, nothing could have prepared me for my arrival in Uganda. There were no familiar points of reference, no parallels or comparisons to be made, nothing to remind me of anywhere I'd ever been. It was just so different. I mean, knock-your-socks-off different.

Everything was brighter, more dramatic. I had once read that, throughout Africa, even the sky seems higher. I had to agree. Dominic chatted animatedly as upbeat Ugandan music blasted from the stereo while Kirsty and I sat gawking like children at every passing peculiarity — of which there were many. A couch and an armchair balanced precariously on the back of a motorbike, cows with horns that looked sure to topple them, hunks of meat hanging from hooks and buzzing with flies in the hot sun, guns everywhere, furniture shops with lounge suites laid out on the street and employees sitting aimlessly on them, frenzied taxi parks, cars indicating one way and moving another, and the biggest, ugliest birds I had ever seen — marabou storks with their bald heads, huge bills, and pale pink gular skin flapping abhorrently from their necks. They were the height of a ten-year-old child with an even greater wingspan, and I watched them circling overhead, desperately hoping that there wouldn't be any in the village.

Kampala itself was a feast for the senses — smells, noises, sights and tastes I had never before experienced. Baskets of bananas balanced on heads, *boda bodas* (local motorbike taxis) weaving precariously through gridlocked traffic, markets overflowing with fresh fruit, chickens running freely, babies wrapped in brightly coloured cloths tied to the backs of tall, proud women, and an overriding sense of movement.

After a night in the city at a local guesthouse, we set out for KAASO the following morning, Cherie now with us. Dressed in what we deemed to be appropriate volunteer travel wear — baggy, oversized cotton clothing and headscarves — we drove south. I watched as urban gave way to rural, concrete buildings became mud huts, power lines passed over the top of villages, and the potholes intensified.

It felt strange to be driving somewhere not found on any map. I had done my research leading up to my departure, reading as much as I could about the East African nation that was soon to become my home. I had studied maps, and while I was unable to find our village on any of them, I did learn about Uganda's overall geography. It is bordered by the Democratic Republic of Congo (DRC) to the west, South

Sudan to the north, Kenya to the east, Tanzania to the south and Rwanda to the south-west. Lake Victoria sits in the south-east corner of Uganda, its shores extending to Kenya and Tanzania. Uganda is divided into over 100 districts; Rakai District (today known as Kyotera District), where we were headed, lay just to the west of Lake Victoria in the southern part of the country. Kabira, the village where KAASO was located, near the swamps of Lake Victoria, was clearly not big enough to justify a dot on a map. Reminding myself that I was not the navigator but a passenger on this journey, I leaned back in my seat and tried to focus on Dominic's latest story.

He was lamenting the fact that there were so few men left as so many had died of HIV/AIDS; women in Uganda grossly outnumbered men. Apparently the government had tried to pass a law permitting only one wife per man but the *women* had protested this, saying that there were not enough men to go around. There was so much I wanted to know and I had so many questions, but my groggy mind was incapable of taking it all in. Although English is the official language of Uganda, there are over 40 tribal languages which are the mother tongues of most Ugandans, and, I was discovering, Ugandan English was very different to the English I knew. While I had been relieved to find that English was so widely spoken, I struggled to decipher Dominic's thick accent and quirky turn of phrase. We three girls were taking it in turns to sit in the front because we were all so exhausted that conversation was draining, even though we were intrigued by what Dominic had to say.

As Dominic continued to talk about the challenges his country faced in the HIV/AIDS crisis, my mind wandered back to the reading I had done over the past few months about

61

this epidemic. It had been impossible to research Uganda without learning about the country's battle with HIV/AIDS and about the government's response — using education to overcome misconceptions — which had been held up throughout Africa and the world as exemplary. Originally known as 'slim disease' due to the rapid weight loss it caused, HIV/AIDS had rapidly spread through East Africa and was commonly associated with sex workers and travelling soldiers, truck drivers, traders and miners who facilitated the spread as they moved through the country.

HIV/AIDS became particularly rampant in the areas surrounding Lake Victoria, including the Rakai District, one of the poorest regions in Uganda. The vast majority of Rakai's population relied on subsistence farming, and the fatal disease wiped out much of the working-age population. By the late 1980s, the prevalence rate of HIV/AIDS in Uganda was estimated to be as high as 30 per cent. There was no treatment or cure available in the country at that time, and the stigma was so great that people refused to be tested; they would rather not know they were sick than risk being shunned by their community. This was a disease associated with promiscuity and prostitution, and the fear of discrimination was greater than the fear of going untreated.

By the time President Yoweri Museveni came to power in Uganda, in 1986, HIV/AIDS had a stranglehold on the country. Museveni launched a major HIV/AIDS-prevention programme focusing on education and openness towards the disease. The programme promoted the ABC approach — Abstain, Be faithful and use Condoms. Weekly HIV/AIDS education lessons were required in schools; and when I first arrived, more than twenty years later, HIV/AIDS awareness was still strongly promoted at educational institutions throughout Uganda. There were books and songs about HIV/AIDS, as well as signs around schools encouraging abstinence, safe sex and avoiding 'bad touches'.

While many other African nations stuck their heads in the sand, pretending that the epidemic was not affecting them, the Ugandan government's widespread education campaign came to be admired by the rest of the world as one of the great success stories in helping reduce the effects and spread of HIV/AIDS. In 2009 there was still a sizable HIV/AIDS problem in Uganda, but this history was an inspiring example of the power of education in tackling seemingly insurmountable problems. And it was through that same deep understanding of the power of education that Dominic and his wife, Rose, had come to establish KAASO.

The volunteer manual had shared their story. Growing up in the small, rural village of Kabira, which came to be known as the 'Capital of the AIDS Highway', Dominic had watched as so many people around him were wiped out, leaving orphaned children in the hands of impoverished grandparents who were struggling to feed their exploding households, never mind educate them.

Doing my research before coming to Uganda, I had been impressed by the country's 'Universal Primary and Secondary Education' system, which offered free education for all. Further reading, however, revealed that the reality was not so rosy. There were still costs expected of parents — uniforms, school supplies, meals — that often proved a barrier to entry. The standard of education was generally low and the dropout rate was high. It was a tragedy when the children were so eager to learn; all they wanted was the chance to go to school.

Determined to give these children the opportunities they deserved, in 1999 Dominic and Rose created KAASO.

The school began with just twelve young orphans who slept in Dominic and Rose's own house. By the end of that first year, the school roll had jumped to 49 children. Classes were taught in a single thatched hut and, although it was hard to make ends meet, they persevered. While they were both teachers themselves, neither Dominic nor Rose received a salary and Dominic worked simultaneously at a government school to help cover costs. Eventually it became clear that if KAASO was to be sustainable, they would need to charge some kind of school fees. Education is hugely valued in Uganda, and as word spread about a school in Rakai where the teaching standard was so high, more and more parents came, asking if their children could also attend. Dominic and Rose accepted their requests, charging them school fees which would offset the cost of the orphans who were unable to pay.

Now, ten years later, there were 623 children at KAASO. Around a third of them were orphans, a third had parents who paid school fees, and then there was a whole raft of those in between who paid some form of fees and made up the rest with donations of food or services. Local farmers paid their children's fees with pails of milk, carpenters fixed desks or repaired bunk beds, grandmothers brought in baskets of tomatoes, avocados or sweet potatoes from their gardens. Somehow, it worked.

Not only did Dominic and Rose run the school, but they also had seven children of their own and managed 19 teachers, five matrons, three cooks, two gardeners and one bow-and-arrow-wielding security guard. KAASO housed 350 boarding students, a community maize mill, various gardens, a Women's Empowerment Group and a piggery project, and there was mention of a library and computer lab. It sounded like an incredible operation and I was excited to be a part of it. There was clearly a great need for education in the village and I was impatient to arrive at the school and start helping however I could. The volunteer manual explained that most classes had between 40 and 60 children, which meant there would no doubt be plenty of opportunities to get into the classrooms and assist the overloaded teachers. I was sure that an extra set of hands would go a long way and I couldn't wait to get started.

As eager as I was to get to KAASO and see how Dominic and Rose's impressive juggling act worked, the 180-kilometre journey from Kampala to the village had so far taken over four hours and we were not yet halfway there. We wove our way slowly south, stopping to visit a seemingly endless parade of Dominic's friends and distant relatives. As we pulled over yet again, I wondered who we might be visiting this time. But this was not another social call. 'Girls,' Dominic said, 'we have now reached the equator!'

I looked out the window to see a white ring with 'EQUATOR' written across the top. 'N' and 'S' were marked on the bottom so you could stand in the middle with one foot in each hemisphere, straddling the two. This fascinated me; I had been brought up on tales of my parents and family friends crossing the equator by boat and the inevitable celebrations that came with it, dressing up as King Neptune and toasting the sea gods. The equator at sea is synonymous with the doldrums — the light winds that plague sailors attempting to journey from one hemisphere to the other. I had listened to stories of people going mad as fickle winds kept them bobbing in one spot for days, even weeks, on end, so to actually make it across the equator was a big deal. And here I was about to simply walk from the northern to the southern hemisphere. Although this equator was nothing but a painted line across a two-lane road, it still felt like a momentous occasion.

We had barely set out again when the car rolled to yet another stop, this time next to a swampy marshland. Travelling with Dominic was like sailing through the doldrums. A man stood on the side of the road holding a bunch of fresh fish tied with banana leaves, and the smell of fish flooded the car as he thrust his dripping catch in through the window.

Kirsty was sitting in the front seat and turned around in horror as Dominic carefully examined each one. 'He's not going to . . . ?' She was a vegetarian and particularly averse to fish. Visions of travelling with a lap full of fish filled my mind. *At least it's better than chickens*, I thought, trying to hide my smile.

'No, look!' Cherie pointed out the window. 'What is he . . . ?'

We jumped out to see the three fish neatly tied to the front of the car, dangling over the number plate.

'This is the Ugandan way,' Dominic explained, laughing as we set off once more. He laughed a lot. I liked him.

By now the sun was burning orange through the trees, and as I watched its downward slide I found myself wondering what would await us at the end of this long journey south. Choosing to volunteer this way meant that there was no formal orientation, no time to acclimatise or get to know the culture before our arrival; we were plunging headlong into it. KAASO had been sporadically receiving volunteers for several years, but few had ever stayed as long as six months. I had deliberately tried not to picture what my new home would be like, for how could I possibly conjure up images of a place that was so far removed from all I'd ever known? I had instead pictured my days helping to ease the teachers' burden in the classrooms and bringing smiles to the children through music. I reminded myself that I was going to *learn* more than I could ever teach, and the philosophy of *Lords of Poverty* echoed in my ears — *Change needs to come from within, not be imposed externally. Take time to think, to listen, to absorb.* I just hoped it wouldn't take too long for me to find my purpose and for things to fall into place.

On the outskirts of a town called Masaka, we stopped for some food and ended up acquiring a new passenger — a man who was travelling to a nearby town with a box of piglets. I had no idea how they were going to fit the box into the boot with all our luggage, the *matooke* and the chicken, but somehow they managed. Back on the road again, I didn't have time to ponder this improbability as my thoughts were soon interrupted by yet another stop. Out the window I could see roadside stalls piled high with huge vegetables and incredible-looking fruit, and I admired the giant green avocados and the fingers of tiny yellow bananas. Assuming that we had pulled over to buy fresh produce, I was unprepared for the sight that met me. This was not a shopping trip; we had been stopped by the police.

'What's going on?' I asked, slightly panicked as a group of men with guns surrounded the car. 'What are they saying?'

Before I had finished speaking, our new travelling companion had jumped out of the car and was standing casually chatting with one policeman while the others circled like vultures, congregating at the front of the car and barring the way. Words passed back and forth until eventually there was an exchange of smiles and handshakes, and we were free to go.

'What was that all about?' Kirsty asked.

'Ah, just road police,' the man with the piglets said, dismissively. 'No problem, just talking.'

'But what did they want?'

'Ah, you know, just some small thing between friends,' he said with a grin.

I looked over at the girls. I had a pretty good idea what that meant. But for what?

'Uh ha!' he exclaimed and nodded towards the front of the car.

I was lost.

Then Cherie started to laugh. 'The fish?'

'Yes! The fish, they cover the number plate. This is against the law.' The man was now laughing.

Kirsty's logical mind was not following. 'But the fish are still there. They pulled you over because the fish were obstructing the number plate and that's illegal. So you gave them some "thing between friends" but didn't move the fish? I don't get it.'

Nor did I, and nor did Cherie. I don't really think Dominic did either. But it was one of the many lessons we would learn — don't search for logic. You won't find it and you'll kill yourself trying. Best just to sit back and let Uganda move to the beat of its own drum, and join in if you can find the rhythm.

The light was fading when Dominic announced we were nearly there. We dropped the man with his box of incredibly well-behaved piglets on the side of the road just before Kyotera, the nearest town to KAASO, and then turned off the main road, trading tar-seal for a dirt track that was all holes and no road. We bounced wildly, grabbing onto whatever we could find as Dominic negotiated potholes so epic that it seemed as if we might disappear into them completely. Children ran to greet the car as we rumbled past, shrieking with delight and horror when they saw our three white faces.

'*Muzungu, muzungu!* How are you, *muzungu?* Bye, *muzungu,* bye, byeeee!'

Muzungu is a Swahili word which literally translates as 'one who wanders aimlessly', originally used to describe the European missionaries and traders in East Africa in the eighteenth century. Nowadays it is a generic term used to refer to any white person, and it was to become our second name in the months to come. We laughed at how shocked they were by our whiteness, and waved through the cloud of dust we were stirring up.

'Eh! They are very happy to see you girls!' Dominic laughed. 'And so the children at KAASO will be too. You will see how much these children love their school — here in Uganda it is some big thing to attend school. These children, even the small ones, they understand that education is their future and they are so eager to learn.

'One time, we had a little girl from the village who lived just across the road from KAASO. She wanted so badly to go to school but the family could not afford. In the end, we arranged they would bring us *matooke* and cassava and the child would go to school. Eh! You should have seen! Her first day she walked all the way to the next village instead of just crossing the road because she wanted everyone to see her in her new uniform so they would know she was going to school!'

We laughed with Dominic, but I felt humbled by the little girl's story. I thought back to the frustrating conversation I'd had with the ignorant girl who assumed that all children would rather be running around playing than going to school. I had a feeling that the next six months were about to prove her horribly wrong.

The evening light was spectacular, and I was overwhelmed by the vivid colours around me: the luminous green banana plantations bathing in the last of the sun, the blue sky overhead turning pink and glowing on the red, red earth. I had never seen colours so vibrant; they were almost luminous. It felt as though the lens on the world had been changed — or at least on the eyes through which I saw it.

'This,' Dominic said, pointing to a rise on the left-hand side, 'is KAASO hill. From the top you can see all the way to Lake Victoria. The volunteers sometimes go there to relax, to lie in the sun. It is a nice place.'

It looked more like a mound than a hill, but I made a mental note to go up one day.

'Ah ha!' Dominic's eyes lit up. 'And this is KAASO ...'

Up ahead there was a metal sign bearing the hand-painted words 'ST PAUL KAASO PRIMARY SCHOOL'. We turned into the school in front of two brick buildings. The iron sheeting on the roofs had rusted and the green paint was peeling in places, but the buildings were decidedly more solid than the mud huts we had passed along the way. Dominic pulled up outside the first building, announcing that this was his home. I could make out the silhouettes of people standing in the half-light, and they slowly stepped forward as we got out of the car.

Rose came first, greeting us with a handshake and welcoming us to KAASO. Tall and slim with carefully sculpted features, her skin was ebony against the yellow scarf that swept her hair back from her face. Her mouth rose in a half-smile that betrayed little and it seemed as if she would take some time to get to know, but she was kind and asked about our journey.

'It was long!' we laughed. 'Dominic seemed to know many people along the way . . .'

'Ah yes, he is always this way. You will become used to it,' she said, her eyes showing her amusement.

Next was Teacher Sarah, opposite to Rose in every way. Everything she did was big and loud. Unlike Rose's willowy figure, Teacher Sarah's was full, and her round face was dominated by a permanent grin. She too had wrapped her hair in a bright scarf and she laughed as she introduced herself.

Little faces were hiding shyly behind Rose's dress, and Dominic drew out their children to meet us. There were six — Derrick, Kevin, Phionah (pronounced 'Fiona'), Rhona, Prima and baby Denise, held in Phionah's arms; the seventh, Joseph, was away at secondary school. Little Prima launched herself at us, engulfing our knees in an affectionate hug. Teacher Sarah shrieked with laughter and said something in Luganda to Rose. A small smile crept across Rose's face and I was struck by how beautiful she was.

'Okay, now I will give you a tour of KAASO!' Dominic announced.

Cherie caught my eye and her face mirrored my own exhaustion; it had been a long couple of days travelling and bed was feeling endlessly appealing, but Dominic insisted and we didn't want to offend him by refusing.

'Don't worry, we will be so fast!' Dominic reassured us, and I couldn't help but smile. It was only day two, but already I had been here long enough to know that nothing happened quickly in Uganda.

From that first tour I remember how suddenly night consumed us. I remember how big it all seemed, much bigger that I'd imagined. I remember the dusty paths, the smell of the piggery, the giant pots of beans, the rows of classrooms, the small faces looking out through the barred windows of the dormitories. I remember walking through a place inexplicably named 'Freedom Square'. Dominic gave a thorough explanation of everything and, even though I wasn't taking much of it in, it felt good to be there.

Looking up, I watched in awe as the stars exploded across the night sky. I had seen starry nights before, but nothing like this. The sky truly *was* higher, the stars were brighter; even the black was blacker. It felt like the world was spinning on a new axis. When I finally tumbled into bed that night, tucking myself in under my mosquito net, I fell asleep with a smile on my lips. In the morning, the sun would rise on my new life in Uganda, my path would unfold before me and everything would fall beautifully into place. At least, that's what I thought would happen. I still had a lot to learn.

CHAPTER FIVE

The following morning I awoke to the sound of roosters crowing. It took a moment to register where I was as I looked up at the mosquito net engulfing me in a holey sea of white. Lying still for a moment, I tried to gather my thoughts. I was on a foam mattress on a narrow wooden frame wedged in between two other beds, also cocooned by mosquito nets — which were 'impregnated for extra protection' — and on each bed was an equally bewildered-looking body: Cherie and Kirsty. I was in Uganda, in a small village called Kabira — as far as I could get from home, in every possible sense. The sun shone brightly through the thin fabric curtains and I could hear the village coming to life outside. It was time to get started.

Everyone was thrilled to have us at KAASO and welcomed us with open arms — then promptly went back to what they were doing. Sure, they had time for us if we asked questions or needed help, but they were all so busy going about their daily tasks that, essentially, we were on our own. We had deliberately chosen to volunteer at a place where we would not have our hands held or be told what to do, and that's exactly what we found. It was up to us to make our own way.

The only trouble was that it was hard to know where to begin. Our arrival in May fell during the school holidays, so there were no classes running. Most of the children had gone back home to their families for the break, and those who didn't have parents went to stay with grandparents, aunts, friends or neighbours. The few children who really had nowhere to go remained at KAASO, along with the school netball team who were training for an upcoming competition. Unsure of quite what to do that first morning, Cherie, Kirsty and I followed the sounds of laughter down towards the school field where a netball game was in full swing.

The field was a huge expanse of rocky grass with banana palms growing wild around the perimeter. Patches of dirt interrupted the greenery and occasional red bricks jutted dangerously out of the earth. Long-horned cows grazed casually among the netballers, who, oblivious, ran around the field under the enthusiastic instruction of their coach. With uncontained delight they invited us to join them, and our squad soon multiplied as we were joined by curious children spilling out from the neighbouring mud-brick houses. The sun was streaked with clouds, but that did little to dampen the scorching sunshine, and after a couple of hours of running around the field we were overheated and exhausted. We made our way back up through the school to the volunteer house. It seemed the logical place to go and the solid brick walls offered cool solace but, standing in the doorway, we felt lost, not sure what to do next.

I had been warned about this by John Howse, an old friend

from university and an inspiring humanitarian, who'd advised me to think about how I wanted my volunteer experience to be and urged me to *go with purpose*. Although I was well aware of the dangers of ignorant foreigners launching themselves into the developing world to 'help' and inadvertently doing more harm than good, I didn't necessarily know how to avoid doing that myself. So I had been grateful to catch up with John on a fortuitous trip to Wellington not long after being accepted at KAASO. He had picked me up in the city and driven me around the waterfront to a windswept rocky cove near Island Bay. Summer was struggling to break its way into the city as we sat with our backs against the rocks, hiding from the buffeting wind and catching up on the past three years.

After finishing university, John had spent a year in South Korea, where he had taught a class full of young children who studied from the wee hours of the morning until long after the sun went down. From there he moved to a Myanmar refugee camp on the Thai border, training Karen refugees fleeing Myanmar military oppression to become English teachers so that they could try to find employment in refugee camps, at schools in Thailand, or back in Myanmar if the situation improved. He stayed on to work with Myanmar advocacy groups as the situation deteriorated during the 2007 Saffron Revolution, the brave protest movement of Myanmar monks against the anti-democratic government regime. John then took a job in Kenya, coordinating and helping settle newly arrived volunteers as part of an international volunteer network, before working with a community-based organisation in Palestine, where the nights were filled with explosions and gunfire and the children he taught would drag themselves, bleary-eyed and exhausted, into his classroom each morning.

I listened in speechless awe as he filled me in on the stories of the people he had met and their incredible tenacity in the face of such unthinkable suffering. I was blown away by all he had seen and done, and urged him to tell me more, swept back in time to the spirited conversations we had shared during our university years.

'The children in Palestine were incredible, as were all the other children I met during my travels and through my work,' he said. 'What hurt me most was knowing their predicament — every night from my apartment I could see and hear the sounds of weapons firing and bombs exploding in their neighbourhoods. I could feel their fear and would amplify that experience to imagine it happening in the room next door. The children were so strong-willed, but they would come to class just so shattered with a weary distance about them. Comforting them could only do so much because they knew that the violence that suspended their freedom and destroyed their innocence would return the following night. They knew what you were going to say — they'd heard it all before — and it had always brought them nothing.' He paused and we sat in silence, looking out across the Cook Strait as a lone yacht battled against the wind, trying to enter the harbour.

'So, you're off to volunteer in Uganda!' He turned to face me. 'It's finally happening. Amazing! I'm so happy for you, Em.'

'Thanks, I'm really excited. It's about time,' I smiled. 'Any fabulous words of wisdom for me?' I asked, pulling my thin cardigan around me, cold in spite of the sunshine.

'Well, there's no singular way to approach it and a lot depends on the culture in your village and the specific project, but there are a couple of pieces of universal advice I'll share with you, things I wish someone had told me when I first headed out into the world. Firstly, I know you're an idealist and that's what makes you you — so please don't change. But one thing you will come to realise is that you can't do everything.

'When I was in South Korea, at the refugee camp in Thailand, and in Palestine, teaching those kids who were so exhausted they could barely keep their eyes open, I began to understand that my role was not to teach them by pushing them — they were already being pushed to the limit — but to try to make them enjoy what they did. And if that meant playing some silly song on my guitar and making them smile, then that was enough. If I could have them associate my classes with enjoyment, make learning a positive thing for them, then that was a success.

'Try to work out what's actually needed of you because it might not be what you first think. It could be as simple as teaching them a song that brings some joy to their tough life. Or it could be something profound, something that changes their life in a fundamental way. But don't be too hard on yourself in the early days. Remember, it's not your world so you need to pause, take a step back and really *listen* to work out how you can best be helpful.'

I nodded, letting his words sink in. I took a handful of sand and let it run slowly through my fingers, humbled by what I was up against.

'But at the same time, it's also important to go with *purpose*. There are so many well-meaning people who go to developing nations with vague intentions of wanting to help or "do good", but they're often not qualified for the job at hand — and there are many who think the mere colour of their skin qualifies them. Believe me, it doesn't. So work out what your purpose is, then go for it once you get there. That will make sure your time in Uganda is really worthwhile.'

I watched the waves crash noisily, the foam-edged water sliding down the rocks and into the churning sea before being sucked out and dumped ashore again. The little yacht had made its way around the headland and was safe in the shelter of the harbour, but I felt exactly the opposite — adrift. I was grateful to have had the chance to talk to John before going to Uganda, but his words had unsettled me. What *was* my purpose?

Education was hugely important to me and I knew I wanted to help in the classrooms, knowing how understaffed the teachers were. I also wanted to write about my experiences, sharing my stories with family and friends back home to help open their eyes to a world beyond their own. But day to day, what would I actually do at a rural school in Uganda? I had tutored during school and university, but I wasn't a trained teacher. I knew little about construction or fixing things, I was not a gardener, and I knew nothing about growing crops. I loved children, but had none of my own. I had no experience on farms and wouldn't know where to begin tending to animals. On top of it all, I was scared of chickens. I had no real purpose. I was at risk of becoming the volunteer who went for the 'experience' — but didn't really do anything useful to help.

Sitting on the beach with John that day, I had felt overwhelmed by the path I was setting myself on, wondering whether I was really cut out for it. And now, as Cherie, Kirsty and I hovered in the KAASO volunteer house like awkward visitors, I was having the same doubts.

Kirsty eventually took the initiative and suggested that we use this time to unpack. 'Well, it's not as if anyone seems to be desperately in need of our help right now, so we may as well get settled in,' she said, shrugging and heading inside to where all our worldly belongings were sprawled across our bedroom floor. Cherie and I followed suit.

The volunteer house contained a dining room with a large, oval wooden table and a set of shelves that held a collection of chipped mugs and plastic plates. The bathroom was just that — a room with a grimy bath that had major drainage issues and taps that could only be decorative, as there was no plumbing connected. Another small room housed a toilet with no seat that flushed only sometimes, after the tank had been manually filled by boys perched atop a rickety wooden ladder, pouring water from yellow plastic jerry cans. There were two bedrooms in the house, but the idea of sleeping alone appealed to no one so the decision had been quickly made that all three of us would share the larger room. It was cramped, but at least we would all be together.

The walls inside the house were painted a minty colour which we nicknamed 'Uganda green', as every second building seemed to have been doused in this same colour. It was as if some paint delivery had gone astray, tins of 'Uganda green' dropping in every village and being adopted with gusto by all who found them.

Our bedroom had a high window facing west towards Dominic and Rose's house, and another larger one looking south across the front lawn towards the main dirt road and the village of Kabira. The village itself consisted of nothing more than a few huts, a small row of eclectic shops, the improbably named 'Atlantic Hotel' (which was actually a stall selling chapattis), and KAASO. Solid metal bars divided the view from our window into a grid of squares, and little faces kept appearing between the bars, creeping through the garden and trying to decipher these strange *muzungu*. We smiled and waved and they shrieked with laughter and then ran away, soon returning as curiosity got the better of them.

An open wardrobe took up most of one wall, with a wooden branch to hang clothes from running the width of it over a couple of uneven shelves. We had come laden with supplies; piles of books, coloured paper, crayons, pencils, stickers and art materials overflowed from our backpacks, along with medical supplies and other donations we had brought from home. We organised these items in neat rows in the back of the wardrobe, excited to have resources to take into the classrooms. Photos of family, friends and Kiwi beaches soon covered the walls, and our new home began to take shape.

The room was crisscrossed with blue string — it looked like a drunken spider had stumbled about madly, weaving a tangled web of blue. Our mosquito nets hung from the strings overhead and we flung our towels, cotton scarves and headscarves over them too, so when you lay in bed you had the impression of an underwater garden of seagrass swaying gently above.

Our packs emptied, we stuffed them under the beds and sat to survey our work. The room looked great; a place I could spend the next six months of my life. It was perfect. In a haphazard, Uganda-green kind of way.

Now that our room was organised I was eager to get under way, but with no classes, no set timetables and no clear roles for us to play, it was still hard to know exactly what to do. Full of enthusiasm and best intentions, we spent those early days wandering around trying to work out how to get involved in the activities taking place throughout the school. There were matrons washing clothes and airing mattresses, cooks preparing meals and fetching water, workers chopping firewood and tending to the gardens — but no one seemed to really need or want our help. So we simply played with the children, introducing them to skipping ropes, bubbles, puzzles and other games we had brought with us. They loved the different activities and fell over themselves to try every one.

We played for hours on end, knowing that the time for games was now — I couldn't begin to imagine how overwhelming it would be once we had over 600 children to contend with. There were only so many little bodies that could jump a skipping rope at one time. In spite of the lack of overriding purpose, however, our days were never empty and life was certainly not dull.

Living in a rural village without electricity or running water was not as hard as I had originally feared either, but there were still a few basic things we needed to learn. Like how to bathe. To me the word 'bathing' conjured up images of Roman baths, flowing fountains, curvy bodies, steamy water and aromatic oils. So when Teacher Sarah told us she was going to teach us how to bathe, I felt excited. However, it didn't take long to work out that the reality of bathing in Uganda was vastly different to my Roman baths fantasy.

Armed with three green plastic tubs, a red plastic mug and several foot-long bars of blue soap, Teacher Sarah took us to the volunteer bathroom and slowly guided us through the process, patiently explaining to three grown women how to wash themselves. I smiled inwardly, wondering what she must have thought of us. Following Teacher Sarah's lead, I used the mug to scoop water sparingly from a big black plastic water barrel that sat in the corner of the bathroom, then pour it into my green bathing tub which would have been just large enough to bathe a six-month-old baby. The day before, I had watched with embarrassment as two small boys staggered into the bathroom, each dragging two 10-litre jerry cans full of freshly collected pond water. They struggled to pull their heavy loads up to the lip of the giant water barrel, but were careful not to spill a drop as they filled the drum for our bathing supply. I vowed to fill it myself from then on, mortified that the very children we had come to help were waiting on us like guests in a hotel.

'Now you take that facecloth, you put it in the water and you use that to make your body so wet.' Teacher Sarah pointed to my facecloth — which was actually a corner cut from my towel as I had forgotten to bring one but was told it would be vital in the bathing process. 'Then soap!' She motioned to the oversized bar of laundry soap that looked like a giant rectangular blue Toblerone bar. 'You put soap on that facecloth and you scrub, scrub, scrub!' She demonstrated vigorous scrubbing motions over her body. 'After, you rinse. Yes, then, eh — you are so clean!'

I looked over at the other girls, who were also eyeing the two inches of cloudy pond water swirling in the bottom of their tubs and wondering how this bathing business was going to go.

'Who wants to go first?' Teacher Sarah asked.

'Sure, I will,' I volunteered. How hard could it be? I had grown up on boats where our daily 'shower' ritual was to dive into the sea, clamber back into the cockpit and soap up with Mama's special Green Apple Shampoo ('best results in salt water' — apparently) and then dive back overboard. Nick and I would be given a quick rinse down with the outdoor shower to wash off the salt and then, *voilà*! Clean little bodies. Surely the boat-bathing of my childhood would hold me in good stead here?

The bathroom vacated, I stripped off and hung my dusty clothes on the nail protruding from the back of the wooden door. Stepping into the bath, I dunked my facecloth in the water and wiped my body down, starting with my face and ending with my muddy toes. I watched the bath slowly turn red as the dust on my skin mixed with the pond water. I ignored that and, using Teacher Sarah's scrubbing technique, managed to work myself up into a fairly decent lather. Now, to rinse. I looked down at my tub, now full of dirty soap suds floating in muddy water. Oh, to be able to dive over the side of my boat now. *I chose to come here*, I reminded myself, and got to work pouring cups of brown foamy water over myself.

Surprisingly, I felt refreshed after bathing; but more than anything, I felt immensely satisfied. The joy of being clean is only truly felt when you have been covered in dust for days and know that the nearest body of swimmable water is hundreds of kilometres away. That said, I decided to leave the challenge of washing my hair for another day.

Later that week we worked on washing our clothes, and I kicked myself when I saw that our water barrel had been miraculously refilled. I vowed to keep a closer eye on the little water fairies. I hated the idea of the children having to look after *us* when we were supposedly here volunteering to help *them*. Clothes washing followed a similar process to bathing, using the same water barrel, the same blue soap and the same bathing tubs. The volunteer manual had warned about the *putzi* fly, which laid its eggs in wet clothes hung out to dry. Your body heat would cause the eggs to hatch and the larvae would burrow into your skin, forming a boil as they grew. To kill the flies, ironing all clothes and bed sheets was recommended. In the absence of an iron, ironing board and electricity, we decided to take our chances.

Washing and bathing mastered, our thoughts turned back to how we could get involved in school life. We set off one morning in search of Rose to see if she needed any help. She was headed towards the maize mill and invited us to join her, so we followed her past the piggery with its foul stench towards the sound of whirring machinery, so loud in the otherwise peaceful village. Donated by the Rotary Club of Halifax, Canada, in conjunction with the Rotary Club of Muyenga in Kampala and the Rotary Foundation, the maize mill was an impressive initiative. Local farmers brought their maize to KAASO, the school bought it from them and then milled it to feed the children. Everyone benefited: the farmers had a guaranteed market and KAASO secured its food supply, thus supporting the local community, which included many of the school's parents.

We stood with Rose as she explained the process and then, much to the amusement of the local workers, we offered to help, keen to be of use rather than just being spectators. Soon we were kneeling in the dirt, sorting maize kernels on wire-mesh frames, sifting out impurities, rocks and beetles. It felt good to be doing something physical, something helpful, and I enjoyed feeling involved in village life, even if just for a moment. However, as eager as I was to find my purpose here, and while everyone appreciated our efforts, it was clear that this was not where our real skills lay. We had no intention of taking the jobs of local workers far better suited to the task, so at the end of the day we waved goodbye and left the maize mill to the people who knew best.

It was only a few days since our arrival, but I was already growing impatient. It had taken so long to get to this point, and now that I was finally here I felt a sense of urgency. I came from a culture that desired results — fast results. I was not used to sitting around idly, waiting for the world to happen; the world I came from pushed you to *make* things happen. I wanted to be part of the community, to feel involved and useful — sooner rather than later. But I reminded myself that the ground here had shifted and I just needed to be patient.

We were due to meet with Dominic the following day, and I was looking forward to speaking with him about our six months at KAASO and the shape they might take. Dominic had barely been around since our arrival — he was a very busy man. Not only was he the Director of KAASO, but he was also the Head Teacher at Kamuganja, a local government school, he cultivated various gardens around the region to help supplement KAASO's food supply, he was the head of mathematics for the whole of Rakai District, he had a constant flow of visitors from the community seeking his advice and assistance, and he had a wife and seven children of his own. I wondered how he managed it all. I felt immensely grateful to him for making time to sit with us and map out a plan for the coming months. As much as we were enjoying our time so far, we didn't want to simply fill our days with small tasks like token netball sessions, rope-skipping, or a day's work at the maize mill. We wanted something bigger, something we could sink our teeth into.

Friday morning dawned with the usual symphony of roosters crowing and children laughing. Our meeting with Dominic was due to start at 'exactly' 8 a.m., so we quickly ate breakfast — milk-less tea and dry, crumbly bread which we spread with 'Blue Band', a strange kind of margarine 'enriched with extra fat' that mysteriously defied the need for refrigeration — then went next door to Dominic and Rose's house for our meeting.

'Good morning, girls,' Rose smiled warmly. 'Please, come inside. How have you slept?'

'Fine, thank you. We're here to see Dominic. We have a meeting with him now.'

'Of course,' Rose nodded slowly, realising that we were still new enough to believe that Dominic would actually be on time. We had not yet learned that 'Africa time' had the flexibility of a rubber band. 'Except, you see,' Rose said, 'I have just spoken to him and he has still not left the government school in Kamuganja. I think he may be some time. Really, I am so sorry for the delay. Perhaps we reschedule this meeting for the afternoon instead?'

Thanking her for her help and trying to hide our disappointment, we stood there dumbly, wondering what to do next. I felt frustration welling up inside me; I wanted to get started. I suddenly remembered reading something about a school library in the volunteer manual. 'Maybe we could help out in the library in the meantime?' I suggested hopefully, not even sure whether this library existed.

'Of course!' Rose smiled broadly. 'I am sure Secretary would love your assistance. You will find her in the office. Thank you for that good work, Madam Emma.'

People in Uganda are hugely polite and titles are very

important. Not only do people use *ssebo* or *nyabo*, sir or madam, to greet each other, but they also refer to each other by their titles. Dominic was known as Director, Rose was Headmistress, the teachers were all called Teacher so-and-so, and Susan, the school secretary, was simply known as Secretary. Not to be left out, we were Madam Emma, Madam Kirsty and Madam Cherie.

The office was located at the front of the school next to the volunteer house, opening out on to the school's grassy lawn and the dusty main road of Kabira. A concrete veranda served as an entryway and we stepped up and gently knocked on the open glass doors. Susan was sitting inside tapping noisily at an old-fashioned typewriter when we entered, her brow furrowed in concentration, her spiral curls bouncing as she hammered the keys. She didn't notice us standing before her and we had to shout to be heard.

'Susan? Susan? SECRETARY! Hi. How are you?'

'I am alright, thank you, *nyabo*. How are you?'

'We're great, thanks,' Cherie replied.

'How can I help you?' Susan asked.

Kirsty took the lead. 'So, we had some free time and we thought we'd come and help you with the library. Maybe organise the shelves for you?'

I looked behind Susan at the chaotic collection of books, piled messily and balanced precariously on rows of sagging wooden shelves.

Susan looked up at us through her long lashes, confused. 'Sure. This is fine, but . . . What do we need to organise?'

Realising that we were risking offence, Cherie stepped in. 'Oh no, it's not that it's *dis*organised, it's just that we thought it would be good to have a look through the books to see what we might use in the classrooms when the children return . . .'

'We won't bother you,' I assured her. 'You look very busy, so please don't mind us. We'll be quiet.'

Nonplussed, Susan shrugged her shoulders and went back to pounding the keys of the typewriter.

Cherie, Kirsty and I split up, each tackling a different section. I went to the back wall and was impressed by the books I found. They were old and not in very good condition, but there was a wide selection — science, mathematics, social studies, English, religion, health. I even found choral books, making notes of songs I could sing with the children in my imagined choir. My excitement grew as I thought of all the possibilities: I could write a school show, run music classes, give guitar lessons. Cherie found a bunch of storybooks and we discussed creating reading groups and setting up 'story time' with the children. All these amazing resources were just sitting there untouched, ready for us to use. I felt myself getting swept away by all there was to do and had to remind myself to proceed slowly, slowly. *There's time for everything, it's still early days.* But that didn't stop me buzzing with the potential of what lay before me.

Susan looked up from time to time as we completely rearranged the shelves, labelling each of the different sections and grouping similar books together. Eventually she stood and abruptly left the room. We stopped and watched her go.

'Oh dear, maybe not off to the best start with Susan,' Cherie said. 'I'm guessing she's not impressed with us taking over and intruding in her world.'

It was probably true. For all our best intentions not to upset the existing order, we had done just that — and we hadn't even been there a week. We had barged in and decided that we would set things 'right' — right according to us. We hadn't asked Susan what she needed; we had decided for her what *we* believed would be most useful. In doing so, I had already broken one of my own rules: change needs to come from *within*, not be imposed externally. We were in a different world to that we were used to and it was inevitable that we would make mistakes along the way, but I was embarrassed by our early blunder. I vowed to find a way to make it up to her.

At lunch I sat quietly, sliding my food around my plate. I was enjoying myself here, but I was starting to feel like a true *muzungu* — 'one who wanders aimlessly'. Having been brought up in a world where plans changed — literally — with the weather, where an unexpected storm could set you off course or require you to alter your destination altogether, I knew how to be flexible. But that didn't prevent the growing impatience I felt. In my naïve fantasies of how I thought my volunteer experience might be, I had imagined that by now I would already have launched into the classrooms and be helping shape the future of these young children. Instead, I had arrived at a school all but empty, in a village that was going about its business just fine without me.

So now I was fighting an internal battle — although I knew I should be patient, it had taken so long for me to get to this point that I didn't want to wait any longer for the path to magically roll out before me. I wanted to launch in and create my own path. But, I had to remind myself, then I would be at risk of doing something unhelpful, unnecessary or inappropriate. My tendency to throw caution to the wind had usually worked well for me in the past, but this was not a place I knew, nor a culture I understood. Despite my keenness to find my purpose, I knew that the best thing to do was to observe, listen and absorb, and have faith that when the time was right I would be able to see the path before me.

CHAPTER SIX

n the end, our meeting with Dominic took place at sunset. He rushed into the school grounds, apologising profusely for his delay, explaining that he had been caught up with parents bringing their children back to school at Kamuganja. Government schools started the term a few days before private schools and KAASO, with no government funding, was classified as 'private'.

We assured him that the delay was no problem, thanked him for his time, and then sat down together at the dining table, sipping cups of hot tea and waiting for the temperamental generator to burst into life. With no electricity in the village, the sporadic power we did get came from a diesel generator that filled our world with light for a few hours each night. Our light was directly proportional to the amount of diesel in the tank; just when we could see no more, someone would fuel the generator and the lights would fire up with brilliant splendour, but equally without warning the diesel would run out, plunging us back into darkness.

'So, girls,' Dominic clasped his hands and leaned forward, 'first, let me please officially welcome you to KAASO. Really, we are so grateful to you for choosing to come to our school. We know that together we will do many wonderful things.' He beamed and I already felt so glad that we had ended up where we did. 'So, tell me, how are you finding the school so far? We want you to feel at home and treat it as such. You volunteers bring so much to our community, our school and our KAASO family and we are ever grateful for that good work.'

We thanked him for his kind words and assured him that we felt most welcome. 'It's amazing here, everyone has been great,' Kirsty said. 'If anything, the only complaint would be that everyone is *too* helpful! We offer to help but they always insist on helping *us* instead.'

Dominic's face crinkled with laughter. 'Eh! That is because you are our guests! We cannot ask guests to work — this is not the Ugandan way!'

We were confused. 'But we came here to *volunteer*,' I said. 'We *want* to help, that's what we're here for.'

Dominic smiled. 'I know, I know. Don't worry, it is a problem that is slowly being resolved. You see, when the volunteers first came to KAASO some years ago — was it 2005? Yes, these first volunteers came and we treated them as our guests. We cooked and cleaned for them, we looked after them and refused their offers to help. Over time, they grew frustrated and bored, wanting to do something and be more helpful. It was then I understood that in your culture, you make your guests do *work!*' He shook his head with amusement. I found myself smiling, realising that the concept of a 'volunteer' did not exist here — family was put to work and guests were treated as royalty. Volunteers fell in a shady grey area, unclassifiable; neither family nor guest.

'I know this is somehow difficult to understand but I assure you, we are getting better,' Dominic said. 'I will speak to everyone and encourage them to let you help. You will see, it will take some time but *mpola mpola* we will get there. Slowly, slowly.'

The generator suddenly roared to life, flooding the room with light and I blinked as my eyes adjusted to the brightness.

I calculated that volunteers had been coming to KAASO for about four years. 'So how did you first start getting volunteers?' I asked.

'Ah ha! You want to know the story?' Dominic's face lit up, always keen for storytelling.

I wanted to hear every story he had. Dominic, and everything about him, fascinated me. We refilled our mugs from the flasks of boiled water, pouring the steaming water over our floating tea leaves, and sat back to listen.

It was 2004 and Dominic was in a photocopy shop in Kampala when he bumped into a friend of his, Venesius. The two got chatting and Venesius told Dominic about an organisation he'd heard of called Kids Worldwide. He had a friend who ran a children's home in Kampala and had been receiving volunteers through this organisation. The children's home had benefited hugely from the donations the volunteers brought, not to mention the extra sets of hands, and Venesius urged Dominic to apply for KAASO to be added to the Kids Worldwide portfolio. Venesius helped Dominic through the application process and together they set up an email address for Dominic, which was to be the contact for all future volunteers coming through Kids Worldwide. Dominic was thrilled when KAASO was accepted — now all he had to do was wait to receive applications. Volunteers from around the globe would soon be flooding to KAASO.

'Every week,' Dominic explained, 'I would make the trip into Kyotera to check my emails, but every week the same — nothing. I thought no one was interested in helping our children, but Rose encouraged me to persevere. She told me that, some day, someone would want to help us. So I continued to travel, back and forth on the *boda* — I did not have a car in those days — but still nothing. Then, some months later, Venesius rang to ask me how the volunteers were going and I had to tell him the sad news that no one wanted to come to KAASO.

'He was surprised and asked if I had been checking my emails and I said, "Of course! Every week I go to the post office and check but every week there is nothing!" And then I heard him laughing.' Dominic grinned.

'"The post office?" Venesius cried. "What are you doing at the post office?" So I explained I was checking my emails — at my PO box where the mail comes to. Well, did he laugh and laugh *so much*! All this time, I had been asking if any mail had been delivered to my PO box — I didn't know that the messages came *inside* the computer! The next time I went to Kampala, I met with Venesius and he took me to an internet cafe. We opened my emails and wow, wow! So many emails!' Dominic exclaimed. 'All these volunteers who had been applying, wanting to come and help our children of KAASO, and for months they had not heard from me. I was so much upset. After that, Venesius gave me a good lesson in emailing and now I am the *kafulu*.' He nodded proudly. 'That means "expert" in Luganda.'

We all laughed, picturing Dominic despondently staring into his empty PO box every week, searching inside for the elusive applications that never came, while volunteers around the world waited for his reply.

'Well, we're very grateful to Venesius for all his help — if it wasn't for him, we would never have found you!' Cherie said.

'Does Venesius still live in Kampala?' I asked, thinking that it would be interesting to visit some other projects and maybe Venesius could put us in touch.

'Eh, that one is not around anymore,' Dominic said slowly, stirring his tea leaves.

The three of us sat quietly, letting his words sink in. What did he mean by 'not around'? What had happened? I desperately wanted to ask but held back, trying not to put my foot in it like we had with Susan. Luckily, I didn't have to wait long.

'It was maybe a year or two ago. He died from AIDS. His wife too. Now their children are orphans and live with their grand, not so far from here,' Dominic explained, using the Ugandan abbreviation for 'grandparent'. 'One of them, Marvin, is a pupil at KAASO but the other, eh — he is not so well, he is also having AIDS. He remains at home with the grand. Maybe Rose will take you to visit them one day.'

'Sure, that would be . . .' I trailed off, unsure of what word to use. Great? Nice? Instead I simply said, 'I'm so sorry to hear.'

'Well, it's almost dinner time,' Kirsty stepped in, in an attempt to keep us on track. 'So I guess we should get our fees sorted, right?' Although we paid nothing but a one-off $30 admin fee to Kids Worldwide, there was a small monthly fee paid directly to KAASO, primarily to cover the cost of our food and board, but also including a built-in donation for the first three months that went towards developing the school in some way. The idea was that volunteers could sit with their project director in-country and decide together what their donation would go towards.

Rose entered the dining room, balancing baby Denise on her hip, and sat down with us to go through the KAASO priority list, freshly printed on Secretary Susan's duplicating machine. As we ran through the various projects, I realised just how huge Dominic and Rose's vision for KAASO was. Priorities ranged from major construction to teacher education to farming projects to simple textbooks. The list seemed endless. The half-finished sick bay needed to be completed, teacher housing built, a permanent children's kitchen constructed to replace the current flax hut, nursery latrines dug, the school property fenced, proper classroom partitioning erected, the piggery extended, and they even had dreams of purchasing a school bus. The number one priority, however, was to build a new dormitory so that the library/computer lab could be used for its original purpose.

'I thought the library was in the office?' Cherie asked.

'Ah, that is the *temporary* library,' Rose explained. 'The dormitory down by Freedom Square — this building was originally built as a library and computer lab but, due to lack of space, we have had to fill this with bunks and children. One day we hope we can have a whole building dedicated only to books and computers, not just for KAASO but the entire community as well.'

I thought about how incredible that would be, but, for now, constructing a dormitory was far beyond our budget. In the end, we decided that our donations would go towards completing the half-finished sick bay. Dominic carefully wrote out receipts for us, promising to account for every shilling in the construction process. We assured him we trusted him, but it was nice to know that such a level of accountability went on.

'Supper must be ready,' Rose said, getting up to leave, readjusting Denise who was now sleeping across her lap. 'I will go and fetch the dishes for us.'

'Please, let us help you,' Cherie said, jumping up before Rose could protest that we were 'guests'.

Rose smiled knowingly. 'Thank you, please. That would be most helpful,' she said, and we gratefully filed out the door.

Over dinner, Rose mentioned that she would be starting to prepare the secondary students for their departure the following week. I was glad that she had brought the subject up, as I had been meaning to ask about these helpful students who were forever checking in on us. There was Ambrose, with his shy smile and sweet nature, who was constantly offering to help. We would laugh and tell him that *we* wanted to help *him*, but he would just shrug his shoulders and smile. Then offer to help again.

There was also Jackie, a spirited girl of fifteen who could usually be found helping in the 'kitchen', a mud-brick hut with a straw-covered floor and a hole cut through the roof to let out the smoke from the cooking fire. And then there was Grace. A close friend of Rose's had recently died, and her daughter, Grace, had come to stay at KAASO as Rose was like a second mother to her, and was helping her through this tough time. All three of these older students were spending their holidays at their former primary school; they had been at KAASO since our arrival.

One afternoon, Ambrose had come to sit with Kirsty and me in the volunteer house, while Cherie drew pictures with some of the younger children outside.

'Soon I will be leaving,' he told us. 'I must go back to my secondary school. Term two is beginning.'

'Oh, we will miss you!' I said. 'Maybe we can come to visit — how far away is your school?'

'It is far — but somehow not so far,' he replied.

Kirsty laughed. 'How far is that, Ambrose?'

He just smiled. 'Some day I will take you there. It is that way,' he said, pointing vaguely north.

'So you came back to KAASO to visit during your break?' Kirsty asked.

Ambrose looked out the window to where Cherie was patiently distributing coloured pencils to a riot of excited children. 'Hmm,' he mumbled and did not elaborate further. Turning his gaze back inside, he spotted Kirsty's laptop sitting on the dining table and his face lit up.

'Do you know how to use those things?' he asked.

'A laptop?' Kirsty asked.

'Yes! Those computers. They teach them at school but I am not so great. It is one of my problems which I struggle with in class.'

'Would you like me to teach you?' Kirsty offered.

'Oh, Madam Kirsty! That would be very wonderful!'

While they cleared the table to make way for the lesson, I went outside to join Cherie and her impromptu drawing class. We passed the rest of the afternoon in a state of hilarious confusion as the children tried to teach us phrases in Luganda, shrieking with delight to hear their native words rolling off our foreign tongues.

That evening, Kirsty showed us the bio Ambrose had written as typing practice:

WHO IS AMBROSE?

I am a Ugandan, aged 16. I was at St Paul KAASO from 2004 up to 2006. Now am at St Henry's College which is a single sex school. I am very happy with my primary school that is KAASO because it has helped me since the death of my father. May the Lord bless the entire community of KAASO.

Special thanks to Madam Kirsty who has helped me during my computer training this holiday. May the Almighty Lord bless you.

'What happened to his dad?' I asked.

'I don't know,' Kirsty replied. 'I didn't want to ask.'

'Do you think that's why those secondary students are here? Because they have nowhere else to go?'

The thought had weighed on my mind, and now, at the dinner table, I took the chance to ask Rose more about these students. 'Rose, what's the story with Ambrose, Jackie and Grace? They've been here the whole time we've been at KAASO. Why don't they go home for the holidays?'

Rose looked at me with a sad smile that was hard to read. 'Mmmm. Some things in Uganda are not so easy,' she said, before taking a large mouthful of *matooke*. When she had finished eating, she simply shook her head. 'KAASO is their home, their family. This is where they come.'

I shook my head slowly, feeling awful that these students had such tough lives, but also grateful that they had Dominic and Rose to care for them.

'So if they have no parents, who pays their school fees at secondary school?' Kirsty asked. I looked over at her. It hadn't even occurred to me that once the children left KAASO, where Dominic and Rose supported those unable to pay school fees, the children would be on their own.

Rose shrugged. 'Sometimes we get some help from sponsors, but usually this job falls on us. The government secondary schools are free but they have their challenges, so many students end up dropping out to work in the fields, or worse — without a family to guide them, girls can be led astray and fall pregnant, or boys can end up in the wrong crowds and get involved in crime. Without education, it is very hard to keep children on the right track. We do what we can and there are some few people who help but, eh. There are so many children. It's not so easy.'

She sounded tired, but the wheels were now turning in my head and I couldn't stop.

'So, sponsorship — I didn't see that on the priority list. Isn't sponsorship a priority, too?' I asked.

Dominic answered for Rose. 'Of course, this is also very important, but we have to think of the bigger picture. Construction can benefit so many children. Sponsorship is only one child.'

'So would you consider construction more important than sponsorship?'

'Really, this is hard to say,' Rose said. 'Both are very important. We cannot just choose one or the other.'

'But if you *had* to choose one?' I knew I sounded like a stubborn child, but I couldn't let it go. I had to know.

Rose sighed, but it was Dominic who spoke. 'Then we would have to say construction. For the greater good.' I could tell from the look on Rose's face that sponsorship was still incredibly important, and realised that it probably fell to her to find the funds to keep these children out of the fields and in class; but I had pushed enough. I went back to my beans.

That night Cherie, Kirsty and I offered to do the dishes, and no one refused. We stood out beneath the stars, wiping the pots and plates with a grimy rag, trying to get suds going with the universal laundry-bathing-dishwashing soap. My head was spinning with the evening's information overload.

'It's incredible what those two have achieved over the past ten years. I don't know how they manage it,' I said, scraping my pumpkin skins into the bucket for the pigs, feeling guilty; Dominic and Rose had eaten theirs. Nothing was wasted here.

'I know, it's amazing,' Cherie agreed. 'How does Rose not get *tired*? You know she's up before sunrise every morning, and she told me that last night she didn't get to bed until 2 a.m. Denise was sick, and she also goes and checks on all the children in the dorms — even though the matrons are there. She's unbelievable.'

'You know what I can't stop thinking about?' Kirsty asked. 'Ambrose. I saw him just before, helping the cook to feed all the younger children. He's a sixteen-year-old boy and he's spending his holidays looking after primary-school children that aren't even his own siblings. I know he doesn't really have a choice, but he still does it with a smile. It's impressive.'

I agreed. 'I wish there was more we could do to help him and the others.'

'I know, but you heard Dominic — the most helpful thing we can do for now is assist with construction and that's just what we're doing,' Cherie said.

I knew she was right, but it still didn't feel like enough. As I flapped the plates dry in the cool night air, I slowly came to the realisation that finding my way in this place wasn't going to be as easy as I'd thought. Nothing here was obvious; it was nuanced in a way that was all new to me. I was starting to see the enormity of the problems this community faced, and I realised that I would have to learn to accept that no matter what I did, it would never be enough. That was already upsetting me. I wanted to be able to solve all the problems of the world — but it seemed that I was going to have to be strong in working out where my help was needed most, as with the case of construction versus sponsorship.

I carried the plates into the mud-brick kitchen, placing them on the metal rack that stood on the hay-covered floor near the entranceway. A part of me was beginning to wonder whether I was really cut out for this. How would I cope for the next six months when faced with the difficult reality of having to choose who to help and who to turn away from? As I walked back to the volunteer house, I paused to look up at the sky and was struck yet again by how bright the twinkling stars were in the thick blanket of night. I reminded myself that I was here now, and I was committed. The only way I was going to find out whether I was up for the challenge was to try.

The following week brought with it the first of the children returning to school after the holidays. They arrived on foot, on the back of bicycles or motorcycles, a rare few by car, all juggling battered metal suitcases. We couldn't wait to meet them, so when Rose suggested we might help at the registration desk which had sprung up on the front lawn outside our room, we practically fell over ourselves to get started. Not only would this introduce us to the children, but it would also be a way for us to meet the teachers who were flooding into the school as well.

The only downside of meeting the teachers was that it emphasised just how inappropriately dressed we were. The volunteer manual had suggested bringing smart clothes for special occasions, so we had assumed that on a day-to-day basis we wouldn't need to wear 'nice' clothes. We were wrong. I cringed every time another teacher walked into the school, the men in jackets and trousers with crisp white shirts and the women in smart blouses with pressed skirts and high heels. As we went over to shake their hands and introduce ourselves, I was embarrassed by our shabby appearance — our baggy T-shirts, long skirts and rubber flip-flops. At least we knew that women should not wear trousers in the village, which the volunteer manual had warned could be seen by the more conservative as an 'invitation to prostitution', but I still wished we had brought smarter clothes.

Secretary Susan was managing the registration desk and, hoping to win her back, we politely offered our services, emphasising that we were happy to do whatever *she* wished. She eyed us warily, then shrugged and said we could help by writing the children's names onto the class lists and ticking off their 'requirements' — the long list of items they were expected to bring each term. We told her we would gladly do whatever she needed, and cheerfully took our positions at the makeshift registration desk.

I didn't realise that such a seemingly simple task could be so difficult and so heart-breaking. So many of the children arrived with so little. We had a list of items the children needed, but we didn't know whether they needed the entire list or just some of the items, and were unsure of how vigilant we had to be. We tried asking Susan. Did the children really require a new hoe each term? Did it matter if they didn't have the full 5 kilograms of sugar? And what if they couldn't afford to pay for it? But to every question she simply answered, 'Of course,' then walked away. Perhaps our faux pas in the library had offended her more than we realised.

As the children flooded in and the lines continued to grow, we tried to do our job as best we could, but it was so upsetting. Often I would ask a child for a basic item on the requirements list — exercise books, pencils, pens and rulers — and be met with a murmured 'I don't have.' We knew we were supposed to charge for any items the children hadn't brought, but many of the parents and guardians simply could not afford to pay. We would ask for 400 shillings — about 15 US cents — for a straw broom and the people could not meet our eyes. We could feel their quiet desperation at their inability to pay.

I was also overwhelmed by how many names there were. As we filled in the children's names on the class lists, I watched the numbers grow until there were 50, 60, 70 students in a single class, with still more children to arrive. The volunteer manual had warned that the classes would be large, but now that I was here it was daunting to think of actually facing so many children in a single class. I realised how huge the need for help was, and could only imagine how grateful the teachers would be for our assistance once classes resumed.

While communication remained a challenge, one redeeming factor was that I had been taking evening Luganda lessons with Phionah, Dominic and Rose's eleven-year-old daughter, which were proving to be immensely helpful. Many of the parents and guardians accompanying their children did not speak English, so I was able to help them with my limited Luganda. Although I spoke French and Spanish, Luganda was vastly different from any other language I had learned. Nonetheless, I persevered; it was important to me to learn some Luganda in an attempt to stick to at least one of my 'rules' of volunteering: *learn the local language.*

At the registration desk, an elderly woman and what I assumed to be her grandchildren arrived and stood nervously before me. I tried to make them feel at ease by putting my Luganda into practice. '*Oli otya, nyabo?*' I greeted the grandmother, asking how she was.

Taken aback, she smiled shyly and replied, '*Gendi, nyabo. Oli otya, nyabo?*' She was fine, how was I?

'*Gendi, nyabo,*' I replied proudly. This was going well.

I asked her the names of the children and was delighted to learn that one of them was called Emma. 'Wow! Which one is called Emma?' I asked. '*Amanya gange enze* Emma,' I added as I pointed to myself, telling them my name was also Emma. 'Which one is Emma? *Gwe?*' I asked, pointing from one child to the next. Wide eyes stared at me blankly. Finally a small boy nodded his head slowly. *He* was called Emma. It turns out that in Uganda Emma is a boy's name. I had to laugh; normally that would have surprised me, but I was quickly learning to just accept things without question.

Moving on, I ran through the list of requirements. I didn't

know how to say jerry can, but I had learned the word for water. 'Do you have a jerry can, you know, for carrying *amazzi*?' I demonstrated pouring water from a jerry can.

The grandmother looked as though I'd just spat in her face and I stared at her in surprise. At the next table, I heard Susan giggling and wondered what I'd done wrong this time. The words were correct; I was doing well. Wasn't I? Where was Phionah when I needed her?

It turned out that my pronunciation was wrong — the word had come out *amaZZI* rather than *aMAzzi*, an important distinction. I had inadvertently told this woman that her grandson needed a jerry can for carrying *faeces* rather than *water*.

That was where my career at the registration desk ended. Feeling defeated, I stepped aside to let Susan take over. Cherie and Kirsty were having the same trouble with the language barrier and, despite our best intentions, we clearly weren't being very helpful. Now at a loss, we drifted around aimlessly, discussing why the children all brought boxes of razor blades, called 'safety blades'. There was nothing safe about them and yet even the tiniest children used them for sharpening pencils, cutting fingernails and shaving heads.

Eventually, Susan assigned us the 'very important' but massively inefficient task of collating the requirements into piles from where they would be put in sacks too heavy to carry, which we then had to drag to the storeroom. While this trip wasn't a long one, it involved traversing the rickety wooden bridge outside the volunteer house, the purpose of which became apparent during the torrential rains which came each day when rivers of mud flowed through the school — I had quickly learned that the Ugandan rainy season was not a non-stop monsoon, but a daily deluge that came and went without warning and was always followed by blinding sunshine. From the bridge we crossed the muddy path that skirted Dominic and Rose's house and went around the corner into the storeroom. We tried to suggest other systems, such as fewer items in each sack or even a wheelbarrow of sorts, but these were all met with frowns from Susan and the teachers she now had helping her. We took that to mean no.

So we continued lugging the overflowing sacks, sweating and stumbling and wondering where all the workers who had previously been lugging sacks had disappeared to. Did they have other urgent jobs to tend to, or had they been sent away in an attempt to give us something to do? It was hard to believe that this was the best use of our time; it felt more like a token way to keep us busy, and I didn't want to be doing token jobs. I had come here motivated by a desire to help educate children in a region wracked by poverty, not to lug sacks around a school. Sure, I had been happy to muck in at the maize mill for a day, and I didn't mind helping with a few sacks here and there, but as the hours slipped by and the sacks continued to pile up, my frustration grew.

I heard a shout and looked over to see Kirsty's leg bleeding; someone had accidentally put a hoe in the sugar sack. I sighed as I watched her angrily toss the hoe aside and tend to her wounded leg. Surely this wasn't what we had come to Uganda to do? I had had grand visions of doing something meaningful, something long-lasting and worthwhile. I wanted to be a force of change in these children's lives, to inspire them and be an influence that resonated for years to come. But then John's words came back to me, echoing in my ears. Yes, he had said to go with purpose, but he had also told me to take the time to work out what was really needed before I launched in. *It's not your world, so pause, take a step back and really* listen *to work out how you can best be helpful.* While collecting school requirements was obviously not the difference I had come to Uganda to make, it was clear that we were not cut out for the registration-desk job; and until classes were under way we should make an effort to help with any jobs that needed to be done. Like lugging sacks. We stuck at it.

Back at the registration desk loading the next lot of sacks, Susan seemed to take particular delight in firing various requirements at our heads as we scrambled under the desk beneath her feet, gathering armfuls of toilet paper and shoe polish. I tried to ignore the box of 'safety blades' that bounced off the back of my head, telling myself that it wasn't intentional and she just wasn't looking where she was throwing. But I knew full well that wasn't true; reconciliation with her was going to be harder than I'd thought.

Soon there was sugar between my toes, my body was sticky with sweat and laundry soap, my clothes were dirty, my hair itchy, my back ached and my face was muddy. Cherie and I did another sugar run, awkwardly lugging the weighty sacks across the school and over the small bridge that led to the storeroom. We swatted away the bees that thronged, but the air filled with their frenzied buzzing. And it wasn't just the bees swarming — the children were really excited to find us at school, and they ran after us, helping us to carry bags of sugar as an excuse to walk with us.

In the storeroom, Cherie and I were in the midst of pouring sugar from a smaller plastic bag into the master supply when the thin plastic split and sugar went flying across the concrete floor. Heavy rain from the previous night had flooded the room, and the water had mixed with dirt to create a muddy pool. The sugar tumbled into the water and we watched with horror as the children dived to the floor. Before we had a chance to stop them, they were scooping handfuls of muddy sugar into their mouths.

'No! No, stop!' I cried desperately. '*Neda!*' I said, as we tried to pull them back, but there was no point. Mud or no mud, it was sugar, a highly sought-after commodity, and they would take what they could get.

'Just leave them,' Cherie sighed, walking away. 'There's not much we can do.' The sun had begun its downward slide, which would all too quickly lead to night. There were more supplies to carry, hoes to collect and sacks to drag, so we turned slowly and left the storeroom swarming with children and sugar and bees.

By nightfall I was utterly exhausted. I had written a list of things to do on my hand, but it had washed off. That was how I felt: washed out. A hot shower would have been bliss, but there was no chance of that, so instead, waiting for the generator to burst into life, I collapsed on my bed and lay in the darkness, sandwiched between the other girls. The only place where we could have a moment to ourselves was our bedroom; even our 'alone' time was shared.

A phone beeped in the darkness. We all jumped, hopeful. It was for Kirsty. Marcos, her boyfriend, asking about her day. Cherie and I lay back, disappointed.

In spite of our best intentions to come to Uganda single and independent, all three of us had met boys just before moving to the village. We had been so certain that we would come here with open hearts and minds, but that had all changed at the last minute; and, in spite of ourselves, we were grateful for our boyfriends' support. Cherie had Mike, a primary-school teacher who was fascinated by her plans to go volunteering in Uganda. Kirsty had started dating Marcos, a Canadian engineer who had wooed her in the final weeks before her departure. And I had fallen for Matt, an Australian superyacht captain I'd met in a marina in Turkey while visiting my parents on board *Sojourn* before coming to Uganda. He was intrigued by my volunteering adventure and made me promise to keep him updated on village life during our six months apart.

As Kirsty wrote back to Marcos, balancing her phone on the windowsill where we could sometimes get enough reception to send a message, I picked up my phone to write to Matt. But I stared at the blank screen, unable to find the words. He, and everyone else I knew, believed that I was coming to Uganda to save the world — or at least to try to change it a little for the better. They all thought I was here doing extraordinary things. How could I explain that my daily reality involved lugging sacks of sugar and soap around, bathing in cupfuls of water from a slimy barrel of pond water which the children filled for me, and dodging boxes of 'safety blades' tossed at my head? Was this really what I'd imagined? I tried to think beyond all that, to take in the wider picture, but I was lost for words. How to describe the look on the children's faces as they arrived empty-handed, their parents' inability to pay, entire families devastated by HIV/AIDS? How to explain that children devoured handfuls of sugar from a muddy floor?

In the end, I gave up trying to put it into words. I tossed my phone aside and made my way out into the night to play with some of the newly arrived children.

CHAPTER SEVEN

A few days later, Cherie, Kirsty and I decided it was time to approach the teachers about helping in the classrooms. The teachers had been back at school almost a week now, which we felt was enough time for them to have settled back in and become used to our presence at KAASO. We spoke to Rose about it, and within an hour she had organised a meeting with the full teaching staff. We stood before them in one of the classrooms and introduced ourselves, explaining where we were from and how excited we were to be at KAASO.

'We would love nothing more than to help you with your classes,' Kirsty explained. 'We are not trained teachers but we all have some kind of teaching experience, and we are willing and able to assist you in any way. We love to be busy, so the more we can help, the better!'

We indicated our preferred subjects but made it clear that we were happy to do whatever would be most useful to them.

'These past few days at the registration desk, we have seen

how enormous your classes are and can only imagine how much work you must have juggling your schedules. So, please, use us to help ease your workload,' Cherie added.

I chimed in at the end. 'We are free to start straight away so please don't hesitate to ask for our help — we're volunteers, not guests — that's what we're here for,' I said, careful to make the distinction clear. 'We're so happy to be at KAASO and can't wait to get started. We look forward to the next six months together.' I sat back down, my face flushed with heat and excitement.

Rose thanked us for our kind words and all the teachers nodded in appreciation, but none of them said a word. Children were still arriving back at school, so we resumed our posts sorting requirements at the registration desk, feeling discouraged by the lack of instant job offers.

'Maybe it will just take a while for them to get used to us,' Cherie suggested. 'They've only just met us and probably need to work out how we can best fit into their teaching schedules.'

I hoped she was right. In spite of my eagerness to begin, I resigned myself to the fact that, once again, we would just have to be patient.

Later that day, I was in the midst of stacking bars of blue laundry soap when I noticed a young woman standing behind the horizontal wooden pole that served as a fence between KAASO and its neighbours. There was a hut behind her, crudely made from mud, pierced by straw and leaves. A billowing, stained curtain served as the hut's door and the roof was thatched. I wondered how it fared during the torrential rains that came each day. The woman had a tiny baby strapped to her back, and when I caught her eye she smiled and waved me over. I was startled; everyone in the village always appeared to be so busy — what could she possibly want with me? Grateful for an excuse to abandon my post, however, I went over and introduced myself in my best Luganda. I was surprised to find that she spoke reasonably good English. Her name was Flora, and she explained that she looked after the old women and children who lived in the crumbling mud hut behind her.

'*Jebale ko, nyabo.*' I thanked her for her good work, and stood, smiling dumbly at my new friend, happy to feel that I was in some small way part of village life just from the mere act of talking to our neighbour.

'I would like to request your help,' she said softly, not meeting my eyes. 'I need to fry some cassava for the evening meal but I have no cooking oil. I cannot afford. Can you help me?'

I looked at the baby strapped to her back, staring up at me with big brown eyes. The curtain behind Flora blew aside long enough for me to catch sight of a tangle of limbs inside the small hut; older women caring for the young children inside.

'Of course!' I agreed, excited by the opportunity to help. 'Not a problem, I will bring it to you this evening.'

She thanked me profusely and I returned to the laundry soap with a smile, feeling satisfied to be helping my new village community. I had just resumed my soap stacking when, all of a sudden, dark clouds swallowed the light, the skies opened up, and without warning it began to pour.

Now, where I came from, people went inside when it rained. There was a deafening clap of thunder and as the first fat drops fell, Cherie, Kirsty and I raced for shelter. We didn't yet fully realise just how valuable water was, as so far we had only experienced the rainy season and were yet to live through the long, hot months of the dry season when water would become increasingly scarce. Safely inside, we were mortified to realise that we had run the wrong way. In Uganda, it seemed, everyone rushed *outside* when the rain started — children hurried into the downpour to bring in washing, babies and mattresses, and buckets, tubs and jerry cans were laid out to catch the rivers of fresh water pouring from the rooftops.

We watched as a little girl came flying over to the volunteer house with a bathing tub, placing it under the flow of water that was gushing off our roof and onto the ground, so many precious drops wasted by our failure to act. I thought of the little water fairies that continued to fill our water barrel when we weren't looking, and cursed myself for being so stupid. Why had I not thought of this? It wasn't as if collecting water was entirely foreign to me. When my parents and I were living on our yacht *Joshua* in New Caledonia, Dad would steer *towards* the rain squalls so that we could all bathe, plugging the cockpit drains with bungs so that it would fill like a bathtub. Our water supply at sea was far from endless, and I was annoyed at myself for not having thought to collect water here as the first drops began to fall. Belatedly launching into action, we raced to the bathroom and grabbed our bathing tubs, then ran out into the rain to try to catch the streams that flooded off our tin roof.

The rain stopped as abruptly as it began, and the dark clouds quickly gave way to brilliant sunshine. The registration desk was reassembled and the requirements continued to stack up on the muddy grass. I looked next door to see Flora and her baby emerge from behind the now-sodden curtain. Somehow the hut had survived the deluge. I waved to her, then took a deep breath and resumed my work.

That evening, I delivered the cooking oil to Flora and she knelt to me in thanks, as was tradition in the Baganda culture of the region. I felt humbled, and assured her that I would be happy to buy her more once she ran out. She thanked me profusely and I returned to the volunteer house feeling virtuous and happy. My self-congratulation quickly evaporated when Rose gently pulled me aside and tactfully suggested that I might check with her before donating things around the village next time. It turned out that my friend Flora was a total con who was just parading around with someone else's baby and didn't look after any old women or children at all. The next morning Flora and her cooking oil were gone, and I never saw them again.

As the days slipped by, we kept offering to assist the teachers in their classrooms but our offers continued to fall on deaf ears. The term was now in full swing and classes had well and truly resumed. We would walk past the overflowing classrooms, looking longingly through the barred windows, desperately hoping to be welcomed in; but it seemed that we were not wanted.

I began to despair, wondering what we were doing wrong. I had had such great visions of quickly becoming enveloped into the school community, but as time passed, my hopes slowly faded and my confidence took a plunge. I began to feel that we could do nothing right: we had upset Susan in the library, our efforts at the registration desk had been pitiful, we still couldn't speak the language properly, we ran the wrong way when it rained, and my attempt to help in the community had failed with the disastrous cooking-oil incident. We couldn't even get the dress code right.

One afternoon, out of desperation, I sat down under a tree and started playing my guitar. I soon found myself swamped with children who were equally desperate to sing — and to see my guitar — so I played and played until I ran out of songs. It wasn't the full schedule of music lessons I had hoped for, but I called it a music lesson anyway because I needed to tell myself that I was doing *something*. It gave me a brief sense of satisfaction, but that's all it was — brief. I wanted more. Kirsty helped the netballers in their training and I continued my afternoon music sessions, but that only left Cherie wondering what *her* purpose was. Emma was the 'music' volunteer, Kirsty was the 'sport' volunteer. What was Cherie? Cracks were starting to form between us and I felt helpless to stop them.

As days turned to weeks, my frustration intensified. What were we even here for? What had we actually achieved since being in Uganda? Sure, the construction of the sick bay was going well thanks to our donations, but we had recently learned that the sick bay would, on completion, be used as a dormitory due to overcrowding. This was upsetting, as malaria season was approaching and already we were starting to see sick children lying around the school, fevers raging, with nowhere to go. But it wasn't just the repurposing of the sick bay that bothered me; it was also that I didn't want to be useful only for the funds I could provide. I was at a rural primary school in Uganda where the classrooms were full to bursting, and I wanted to be of help. There were 98 children in Primary Three (P3) alone, and the other day I had walked past the classroom to find there wasn't even a teacher in it. I walked to the next class and found the same situation there. Eventually, I realised that all the teachers were having a staff meeting so the entire school was without teachers. Why couldn't they have asked us to help? At that point I would have happily taken on a class of 200 children!

Even though I knew that I would learn more than I would teach during my six months here and this philosophy remained important to me, it felt as though getting into the classrooms was the key to our understanding of everything. If we could just get inside, everything would make sense, our purpose would come clear and the seemingly impenetrable world of KAASO would be unlocked.

I began to wonder *why* the teachers didn't want us to help. Did they still view us as guests, like Dominic had explained? Did they think we weren't up to the task? Or, worse, was this just a classic example of foreigners imposing themselves on a community that didn't want them or have any use for them?

One night I lay awake in bed, trying to work out how we were going to find our way. It had now been more than a month and we were still not in the classrooms. I could hardly believe it. I was exhausted from trying so hard and feeling like I was failing at everything I attempted. In my darker moments, I began to wonder what the point of us even being there was. Cocooned within my mosquito net, tears escaped, slipping down my cheeks as I stared up into the darkness. Why was this so hard? I closed my eyes and let myself be washed away to the world I had left behind, a world that embraced me, that made sense to me.

I had always had such a strong sense of community, growing up in my incredibly close-knit family and travelling the world with our extended America's Cup family. I longed for the old sense of belonging I used to feel. Not this aching dislocation of being in a place where we spent our days forever on the outside, peering hopefully into the classrooms, wondering if today would be the day we would be invited inside. We had joined Dominic on some of his trips down to the government school at Kamuganja and, as much as we loved playing with the children there, we still felt like spectators, outsiders, merely visitors who would leave when the sun went down. I so badly wanted to be a part of things, to immerse myself in the Ugandan way of life, to be on the *inside*.

I felt desperately lonely, too. I missed my family, I missed Matt, I missed my friends. I missed everyone I'd ever known. I missed sailing, I missed being out on the ocean. This landlocked existence was starting to close in on me. A little voice in my head began to wonder whether I could handle living with such futility and lack of direction for six months. How long would it be before a light appeared at the end of this long, dark tunnel? I tried to be positive, telling myself that there was nowhere I'd rather be, that everything would be alright — trying to make myself believe my own words.

But everything was not alright. The next morning we were due for our weekly meeting with Dominic, and when he arrived at the volunteer house he was looking uncharacteristically serious.

'Good morning, Dominic,' Cherie greeted him. 'Would you like some tea?'

He accepted it with thanks and sat down.

'Is everything okay?' Kirsty asked. 'Shall we start?'

'Yes, of course! Everything is going on well. Let us begin,' he said, flashing his bright smile.

As usual, Dominic had written up an agenda for our meeting and he began to run through it, updating us on the progress of the sick bay and informing us of the upcoming mid-term examinations. However, it was clear that there was something else on his mind. He shuffled his papers, not meeting our eyes as his smile slowly faded. He paused for a moment, looking uncomfortable, then cleared his throat and spoke.

'We are experiencing a small problem between the teaching staff and the volunteers,' he began. I looked from Cherie to Kirsty, unsure of where this was leading. We were the only volunteers at KAASO. 'I do not want to offend you girls because we are so grateful for all you have done so far, but the teachers have asked me to pass on to you the message that they are somehow not so happy. They are complaining that you are unwilling to help them in their classrooms and they wish to know why you will not be helpful. I am sorry to be sharing this difficult news.'

I could not believe I was hearing this.

'But that's crazy!' Kirsty cried. 'We've been asking them every single day if we can help, and no one seems to want us to go near their classrooms!'

'We'd *love* to help them, that's all we want to do. We've tried so many times but we didn't want to just barge in if we weren't invited!' I added.

'Ah, I see,' Dominic said, nodding, but I wasn't sure he really did see. 'Well, they are going to make a schedule of which classes you will teach. They are working on this and soon they will give it to you. I think it's good, no?'

'That's perfect!' I said. 'Whenever they are ready, we are ready.'

'The sooner the better!' Cherie added.

'OK, great. I am sorry for this unhappy news,' Dominic said, standing to leave. 'But we will make improvements to the situation. In no time you will be helping in our classes. It will be such a good thing for KAASO!'

'That was always the plan . . .' I mumbled, shaking my head in disbelief.

The three of us sat in stunned silence watching him go. How was this possible? I knew we were wading our way through a minefield of misunderstandings, but this was far beyond anything I had imagined. All the time we had been offering to help, had the teachers really not understood us? Was the miscommunication so great that they honestly believed we didn't want to help? I couldn't even begin to get my head around it. *Don't search for logic*, I reminded myself, but I was still floored by the extent of our disconnect.

However, as maddening as it was to think that the teachers were upset with us for not offering assistance, the promise of finally receiving a teaching schedule was enough to motivate us through the following days. We busied ourselves, doing washing, sweeping out the volunteer house and organising our supplies, ready for the moment — any day now — that we would be invited into the classrooms.

The rainy season had well and truly given way to the blistering heat of the dry season and our days were now full of hot, dusty sunshine. We were a stone's throw from the equator and the sun's proximity was felt. Filling tubs of water one morning in preparation for my laundry scrubbing, I thought back on my life just one year ago. I was living on a yacht in the Greek Islands, sailing from island to island. The summer heat in Greece was comparable to that of Uganda, but in Greece when it was hot I wore a bikini and swam in the sea. In Uganda when it was hot I wore long clothing and was just, well, hot. Matt sent me a message saying the water-maker on his superyacht was not working, and I laughed and told him to fix it and send it my way, dreaming about this giant contraption that could suck in water from Lake Victoria and spit out clean, fresh water for drinking and bathing.

As the days went by we tried to stay positive, waiting for the much-anticipated moment when the teaching schedule would be delivered to us. After four days, our hopes began to fade. After one week, we were climbing the walls. In the end, the teachers never came to us with their promised schedule. So one day — exasperated to the point of insanity — we simply sat down and divided the classes between the three of us.

One glorious sunny morning in the middle of June, I marched into each of my classes and announced to the teachers that I would be helping them from now on. I held my breath and waited to be sent away. The teachers grinned, and opened their arms in welcome. They were thrilled. When could I start? I almost screamed with frustration and delight. All the time we'd been trying so hard not to impose ourselves on them, the teachers had simply been waiting for us to be more assertive. If only we'd known that all we needed to do was bowl into a class and we'd find ourselves teaching it!

But there was no point dwelling on the past. I filled my schedule each day with as many classes as I could squeeze in and threw myself into every lesson with enthusiastic delight, ecstatic to finally be in the classrooms. I quickly came to adapt to the rhythm of school life, recognising the need to be flexible. I learned not to get upset when I turned up with my guitar to teach music only to find that it was now a maths lesson, or when I'd planned a PE class only to find myself marking English exams. I simply nodded and changed tack. By the end of the day my diary would be illegible with all the modifications to my timetable, but at least I was in the classrooms now. We had finally become a part of school life without trampling on anyone's toes, and it felt amazing. This was the sense of purpose I had long been searching for.

P1 quickly became my favourite class. Teacher Noelle welcomed me warmly, and before I knew it I had lessons lined up every day. One morning I was at the volunteer house getting ready to go down to P1 to teach the children colours. I was in the midst of collecting multi-coloured items from around our bedroom when Prima, Dominic and Rose's three-year-old daughter, appeared in the doorway, dressed in nothing but a grubby T-shirt. Prima-no-pants. She giggled as I wrapped her in colourful ribbons.

'Are you going to help Madam Emma teach P1?' I asked. 'Yes? Great, thanks! Or maybe you prefer to help Madam Kirsty with her science class . . . ?' I looked across the room with a grin.

'Uh, thanks, but Madam Kirsty has enough on her plate dealing with the rest of her over-excited children, thank you *nyabo*!' Kirsty shook her head, backing away.

I looked at Prima and shrugged my shoulders. 'Looks like you're with me.'

We entered the P1 classroom to a hurricane of cheers. The children were so excited to have volunteers in their classrooms and I couldn't help but shake my head in wonder that it had taken so long. The P1 children picked up the colour lesson well and seemed to understand most of what I said, which was a small miracle given my Kiwi accent and their five-year-old Ugandan English. From there I went to teach English to an incredibly diligent P6 class, stopping by afterwards to help Cherie with P3 music. I was half-dreading P3 with its 98 children and Teacher Fred, who was lovely but often absent, but I couldn't let Cherie do it on her own; the previous lesson had turned into a small riot when Teacher Fred had disappeared and the lesson had disintegrated into chaos, leaving us trying to administer crowd control while I held my guitar over my head. But today Teacher Fred stayed to sing with us and the lesson was a great success, even if I had lost my voice by the end of it.

I was walking back to the volunteer house when a little girl came running after me. She slipped a note into my hand, then quickly turned and ran away. I recognised her as Brenda, an incredibly shy girl from my P1 class who struggled to keep up with the lessons. I watched her go, surprised at her boldness and wondering what she wanted.

Back in our room I collapsed on my bed and unfolded the smudged scrap of paper. The note was elaborately decorated with colourful flowers and read:

I like Madm Emm so much I love

Madm Emm get reds and yellos and beuls and pinks an black

I love you so much. This is you flower

I grinned. My colours lesson had clearly paid off. It made my day.

For most of the classes I was free to plan my own lessons, but for the P7 students, in their last year of primary school, it was a different story. There was an extensive curriculum to cover and the children took their studies incredibly seriously, aware that good results in their Primary Leaving Examinations were vital for future success beyond KAASO. To get into a decent secondary school, the children needed top results in their examinations and the teachers pushed their students hard to achieve. KAASO's high teaching standard was known throughout the district and was the reason so many parents sent their children to the school. These fee-paying parents were vital for KAASO's survival: it was their funds that enabled the school to continue its mission of supporting orphans and underprivileged children.

Arriving in the P7 classroom was always one of my favourite moments of the day. I loved walking up the concrete ramp to be met by 48 smiling faces, greeting me and welcoming me into their classroom. Teacher Beda and I would go through reading comprehension and literature questions with the students, and I often helped with marking, amazed by the number of practice exams the children did.

Cherie had the most teaching experience of the three of us, having studied early childhood education, and she reminded me not to have favourites — but it was hard in this particular class. Sitting in the front row was a boy with shining eyes who hung off my every word. He had a permanent smile glued to his face and was forever leaping up to help me wipe the dusty chalk off the blackboard. Every lesson he would make sure that there was fresh chalk waiting for me, and he would always offer to carry my bag of books back to the volunteer house. He was the smartest boy there — not just because he was the top of his class in almost every subject, but because he understood that in a class of 48 students with one overworked teacher, you needed to be in the front row, you needed to stand out. He was an orphan from the village, with very few opportunities and the world stacked against him. But he knew that every little thing he could pick up along the way might just help his chances to succeed in life, and he would do all he could to improve his situation. This was the boy who was to become the axis of change, the turning point in my life. After him, nothing would ever be the same.

The boy's name was Henry.

CHAPTER EIGHT

The dust blew in through the open windows of the car, coming to rest on my sticky face, where it would probably remain until my evening bucket bath — but I didn't mind. We were on our way south to the government school at Kamuganja for a fund-raising function, and nothing could wipe away my smile. Everything at KAASO was finally in its place. Our teaching success had buoyed us with a newfound energy, and life at KAASO was full and fulfilling. Now I awoke each morning with a sense of purpose, excited to find what would await me in the classrooms. While so much about our little corner of Uganda continued to spin, throw and baffle me, I finally felt like we were on the inside. We had made it.

I looked forward to my lessons each day. I spent most of my time in P1 and P7, and quickly fell in love with both classes. I enjoyed watching the P1 children grasp new words and concepts, seeing their little faces brighten when I'd tell them we were going to hold a spelling bee, knowing full well that they had no idea what a spelling bee was. I had a soft spot for Brenda, the little girl who had brought me the colours note. She had big brown eyes and a smile that made me melt, and I would spend hours after class with her, coaching her through her lessons, explaining where she had gone wrong and trying to make light of the red crosses that covered her page. She struggled to understand and was often at the bottom of the class, but her quiet determination compelled me to persevere.

In P7, I continued to help Teacher Beda with his English lessons. After class, Henry would often come back to the volunteer house with me. He was enthralled by my seemingly endless stationery supplies and brought his torn schoolbooks for me to tape up, which I would do gladly, knowing that it was also an excuse to spend time together. We developed a real connection, and I would listen, humbled, as he spoke passionately about his dreams of becoming a doctor and helping people less fortunate than himself.

My afternoon music sessions had become a regular occurrence, and a devoted group would be waiting for me once their chores were completed. The children were all in different classes, but once the music started, age barriers melted away. There was Immy from P3, who was always the first to arrive, followed by a shy girl from P5 called Stellah, who would sit quietly at first and then light up when she began to sing. Phionah, Dominic and Rose's daughter, would come flying over from the P6 classroom as I strummed the first chords, and little Brenda would slip into our circle, trying to keep up with the older girls reading the song sheets I had written on manila posters.

Amidst the coffee beans laid out to dry in the sun, we would sit in the shade of what came to be known as the music tree, and sing while day-scholars flowed out of the school gates to commence their long walk home. As the sky slowly filled with the streaky red of sunset, we sang and played until night stole the light away.

I had even won Susan over by offering to help with her mountain of typing. She showed me how to align the paper and feed it into the archaic typewriter, reminding me to be sure to give the keys a good 'WHACK!' to get through the three layers of duplicating paper. Once I got the hang of it, I found I actually quite enjoyed it — it was fascinating reading the government-issued exam papers and satisfying to see the pile of typing diminish, knowing that I was now doing something genuinely helpful for Susan. But what I loved most was the look of admiration on her face as she watched my fingers fly over the keys, the staccato rhythm humming like sweet music through the office.

'Oh wow, Madam Emma. You are so fast! This is very wonderful.'

I would beam back at her, warmed by her praise, feeling relieved that I had finally put things right.

Another wave of dust exploded through the window as we hit a giant pothole and I braced myself against Cherie, sitting next to me in the back seat of Dominic's car. We had commissioned Dominic's sister, a local tailor, to make us new clothes, and at last we felt like we looked smart enough to represent KAASO. We had even splashed out on second-hand sandals in the Kyotera markets, an upgrade from our rubber flip-flops.

As we pulled into the grounds of the government school, we were met by hundreds of children who were clapping and cheering our arrival. Dominic stopped the car so that Cherie,

Kirsty and I could get out and walk among them, and we were quickly swamped by children, who grabbed our hands and squealed with excitement.

The children sang songs of welcome, then shepherded us into a classroom where all the desks in the school had been lined up in preparation for the fund-raiser. The classroom was largely barren, the concrete walls dotted with tatty manila posters containing faded lessons. At the front of the room was a couch and two worn armchairs next to a table draped with a lace doily. Someone had written: 'You're most welcome Ladies and Gentlemen' on the blackboard and illustrated it with chalk-drawn pictures.

The fund-raiser was to raise money to build a kitchen — a mud-brick hut in which to cook porridge over an open fire — and it seemed that the whole village had come to the event. All the parents and community members had been invited and would be asked to give what they could, either by bidding in the auction or by donating what little money they could spare. The region was incredibly poor, but Kamuganja was a government school where parents were not required to pay school fees, so whatever they gave at this fund-raiser would be their small contribution towards their child's education. Most of them felt a responsibility to give at least something.

The children directed us to our seats in the front row, and we had just sat down when the Rakai District Chairman entered the room. Dressed smartly in a navy suit and purple shirt, he greeted us warmly and thanked us for our attendance, before taking his seat on the couch of honour. His bodyguard stood behind him and leaned against the wall, cradling his gun.

Dominic stood and welcomed everyone, acknowledging the Chairman and thanking him for taking the time to come all the way to Kamuganja. When Dominic invited his VIP guest forward, the room filled with enthusiastic applause. The Chairman stood, slowly surveying the crowd, before his eyes came to rest on our white faces and he began to speak in English.

'Our guests from New Zealand, please, you are most welcome. I am happy to see you. Director has told me much about the good things you are doing and we are very excited about your presence here. It's not usual to have people from the developed world staying in these remote areas in our poor environment where you could get malaria.' He paused, then added with a grin. 'I hope you don't get malaria!'

I thought of all the children who had been lying around the school these past few weeks, burning with malarial fever, waiting for the school nurse's weekly visit to receive treatment. I felt both guilty and grateful for my daily malaria pills that kept me safe from the disease that took almost a million lives on the African continent each year.

'As you are aware,' the Chairman went on, 'the government has introduced Universal Primary Education in Uganda and this has helped us a lot. When I started eight years ago in Rakai District, the enrolment was only 60,000 students but now it has jumped to 160,000. Children who would otherwise not have gone to school can now attend for free. This is a very good thing.'

As impressed as I was with the rise in enrolment, I couldn't help but think about the government schools I'd seen here — the lack of resources and the understaffing. The Chairman, who must have read my thoughts, continued.

'Nonetheless, we still have our challenges,' he said. 'We suffered through bad governments during Amin's time when many resources were wasted, and although numerous developments have happened since Museveni's government came into power, most of our people remain poor. The challenges we face in education are not because we are unwilling to educate our children, but largely because of rampant poverty.

'There is a high dropout rate, especially among girls, which is a major challenge. When they leave school early without acquiring skills, without that capacity to say no to sex, then they are more vulnerable to HIV/AIDS. This epidemic has created so many orphans who have no one to care for them. These children can't even afford uniforms, let alone an exercise book. In some cases, they can't afford a pencil, which is about 2 US cents or less.'

The Chairman caught my eye and I looked away, unable to hold his gaze. I pictured the families lined up at the registration desk; I understood what he was talking about and it fell heavily upon me.

'Another challenge we face is that very few of our schools have got computer training facilities. I know that you might think, *Why should a leader in a poor country ask for computers?* Well, I will tell you. Computers have become part and parcel of our life and without them we find that we are trapped between the developed world and the backward world.' I thought of Ambrose and his eagerness for Kirsty's computer lessons, hungry to learn, to move forward.

'And how do we power these computers, you may be wondering? Well, even in the absence of electricity, we can use solar power,' the Chairman explained. On the road to Kamuganja, tall power lines marched south without a thought for the villages they bypassed below; although most Ugandans did not have electricity, it was being exported to neighbouring countries where higher revenues could be found. However, across the nation, solar energy was being harnessed with great success by those who could afford the panels. Just a few days earlier, solar panels had been installed at KAASO thanks to a previous volunteer's two-year fund-raising project. The school's lights and power now came entirely from solar energy, saving huge sums of money on costly fuel for the generator. 'You can see we have a lot of sunshine in Uganda; even after a heavy shower the sun will come out.

'So I would like to make a passionate appeal to you: I request that you become our ambassadors in your country and around the world. Wherever you go, speak to your communities about Rakai District and please, attract some assistance for us. The world has become a global village and we need to move forward because if we don't, our children will never become competitive. When God has given you plenty, it is also good to remember that there are others who are not so lucky. If people in the West sacrificed just a dollar each, it would make wonders for the children in Africa. I thank you for coming here and I thank you for caring. Please, do not forget us. *Webale nyo.*'

My heart was pounding as the Chairman switched to Luganda to address the rest of the crowd who had waited patiently through his English speech, most of them not understanding a word. His plea for help had struck a chord, and I was deeply moved. It brought me back to the words that had unsettled me over the past few years: *With great wealth comes great responsibility.* Now, here in Uganda, the Chairman was echoing that same sentiment, reminding those who had been given plenty to help those who were not so fortunate.

Speak to your communities about Rakai District, he had urged. *Do not forget us.*

The fund-raiser concluded with an auction and I watched in a daze as several bunches of *matooke* and two terrified chickens were paraded around the room. I pressed a wad of shillings into the donations basket that appeared before me and the teacher passing it around thanked me profusely, but I was a million miles away. Dominic gave a final speech, thanking everyone for the support and graciously acknowledging a generous donation from the Chairman. He announced that the fund-raiser had generated over one million Ugandan shillings, almost US$500 at that time, and the room erupted in cheers. I clapped politely, then excused myself and went outside to sit on the concrete veranda.

I looked up at the glowing sky, where streaks of red and orange blazed a trail as the sun fell towards the horizon. I was overwhelmed by the Chairman's words and the responsibility I felt on hearing them. There were so many worthy causes to support here. Although Dominic and Rose helped to guide us when we were lost, steering us towards those most deserving, those most in need, it made me sick knowing that we had the power — the money — to decide whether a child went to school, whether or not they would eat, or what their future held. I didn't understand how the world could allow such disparities to exist; how could some people have everything while others couldn't even afford a pencil? I had to believe that it was a simple lack of awareness — that if people knew what was happening in places like this they would do everything in their power to help, to lessen the gap.

Cherie came and sat with me and I tried to explain the guilt I felt, the obligation to help each and every person we came across. She listened, then spoke gently: 'Ems, we who choose to come here have to live with the fact that there are more people in need than we can ever help. You cannot give money to every single person you meet — but then, yes, you do have to live with that guilt. It's a choice we make by coming here, and most people will never be put in that position. The very fact that we're forced to think about it is something in itself.'

I knew she was right, but that didn't make it easier to know that the stash of shillings under my bed that I had saved for my time in Uganda was more than some people here would have in their lifetime. It all came back to the accident of birth. What had I done to deserve this position of privilege? My lucky accident had, in a way, come to feel like a burden, and I couldn't stop feeling so terribly guilty for not doing more.

The Chairman's words continued to ring in my ears during the long, bumpy drive back to KAASO, and stayed with me in the days and weeks that followed. I was haunted by the weight of the responsibility I felt, and as much as I was enjoying finally being a part of school life, I knew that just being in the classrooms was not enough. In my early days at KAASO, all I had wanted was to start doing something and feel useful, but now I realised that I had to go deeper. I had to do more.

Since arriving in Uganda, I had been writing extensive emails to friends and family around the world about my experiences, and had received an overwhelming response from those interested in supporting the school. People I had never met emailed me to say that a friend of a friend was forwarding on my emails and they were fascinated by my story and keen to help. I was blown away by their support. For two months I had thanked them for their messages and added them to my ever-growing group email list. But the Chairman had stirred something within me and now it was time to translate words into action.

Ever since our very first meeting with Dominic, the construction of a new dormitory had remained number one on KAASO's priority list. The building intended as the library and computer lab was currently being used as a dormitory to house 100 girls, much like the now-completed sick bay, which had already been packed with triple-decker bunks to help accommodate the school's bulging population. Volunteers the previous year had begun construction on a new dormitory to free up the library/computer lab, but the project had ground to a halt when funds ran dry. Now, the unfinished dormitory was little more than a collection of bricks strangled by overgrown weeds and long grass. It stood half-heartedly at the edge of Freedom Square, sandwiched between classrooms and other dorms that towered over the incomplete walls. Here was our chance to do something long-lasting, something that would leave a mark on KAASO and help benefit the wider community. It was an ambitious undertaking, but Cherie and Kirsty and I made a decision: we would finish building the dormitory.

We sat with Dominic for hours, piecing together a budget and adding up the figures required to bring this dream to life. We priced out bags of cement, doors, window frames, iron sheeting, roofing poles, labour; everything, right down to the last nail. When the final cost came to more than US$10,000, I wondered what kind of expectations we were creating; our fund-raising plan consisted of little more than sending an email appeal to family and friends. Although between the three of us we knew we could reach a lot of people, it was still an awful lot of money; but anything we could raise was better than nothing, and we had to at least try.

We got to work. We wrote to everyone we knew, outlining the motivation for our fund-raiser and explaining what we hoped to achieve. 'As strange as it may seem for children in rural Uganda to need a computer lab,' I wrote, 'you would be surprised at how great the need is. The children from KAASO who are lucky enough to go on to secondary school end up top of their classes in everything — yet they are failing their computer classes for they have barely even seen a computer before. Around the world, computers are becoming indispensable and Uganda is no exception. At a recent fund-raiser, the District Chairman made a passionate appeal to us: Please help our children to move forward so that we do not become backwards. The world is now a global village, help us to join it.'

I outlined the cost of the project, breaking it down to individual items that people could contribute: for $4 they could buy a roofing pole; for $30, a sack of cement.

'I understand this is a massive undertaking,' I concluded, 'but it would be amazing if together we could help fulfil this major priority for the school, something that would be remembered forever. Many thanks in advance for your support — past, present and future.' It was a long shot, but I had faith that somehow we could do it.

We were not disappointed. By the time our fund-raising

emails had registered as 'sent' from the painfully slow internet cafe in Kyotera, our first donation of $100 had already come through. In the weeks that followed, donations continued to flow in, anything from $30 to $300, and we excitedly tracked their progress on a hand-drawn wall chart in our bedroom. The new dormitory came to be known as 'Kiwi House' because Cherie, Kirsty and I were always referred to as the 'Kiwi Girls'. Dominic would grin every time we sat down for a construction update, telling us that, 'This Kiwi House is going to be the best building in all of KAASO.' It was satisfying to see progress being made; I loved going down to Freedom Square to watch the workmen lining up roofing poles and mixing concrete with their bare feet.

As the fund-raiser continued, Kirsty's time at KAASO came to a close. She had only ever intended to spend three months in Uganda and had a job soon starting in Cambridge, England, where she was moving with Marcos, who was about to begin his Master's degree. I was sad to see her go; and her departure also reminded me just how quickly time would fly — and how much there was left to do. The official opening ceremony of Kiwi House was planned for the school's Visiting Day in October, and there was still a lot of money to be found between now and then.

Back in the UK, Kirsty helped solicit funds, while Cherie and I worked hard to keep donations coming in from our end, sending email updates and photos of the construction as Kiwi House took shape. Money arrived in large and small bursts from family members, colleagues, friends scattered around the globe and, so often in my case, from friends in the sailing community.

One day I received an email from Tom Schnackenberg

and his wife, Annie. Tom is the man who originally asked Dad to join the New Zealand Challenge in 1988, involving our family in the America's Cup for the first time. He and Annie had been deeply moved by my words and had been following my experiences closely over the past months. Now, Annie shared with me the story of her parents, a missionary couple who had moved to Vanuatu, an island group not far from New Caledonia in the South Pacific, in 1943. Tragically, Annie's mother had contracted malaria and died on a remote island when Annie was just nine months old. The stories I had been sharing about the children at KAASO suffering from malaria had struck a chord with her.

'You are an inspiration,' Annie wrote. 'We forward your emails on to our children so that all of us are aware of your absolute dedication. Your descriptions of the huge challenges you and your incredible children face every day are so much like those Dad had told me — amazing that all these years later, the challenges still seem so similar. We are so fortunate to have you, who not just had a vision, but *did* it instead of just dreaming about it.' She signed off saying that she and Tom had deposited $1000 into our fund-raising account and wished us all the best for Kiwi House. I was speechless. I'd had no idea of Annie's family history, and was touched that my stories had resonated so strongly with her. It was a reminder of the importance of personal connections and that seemingly disparate worlds are not always so very far apart.

I was on a high. Funds were rolling in, bricks were being laid, our classes continued to inspire, and I was buoyed by the love and support flooding in from around the globe. I felt on top of the world. I would leave KAASO having made a tangible difference, having found my purpose.

Then Henry arrived at my doorstep with his letter.

His request for sponsorship knocked me off course, shattering the peace I had found and shaking my belief that I was doing enough. The fact that Kirsty had recently agreed to sponsor Ambrose made me feel worse. Ambrose was studying at St Henry's College, one of the top secondary schools in Uganda — where Henry wished to study — and although he was incredibly intelligent and deserved to be at a good school, the fees were crippling for Dominic and Rose. So Kirsty, together with her family, agreed to help towards Ambrose's education. I admired her greatly for it, but I was still so focused on the dormitory fund-raiser; and besides, she now had a full-time job in the UK. What did I have? Three months left in the village, and then no job to go to. And in my heart there was still that old, familiar fear of commitment, that held me back from saying, 'Yes! Count me in for the next six years. I don't know where I'll be or what I'll be doing, but sure, I can take on a twelve-year-old boy, no worries.'

I just couldn't do it. I hated myself for turning Henry down, but at the time I simply couldn't see any other way. I had always refused to agree to something if I wasn't certain that I could honour my commitment.

The way Henry took my refusal so graciously broke my heart. He was so accepting of the hardships he endured; it was humbling to watch. Like so many of the children at KAASO, Henry was a survivor, brought up on a diet of resilience and tenacity, and he always managed to maintain such hope and positivity despite the challenges he faced. Even so, I didn't want to think about what this meant for his future, the dreams he had shared with me. I threw myself into the dormitory fund-raiser, trying to bury my guilt.

Kiwi House wasn't the only thing keeping me busy. During my afternoon music sessions, an idea had formed. I would write, direct, rehearse, orchestrate and stage a school show. As a child I had performed in dozens of productions, and they had helped transform me from a shy child into a confident teenager, buoyed by the appreciation of an enthusiastic audience. I wanted the children here to have the same opportunity. I ran the idea by Rose and Dominic, who responded with overwhelming enthusiasm, and before I knew it I was hammering the keys of Susan's typewriter, writing my first play: a musical, no less — *The Wizard of Mwanza*.

It was an African adaptation of *The Wizard of Oz*, set in Kabira rather than Kansas, and in a jungle not a forest. The Emerald City was the town of Mwanza on the shores of Lake Victoria in Tanzania, and the yellow brick road was a red dirt road back to KAASO. It was to be a pantomime of sorts, incorporating all the songs we had sung over the previous months, and would be performed on Visiting Day just before the opening of Kiwi House, for the parents and guardians who came to visit their children. My hours helping Susan with her typing paid off, and she agreed to duplicate the scripts, which I proudly distributed to the new cast. I had worried that perhaps my idea was a little over-ambitious, but the cast was ecstatic, and as I outlined the play to a room full of grinning faces I realised they were up to the task.

Most of the cast was made up from my music-tree choir. Phionah was to play Dorothy, Immy was cast as Glinda the good witch, and I had created a role as Dorothy's best friend for Stellah, hoping to draw her out of her shell. The youngest children would make a cameo appearance singing 'Twinkle, Twinkle, Little Star', and Brenda danced with delight when I told her she would be among the performers. With only five weeks until opening night, there was no time to waste and rehearsals began immediately.

The rehearsals were another lesson in patience, as the children were often busy in the evenings doing chores, fetching water from the pond or attending evening classes. I had drawn up a careful rehearsal schedule, but this was quickly abandoned and replaced by a new strategy: the children would come and find me whenever they were free to rehearse.

One afternoon, just as I was arriving back at the volunteer house from a music class, Rose appeared on the doorstep with a wide smile, jingling a set of keys. 'Kiwi House is complete,' she announced. 'Would the Kiwi Girls like to take a tour?'

Cherie and I grinned, unable to contain our excitement as we followed her down through the school and watched as she unlocked the heavy padlock on the iron door. Being a construction site, the building was locked when the workers left each evening. Now the dormitory was complete, and as we walked around I was struck by the enormity of it. The high roof was crisscrossed with wooden poles, holding up rows of gleaming iron sheets. The floor had been plastered smooth, all the walls were painted Uganda green, and the windows even had panes of glass. There were two small rooms off the main dormitory for the matrons to sleep in; previously they had slept in a corner of the dorm cordoned off by flimsy flax matting, which fell down constantly. For the first time, the matrons would have a room of their own.

'Rose, it's beautiful!' we said.

'A lasting legacy from our Kiwi Girls,' Rose beamed. 'It is thanks to you we have this!'

Looking around, the realisation of how important this was, not just for KAASO but for the entire community, began to sink in. Moving the girls into Kiwi House meant that there would soon be a functioning library and computer lab for the school and surrounding villages. We had secured funding from the East Coast Bays Rotary Club in New Zealand to fully furnish the library and computer lab, and a local carpenter was already at work constructing shelves, tables, desks and stools. The pile of old laptops — donations from past volunteers — that was currently sitting in the office would soon be set up, and the books from the 'library' that we had once tried to organise could now be transplanted and properly displayed in a more accessible place.

I thought back to the Chairman's words, imploring us to try to attract assistance to help their children move forward in the world's global village. As my eyes scanned down the plaque that listed the names of everyone who had donated to the dormitory construction, I felt that we had, in some small way, done him proud.

Visiting Day dawned with a frenzy of sweeping, cleaning, washing, scrubbing and tidying as the children prepared both themselves and the school for the arrival of their visitors, and for *The Wizard of Mwanza*. As people flooded into the 'theatre' — three classrooms with the flax matting removed to convert them into one large hall — I looked out across the hundreds of faces and suddenly felt nervous. I popped outside to check that the performers were ready, then took my seat in the front row, where my guitar and I were to provide the accompaniment. I nodded to the two little stagehands, to signal that it was time to start, and they dragged my bed sheets — our makeshift curtains — along the rope they were hanging from. We were under way.

The opening scene began and I picked up my guitar. I put my ear to the strings and quietly strummed the first chord, then froze in panic. It sounded terrible. I plucked the strings one by one, and my heart sank as I realised that in the few minutes I'd been outside, the curious children in the front row had turned the tuning pegs and now my guitar was wildly out of tune. I spent the first scene frantically trying to re-tune it, knowing that I had only a matter of minutes before Dorothy would start singing 'Over the Rainbow'. I managed to get it vaguely in tune, deciding that it was close enough and there was enough going on for people not to notice my slightly wayward chords.

In the end, none of that mattered as the children danced and sang their way around the stage, loving every second. Stellah came out of herself, performing better than I'd ever seen before, and the little choir of twinkling stars were a hit with Cherie's hand-painted silver stars tied to their foreheads, Brenda beaming among them. The audience roared with laughter at Dominic in his wizard's cape as he soared across the room, sending the girls, along with two little stagehands and a cardboard Kiwi House, flying back to KAASO. As the last song finished and the children came forward to take their bows, tears rolled down my cheeks. We had done it. The children waltzed off stage, high with exhilaration, and as I looked around the sea of delighted faces in the audience, impressed by their talented children, I thought I might burst with pride.

I went outside to congratulate the children on their performance, but there was little time to celebrate our success as the crowd was already gathering for the official opening of Kiwi House. Together with the children, Cherie and I had made paper chains that ran the length of the veranda, and balloons were swaying in the banana palms that had been freshly planted at the entrance. Cherie had painted 'Kiwi House' over the door, with kiwi birds painted on either side. A blue ribbon was tied across the doorway and a little girl stood with a pair of scissors at the ready.

John Mpagi, a prominent member of the Rotary Club of Muyenga and a huge supporter of KAASO, arrived from Kampala, looking immaculate in his charcoal suit and smart red tie, his shoes shined until they reflected the smiles of the waiting crowd. He gave a moving speech about how incredible it was that three girls all the way from New Zealand had been so passionate about this school to raise such a huge amount of money. He asked us to pass on his immense gratitude to all who had contributed and to let them know that they would forever be welcomed with open arms in Kabira. It was unanimously agreed that Kiwi House was the most impressive building at KAASO, raising the standard of the school as a whole.

John cut the ribbon to rapturous applause, and we were soon overwhelmed by heartfelt congratulations and thanks from countless parents, guardians and locals from the surrounding villages. I felt wholly embraced by the people around me and so proud that my community of family and friends around the world had helped to make this happen. A window, a roofing pole, a bag of cement, a box of nails. Each and every donation had added a part to this whole. I wished that they could all be here for this moment, to feel the crushing gratitude that left your eyes wet and your cheeks aching from smiling.

Visiting Day was full of emotion. I experienced a heart-breaking mixture of joy and sorrow, watching as some children were reunited with family members while others stood waiting at the gate all day for those who never came. It was hard to know who even had a family, as the orphans at KAASO were never singled out from the rest. I had begun to worry that Brenda might be an orphan, so I was thrilled to find her walking hand-in-hand with her mother. She shyly introduced me; I could see the adoration in her face as she looked up at her mother, explaining in Luganda that I was her teacher and the one with the *endingidi* — the guitar.

While it made me so happy to see some children sharing picnics with their families around the school, it killed me to watch the ones for whom no one came. Cherie and I did our best to 'visit' with all the children who had no one, reading their report cards and sharing in the meals that KAASO had provided for them, but nothing could fill the void of an absent parent.

Later that evening, when most of the families had begun their journeys home, Brenda came and found me. She stood clutching a grubby blue-and-white chequered handkerchief, her eyes glowing.

'What's that, Brenda?' I asked, pointing to the handkerchief she so clearly wanted to show me.

She lowered her head and smiled at her hands, then very gently unfolded the handkerchief. Inside was a 500-shilling coin, less than 20 US cents. She picked it up and held it out to me.

'*Mandazi*,' she whispered. A kind of deep-fried bread, the Ugandan version of a doughnut.

I smiled and leaned down conspiratorially. 'How many?'

She held up one finger.

I nodded solemnly and she slipped her hand in mine, walking with me until we reached the road where she stopped, knowing that she must wait inside the school grounds. I went across to the row of shops and bought a *mandazi* for 100 shillings, then came back and handed her the change and her precious doughnut. She thanked me and carefully wrapped the coins back in her handkerchief, returning them to the safety of her pocket. Then, with a wide smile, she took the tiny doughnut and tore it in half, holding out my portion to me.

'Oh, no, no, no!' I cried. She looked distressed, and I knelt down to her. 'Thank you so much, Brenda, you are very, very kind. But I want *you* to have this. *Webale nyo*, I . . . I . . .' I searched for an excuse she would find acceptable. 'I have already had one!'

She nodded her head knowingly; if I had already had a doughnut, then she could accept my refusal. But in a school of more than 600 children you are never alone for long, and she was quickly surrounded. I stood back and watched in awe as she broke her doughnut into dozens of pieces, distributing them to her newfound friends.

I felt a rush of love for Brenda and all the children at KAASO. In a world with so little, every simple pleasure was appreciated, celebrated, savoured. Nothing was wasted. I looked at Brenda's glowing smile, her eyes alight with the excitement of the day: the thrill of having her mother come to visit and knowing that she had seen Brenda perform on stage was already huge — and now a *doughnut*! There was such generosity of spirit, too; all she had, she shared — her joy, her doughnut — not minding if she only got a sliver. As the final crumbs disappeared into waiting mouths, I watched Brenda's face, full of such happiness, such possibility, and the hope that I continued to find in so many children. It humbled me, and filled me with hope of my own. Standing there with Brenda, I believed that, somehow, there would be a bright future for all of these children.

I left the happy group and headed back to the volunteer house. I was on such a high, humming as I walked, that I almost missed Stellah, sitting alone, barely visible under the music tree. I went over to congratulate her on her performance.

'Stellah! Well done today, you were fantastic! Did you enjoy yourself? You looked like you were loving it on stage!' She raised her eyes to meet mine, and I saw that they were full of tears. 'Hey! What's wrong? Come here.' I sat down next to her, wrapping my arms around her thin shoulders.

She fiercely wiped away her fat tears, lips pressed together. In her hands she held her school report, unopened, and the realisation slowly dawned on me: no one had come for her.

I gently took the envelope from her hands. 'Can I see this?' I asked, and she nodded, her eyes fixed on the ground. Her report was impressive: at least 90 per cent in every subject with glowing remarks from all her teachers. 'Stellah, this is incredible! You must be one of the top students in P5! You should be very proud of yourself — I certainly am. And there I was thinking you were going to be a famous actress — now I realise you're going to be a rocket scientist instead!' I drew her close and she managed a half-smile through her tears.

I walked her slowly back to her dormitory and we stopped at the doorway.

'Good night, Stellah. You were a true star today and don't ever forget how proud I am of you.' I was about to add that I was sure her family would be proud too, but then realised that I didn't know if she even had a family. I just hugged her instead.

'Thank you, Madam Emma,' she said with a sad smile. 'Thank you for organising that show and for all you have done for KAASO. We are so grateful. I wish you a good night.' She let herself into the dormitory, while I remained on the doorstep, staring at the closed door. Hot tears rolled down my cheeks as I stood there in the darkness. Joy and sorrow lived in such close proximity here, and it was painful to be slammed with aching heart-break after so much happiness. I pictured Brenda, so full of hope and possibility, holding her mother's hand, the world at her feet. And then there was Stellah, sitting alone, waiting all day for a visitor who never came. The juxtaposition was hard to bear.

Stellah was only eleven years old; she was too young to be without parents. She deserved a loving, caring family to support and encourage her, as I'd had. I felt I needed to give her a hundred hugs to make up for all those she had missed. And yet, astoundingly, in the midst of her sadness she still thought to thank me, to be grateful for my help. But what was I doing to help her?

As I walked back to the volunteer house, I slowly began to understand that I wasn't going to forget these faces, these stories, this aching injustice. I would carry these children with me, and they would remain in my heart long after I left the village.

I collapsed on my bed next to Cherie and we lay side by side, letting the day wash over us, sharing our stories of happiness and heartache. Suddenly my phone's garish ring made us jump, and I raced outside to find reception as I answered the call from an unknown number. It was my parents, calling from the satellite phone on their boat, *Sojourn*, out at sea halfway between Gibraltar and Lanzarote, off the coast of Morocco. They had called to hear about Kiwi House and *The Wizard of Mwanza* and I rattled through the events of the day, tripping over myself to get the words out before the line went dead. The wind was whipping across the boat, making it hard for me to hear my parents, but I closed my eyes and let myself be engulfed by their familiar voices coming fragmented down the line. They listened to my stories, showering me with praise for all I had done; I thanked them, but felt unsettled. I pictured their boat out at sea, skirting around the African coast — all three of us making our way on opposite sides of the same continent.

Yes, it had been a phenomenal day. I had seen my dreams come to life in both Kiwi House and the school show, and I knew that I should feel immensely proud and worthy of my parents' admiration. But there was an image that stuck with me, stopping me from fully celebrating the day's achievements: Stellah, sitting under the tree in the half-light, her tears slowly falling on her unopened report card. That image then merged into another and now it was Henry, standing in the doorway with a letter requesting sponsorship, a hopeful request from a boy I had come to care about so much. And there was me, saying no.

The phone cut out, and all of a sudden I felt a jolt, an instant burst of clarity in which everything seemed obvious. Gramps's words from all those years ago came flooding back to me: *If you feel so strongly, then why don't you go and do something about it?* Despite my own uncertain future, I realised that one thing was certain — I *wanted* to do something about the children I saw before me; I didn't want to forget these faces.

I stared at my phone, willing my shaking hands to redial the number, but hesitating. Did I really understand the enormity of what I was about to take on? It had been a long day, and I was exhausted. I looked up at the canopy of stars overhead, shining brilliantly in the night sky. They reminded me of the children singing their twinkle twinkles, their glittering faces like little stars, full of hope. I so badly wanted to do this, but I knew that once I did there would be no going back.

I stepped off the mound of dirt on which I stood balanced with my phone to get reception, and stumbled over the uneven path back through the darkness to the volunteer house. I was still riding the emotional wave of Visiting Day, and I needed to think clearly and rationally; I needed the light of day. Cherie was asleep by the time I got back to our room and I crawled into bed, enveloped in a blanket of white beneath my mosquito net. I squeezed my eyes shut, hoping that the roosters that heralded the dawn would bring with them the clarity and strength I needed to follow through with the decision that lay in my heart.

CHAPTER
NINE

For the first time since arriving in Uganda, I awoke before the roosters. Sleep had been slow to come, but when it did, it had overtaken me completely. I awoke with a profound sense of clarity. Overnight, I understood what I needed to do. Like Dorothy and her ruby slippers, the answer had been there all along; I just hadn't realised it. It had taken almost six months, but now, in my last two weeks at KAASO, everything suddenly became clear.

Lying in the half-light of dawn, I made a vow that I would come back to Uganda before Stellah left KAASO. She had just finished P5, so that gave me two years to get myself into a position where I could make a financial commitment to her — to let her know that she was not alone, that I would sponsor her. But before that reality unfolded, there was someone who needed my help right now, someone who didn't have two years to wait. As the roosters began to crow, my peace was replaced by renewed impatience. I knew what I had to do, and there was no more time to waste.

I got up and ran outside. The hot, dusty months of the dry season had given way to a second rainy season and the early-morning sky was streaked with dark clouds. Occasional flashes of lightning illuminated the banana plantations. Children were sweeping up the remnants of Visiting Day's excitement and called out to me in greeting, but I just waved and kept moving towards the mound of dirt where I was most likely to get the clear phone reception I needed.

My hands were shaking as I dialled the number, an absurdly long thing that seemed to have far too many zeros. I held my breath, eyeing the heavy skies, willing the rain to hold off as I waited for the line to connect. I tried to imagine the signal, the message I had to get through, winging its way up and out of the village, shooting north-west across the African continent, bouncing off a satellite in orbit and back down to Earth, trying to locate the mast of *Sojourn* bobbing out on the ocean.

Nothing.

I hung up and dialled again, watching as children began to prepare for the oncoming downpour by moving tattered foam mattresses inside and lining up jerry cans to collect the precious cascades of water that would soon be flowing from tin roofs. The dial tone startled me, a distant sound tumbling down the line, a miracle of technology. Above the banana plantation where I stood, a lightning bolt struck and I silently begged my parents to pick up.

Suddenly I was blanketed by the warm calm of my dad's voice. 'Ems! How are you? We were up on deck and almost didn't hear the phone. Is everything alright?'

My heart was pounding as I tried to form the words, quickly reassuring him and Mama, who I knew would be hovering over his shoulder, that I was fine and not to be alarmed by my call, even though we had spoken only yesterday.

Dad, sensing that there was something on my mind, got down to business. 'So, what's happening, Ems?'

I smiled in spite of myself. As far as advice went, it was Mama I rang for the emotional, Dad for the practical. He loved nothing more than to help guide my brother and me through life's major decisions; but now, for the first time in my 26 years, I was asking not for his advice but for his financial support.

'Daddy-o, you know me. I wear my heart on my sleeve and I've spent the past six months trying to be of use, to do something worthwhile, and I know you'll say I've already done so much — but there's something really important I need to do before I leave here and I'm not sure I can do it on my own,' I spoke quickly, acutely aware that the line could cut out at any minute.

'We're listening, Ems.'

'You remember me telling you about Henry?' I asked. 'The boy in my P7 class who I adore, the one who's about to finish his last year of primary school and who wants to become a doctor? Remember I told you about that letter . . .'

The connection faltered and I realised with panic that I had less time than I thought. 'I need your help. I can't leave here without knowing Henry's going to be okay. I thought I could, but I just can't. The thing is, I don't know if I can manage his full sponsorship on my own and I can't say yes without being sure I can see this through till the end.' I had always prided myself on being independent, so it killed me to have to ask my parents for money; but I needed to know that I could stand by the promise I was about to make, no matter what. 'Will you help me sponsor Henry? I'm sure I can manage half the fees if you'll put in the other half ...'

In the background I could hear Mama asking what was happening with Henry and I couldn't help but smile, picturing Dad shushing her, motioning with his hand that he had it under control, as he always did.

Without hesitation, Dad said, 'We would love to sponsor Henry with you.'

I was overcome by a wave of gratitude and relief. In spite of our globe-trotting childhood and the encouragement we'd had to spread our wings and fly, Mama and Dad had made sure to give my brother and me a good grounding in life. They were passionate about education and helped support us through our university degrees, while still requiring us to work through our years of study to ensure that we understood the value of money. Now I was asking them to extend their support beyond their own family and to educate a boy they had never met, and the fact they had such faith in me to agree without question meant a lot.

The first drops of rain had started to fall; soon the skies would open and torrents would flow, turning dirt paths to rivers of mud. Thanking my parents profusely and telling them we'd chat when they reached landfall in Lanzarote, I hung up and raced to tell Henry the good news. I flew across the rickety bridge and along the muddy paths, trails of mud flicking up my back as I ran, but nothing could dampen my elation. I arrived outside the classroom dripping and out of breath, and hadn't even reached the iron door before Henry came running out to meet me.

'Madam Emma! Please, come inside. You are going to be so wet!' he laughed, turning to escort me into the classroom. Rows of wooden desks lined the concrete floor and the children, packed like sardines, looked up with excitement when they caught sight of me, waving and calling out in greeting.

'Thanks, Henry, but it's okay. Let's stay out here — I need to talk to you alone. The rain doesn't bother me.'

He looked puzzled, but simply grinned and waited patiently.

'Henry, my parents and I are going to sponsor you through secondary school.'

He stared at me in disbelief.

'We're going to sponsor you, Henry,' I repeated gently. 'I've just spoken to my parents and they've agreed to help. You can continue your studies at secondary school.'

I watched as the raindrops rolled down his shaved head and past his ears, falling on the shoulders of his thin blue shirt as he stood transfixed, speechless, eyes wide open. There was a classroom of almost 50 children behind him but the world felt silent, as if time was standing still. All I could hear was my own heart beating and all I could smell was the steam rising from the warm earth, and all I could see were the tears of rain sliding down Henry's face.

Suddenly he erupted into an enormous smile that lit the world like a lightning bolt, and he launched himself at me in a forceful hug.

'Eh! Madam Emma, that is really wonderful! Wow . . .' He shook his head and paused, then the reality of my words dawned on him all over again. 'So you mean . . . ?'

I nodded.

'Really?! That is just so GREAT! Thank you so *much* to you and these loving parents. Eh, they must be very good people!'

'They *are* good people, Henry. One day you'll meet them and they will love you.'

'Oh, Madam Emma, I cannot believe . . .' he trailed off. 'Thank you so, so much!'

'It is our absolute pleasure, Henry. You deserve it, you really do.'

'Eh, Madam Emma, I am going to make you *so* proud!'

I smiled. 'You already do, Henry.' I hugged him and sent him back to class — the twelve-year-old boy who had stolen my heart.

The rain intensified but I just stood there, watching him through the barred and glassless windows of the classroom, wanting to stamp this moment forever in my mind. I was thrilled that Henry would be continuing his education beyond primary school, but at the same time it was humbling to be so appreciated for providing something that every child should have the right to. I was acutely aware that it was only because of a lucky accident that I was able, with a single phone call, to alter the course of history for this remarkable young boy; my happiness at being able to change Henry's world was bittersweet, undercut by guilt at having the ability to do so.

Nonetheless, I was on a high as I skidded back up through the mud to share the news with Rose. She clapped for joy, did a little thank-you dance, then poured me a cup of tea.

'Rose,' I said, 'are there many more like Henry? You know, children that need help. And if so, how many?'

'Mmm,' Rose said slowly, 'that is a big question.' She took a careful sip of tea. 'I must be honest and tell you that there are many. It is hard to give the exact number but it is many.'

'I thought so,' I said, my elation quickly fading. 'I gather that Stellah is on her own and I assume there must be others. I just hoped there weren't too many . . .'

'Ah, Stellah. Her family . . . It is complicated.' While the rain continued to fall outside, Rose told me Stellah's story. The second-born in a family of six children, Stellah grew up in a remote village. Her father, still alive today, was an alcoholic who had more children than he could count to different mothers. He treated them all badly and was an abusive, violent man. Eventually, Stellah's mother ran away to work as a maid for a wealthy man in Kampala, leaving Stellah and her sister at KAASO. Stellah's sister was now being sponsored at secondary school by a past volunteer, but Stellah, despite both parents being alive, had no support and was entirely dependent on KAASO to fund her education.

I listened, shocked by the realisation that sometimes having parents could be worse than having none at all.

'The mother, she does what she can,' Rose said. 'But eh, it is not so easy. When you are living as a maid in someone's house, they don't want you to bring your children. The mother is paid so little she cannot even afford the transport to come and visit Stellah at KAASO. That is the situation.'

I didn't want to share my intention to sponsor Stellah with Rose just yet, but I asked if she could put together a list for me of this year's P7 students who would not make it to secondary school without help.

'Of course,' she said, 'you shall have the list by the end of the week. Thank you for that kind heart.'

I left with mixed emotions — it felt good to have made Rose proud, and yet there was a part of me that was worried about what I was getting myself into, wondering what might await me on Rose's list. But I reminded myself that I hadn't promised anything yet — I had merely made an enquiry. The only firm commitment I had made so far was to Henry.

The following night, I screened *The Wizard of Mwanza* on a clunky old TV to a crowd of hysterically excited children — Kyotera's local photographer, Bosco, had recorded the performance on a '90s camcorder. The children shrieked with laughter as they watched themselves singing and dancing around the stage. Brenda found me amidst the thronging bodies and crawled into my arms. She'd had a cough for some time now, and while she had appeared to be feeling better on Visiting Day, now she seemed to be getting worse.

In spite of the hacking coughs that wracked her body, she insisted on watching until the end. When the play was over, I walked her back to the nursery dorm. The solar lighting had gone out and I used my torch to light the way. In the dim beam of light we entered the dormitory and I followed Brenda to her triple-decker bunk bed. She slowly undressed, stripping down to her underwear — except she had no underwear. All that remained was a tattered elastic band around her tiny waist. I helped her onto the middle bunk and went to tuck her in, but there were no sheets on the bed — just a scratchy woollen blanket, and when I pulled it over her it was damp. I remembered Rose telling me that the girl in the bunk above often wet the bed and it would leak down onto Brenda's mattress.

Brenda launched into another coughing fit and I rubbed her back, wondering where that joyful little girl from Visiting Day had gone. This was the same girl who, just a few days earlier, had had it all — a visit from her mother, a 500-shilling coin, a doughnut and dozens of friends to share it with. And now here she was, coughing beneath a soggy blanket under a girl who wet the bed.

'*Webale nyo*, Madam Emma,' she murmured, her voice hoarse.

'*Kale, nyabo. Sula buluunji, nyabo*,' I said, fighting back tears as I wished her a good night. She gave me a half-smile, her eyes battling to stay open while I stood next to her, my hand on hers until sleep overtook her.

I hoped with all my heart that Brenda would get better; but in the days that followed, her condition deteriorated. One morning I found her sobbing in P1 with Teacher Noelle, who said she was 'paining' everywhere — her eyes, arms, legs and head. I couldn't bear to watch her suffer anymore, so I scooped her fragile little body up in my arms and went to find Rose.

Rose took one look at her and nodded. 'She must go home. We will send her to her mother in Kyotera.'

The nursery matron packed Brenda's small metal suitcase containing all her worldly possessions, while Cherie and I waited with Brenda in the volunteer house for her *boda* to come. We read her stories until she fell asleep, then simply sat and watched her as she laboured through each breath. When Rose came to say that it was time for Brenda to leave, we woke her gently. I hugged her goodbye, holding her close as my tears tumbled down the back of her thin dress. She tried to speak, but her throat was raw and her eyes were heavy.

We walked outside to where the *boda* was waiting. The driver hoisted her onto the seat behind him and she wrapped her arms around his waist, resting her head against his back. Then, with a tired smile and a wave, she was gone, weaving up the road, around the bend and out of sight. I wondered whether I'd ever see her again. Even if I did come back within two years, would she still be here? How would I ever find her if she didn't return to KAASO? And what if her sickness was something serious? Brenda was my friend and I would miss her terribly, but there was nothing I could do except let her go and hope that one day we would meet again.

I walked slowly back into the school, struggling to accept our premature goodbye. I was so lost in my thoughts that I almost didn't notice Rose standing outside the volunteer house, waiting. Her list was ready. Summoning all my strength, I followed her into the dining room and we sat down together. When she pulled out her immaculately written list, I could barely hide my despair when I caught sight of the names, each carefully numbered in the margin. There were eighteen of them.

One by one, we went through the story of each child, their family history, their economic situation, their academic record, their prospects and their aspirations. The list contained children abandoned by their parents, orphans brought up by elderly grandparents, children with twelve siblings and parents who survived on subsistence farming, those with mothers who sold pancakes on the side of the road to raise funds for school fees, or with parents battling HIV/AIDS. Each story rolled into another more tragic than the last and I scribbled furiously, trying to gather as much information as I could.

We were just over halfway through the list when Rose paused and looked over at me. I was biting the inside of my mouth, trying to quell the flood of emotion that threatened to overtake me. It was a battle I was losing.

Rose motioned for me to put my pen down, and she spoke gently. 'When Dominic and I first started KAASO ten years ago, the situation was very bad. There were so many orphans, so many people in such need, and they would come, asking for our help. Dominic and I would say to each other, "How can we choose? How do we decide who we can help and who we cannot?" It was so difficult to turn people away when it seemed they all needed assistance in their own way.'

'I don't know how you did it. How did it not break you?' I asked, wondering how I would have survived when I could barely make it through a single list without wanting to burst into tears.

Rose smiled. 'You remember Dominic's words from our very first meeting? "We must think of the greater good." He was talking about construction then, but it also applies to the children here. Dominic and I listened to all the stories and we felt the pain of each of them, but we had to be very strong, to only select those most in need. If we had acted with our emotions for every child, every story of hardship and struggle, then KAASO never would have lasted. And in that case, none of these children you see here today would have received an education. If you want to survive in a world of such challenges, you must act with your head not your heart. You cannot be pulled by every child, every story, or you will lose yourself. Over time, we learned that we could only do what we could do. And we came to accept that what little we did, that had to be enough.'

I thought of the strength it must have taken to be selective, to not be swept away by each incoming tide of tragedy they faced, especially in those early days. If they had let themselves be consumed by every struggle, it surely would have broken them, and KAASO would have collapsed. It was Dominic and Rose's ability to think of the bigger picture that had made KAASO possible in the face of such hardship.

'I understand it's very difficult,' Rose said, 'and there is much sadness in these stories. But remember there is also hope. These children have been given the chance of an education at KAASO and for that they are so very grateful. Anything we can give them from here is a blessing. We can't do everything, but we can do *something*.'

Rose's words triggered a memory from my childhood. It had been my first realisation that we were not all born equal and that sometimes there was only so much you could do. I was eight years old, and on a Mexican roadside. My family was living in San Diego at the time, during the 1992 America's Cup, and we would often make trips down to Tijuana, just a short drive south of the border.

One night in Tijuana, my family had all gone into a restaurant for dinner but I had been unable to get past the front entrance where I had stopped in my tracks, fixated. A girl my age was stringing together intricate mobiles made from coloured beads and shells. I watched as her fingers worked deftly, the strings like music in her hands. She glanced up at me, a shy smile, and then went back to her work. I was captivated; I had to have one of her mobiles.

Mama had come hurrying back outside, frantically scanning the crowded street. Relieved, she smiled when she spotted me crouched down on the ground next to my new friend; wherever I went I was always finding lost souls to add to my collection of childhood imaginary friends. I was thrilled when Mama agreed to buy me one of the girl's mobiles; I slowly studied each one, carefully weighing up my choices before settling on one that had bright blue beads mixed in with white shells.

Mama paid the girl and thanked her, then guided me into the crowded restaurant where my dad and brother were seated on colourful wooden chairs, surveying the giant menus that overflowed with various combinations of beans, rice and guacamole. A mariachi band serenaded us as we ate and I proudly showed off my new mobile to Nick, but he was far more interested in the enormous burrito that had appeared before him than my piece of local craft.

It was dark when we went to leave the restaurant, and Nick and I were looking forward to sleeping in the car on the drive home. We stepped outside, and almost tripped over my little friend who was still sitting there making mobiles. I was horrified. All that time we had been sitting inside eating, drinking and laughing, talking together as a family, she had been sitting outside, alone — and no doubt hungry — on the concrete steps.

'Mama, why hasn't she gone home yet? Where are her parents?' I asked, worried.

'I don't know, Ems, but I'm sure she'll be heading home soon. Come on, let's get you kids in the car,' she said, taking my hand.

'No! Wait!' I was upset. 'We can't just leave her here. Has she had dinner yet? What if she doesn't know the way back home?'

Dad bent down to meet my eyes. 'Emma-lou, I'm sure she is just waiting for her daddy to come and pick her up soon. He told her to stay where he left her so we should just let her be.'

I studied his face, unconvinced. 'Well, we should at least wait a bit so she's not lonely,' I insisted.

Nick was getting fidgety, so Dad went to get the car while

Mama waited with us and the little girl continued with her craft, oblivious to my worries. By the time we left, we'd bought two more mobiles. If I'd had my way we would have bought her entire stock, and taken her with us too, but I had to believe that Dad was right and there was someone coming for her soon. At the time I didn't understand that buying her mobiles was all we could do for this little girl; I was still too young to accept that we couldn't take her home with us. I remember crossing the border that night, my face pressed to the window, watching people lined up waiting to make a run for it. It was my first vivid memory of being confronted with poverty and injustice and feeling powerless to do anything about it.

That moment in Tijuana never left me. Now, sitting with Rose, I thought back on those two little girls — the one from Tijuana with the dancing hands making her mobiles on the street, and the one from New Zealand with the searching eyes who couldn't get the other girl out of her head. As Rose continued with the rest of the children's stories, I slowly began to understand that even if I could help just one child, it would be something.

When Rose had finished, we sat in companionable silence. I was humbled by her wisdom, her level-headedness, her insight, and the dedication she had to this community. She was only 36 years old, ten years older than me, and yet it seemed that she'd lived a hundred lifetimes already. If I learned nothing else in my six months in Uganda, I hoped I could learn to be a little like Rose.

Eventually, I broke the silence to ask the question I had been dreading.

'Rose, can we . . . *rank* them? In terms of their . . . well, their neediness?'

She nodded, a slow smile forming. I had understood.

'We will do it,' she said.

'For the greater good,' I said, with a smile.

So we sat, the future of these children in our hands; and, with the stroke of a pen, determined their fate. As I had done with the fund-raising for Kiwi House, my sponsor-seeking plan consisted of simply sharing Henry's story and my family's sponsorship of him with my group email list, hoping that it might spur on others to sponsor a child. I had no idea how many sponsors I'd be able to find — if any — but at least I would know which children needed help the most. I could start with them. It was better than nothing.

While the new sponsorship drive meant that my journey with Dominic and Rose was far from over, my time at KAASO was coming to an end. Henry had left to sit his final Primary Leaving Examinations, promising to try his 'level best' to make my family and me proud. I had watched him go, turning around to flash his brilliant smile, and I felt so full of hope for his bright future — and privileged to know that I would now be part of it.

Saying goodbye to my music-tree choir was not so easy. I had taught them 'Leaving on a Jet Plane', and I couldn't stop the tears from falling as their little voices rang out, so full of emotion. Stellah started sobbing as she sang, and I looked around to find most of the children in tears. *Why am I singing this?* I thought. It was more than I could bear. I stopped mid-song, but they insisted we continue.

'Madam Emma, this song is our *favourite*! Please let us sing.'

So we did, and while I tried to simply focus on the beauty of their voices, all I could think about was how much I was going to miss them. We sang until it was dark, and then Stellah, Immy and Phionah walked me back to the volunteer house. Stellah threw her arms around me and then slipped me a note before running to catch up with the other girls.

Her words blurred on the page as I lay in bed that night reading by torchlight:

Dear Madam Emma,

I will miss you so much. Please don't go.

I love you with all my heart.

On the morning of our departure, I struggled to close my exploding backpack. Although I had left all the clothes I had brought to Uganda with Rose to distribute to those who needed them most, I had been gifted a mountain of mats, baskets, beads, letters and hand-drawn pictures by the children and friends from the local community, which meant that I was leaving with almost as much as I had arrived with.

The rain outside was coming down in sheets. I watched out the window as the children ran around collecting water, and thought back to the days when we had run inside when it rained while the rest of the school was running out into the deluge. We had felt like such outsiders, so lost as to how we could be helpful. Then a breakthrough in the classrooms had turned our fate around. We had built a dormitory that would forever bear our name, and now I had Henry, keeping me tied to KAASO for years to come. Over the past six months this place had come to feel like home, and leaving brought such a deep sadness within me that it made my bones ache.

As Cherie and I loaded our packs into the back of Dominic's car, the children began to gather. They milled about excitedly at first, then confusedly, and when the realisation dawned on them that we were actually leaving for good, their faces crumbled. Susan, the matrons and all the teachers were there to say goodbye, and I felt overwhelmed as I looked from one to the other, trying to remember every detail through brimming eyes. I said all my goodbyes with a heavy heart, but leaving Rose was by far the hardest. How to farewell this woman who had become like a sister, a guide, an interpreter, an inspiration and a best friend? When I walked over to her, she smiled and said simply, 'There are no words to express everything in my heart. We will meet.'

I hugged her tightly and, even though a fresh stream of tears escaped me, I knew she was right. There was dust here that wouldn't wash off, smiles that wouldn't fade, and laughter that couldn't be silenced. And now I had a connection that couldn't be broken: the list of children needing sponsors was carefully folded in my journal.

I was just about to get into the car when I caught sight of Stellah, standing alone under the music tree. She was clutching a roll of manila sheets — the songs we had sung together, which I had left with her to keep our choir going. I went over to her and gave her one last hug. Her shoulders shook, and I battled to keep my voice steady as I whispered three words in her ear. She looked up at me in surprise, and I nodded. A small smile spread across her face through her tears.

Dominic called out to me that it was time to leave, and I

gave Stellah one final squeeze and jumped in the car. As we pulled out of KAASO, I thought about the commitment I had just made. There was no going back now and I knew it. But it felt right.

I had come to Uganda hoping to contribute in some small way. I had thought that if I did nothing more than draw some smiles and sing a few songs, I would be happy. What I didn't realise was that being here would completely and fundamentally change me; that it would not be enough just to spend six months as a one-off volunteer. Uganda had opened my eyes to a world beyond my own; and now that it was part of me, part of my history, part of my soul, I was committed. And that no longer scared me.

I had learned more in these past months than in any other time in my life; the growth curve had been exponential. Now the winds of change were blowing me towards new horizons. While I didn't want to leave African soil, I knew I had to go — but I also knew that this was not the end.

Driving through the village, the words I had spoken to Stellah rang through my mind. Dominic's music was blaring from the stereo, a typically upbeat Ugandan tune that made it impossible to feel sad. There was an overriding rhythm that pervaded all aspects of life here and I had come to learn that even in times of sadness, people laughed. So I smiled as I looked out across the banana plantations, my own words following me on the long drive north. I'd made promise, a vow:

'*I'll come back.*'

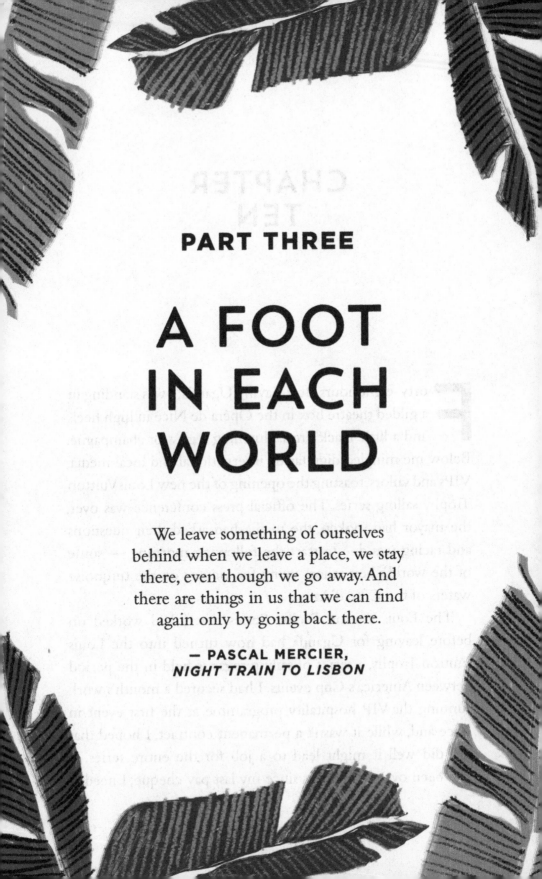

PART THREE

A FOOT IN EACH WORLD

We leave something of ourselves
behind when we leave a place, we stay
there, even though we go away. And
there are things in us that we can find
again only by going back there.

— PASCAL MERCIER,
NIGHT TRAIN TO LISBON

CHAPTER
TEN

F orty-eight hours after leaving Uganda, I was standing in
a gilded theatre box in the Opéra de Nice in high heels
and a little black dress, clutching a glass of champagne.
Below me mingled dignitaries, international and local media,
VIPs and sailors, toasting the opening of the new Louis Vuitton
Trophy sailing series. The official press conference was over,
the mayor had spoken, the media had asked their questions
and racing was due to start the following morning — some
of the world's best sailors vying for victory on the turquoise
waters of the Côte d'Azur.

The Louis Vuitton Pacific Series that I had worked on
before leaving for Uganda had now turned into the Louis
Vuitton Trophy, a series of sailing regattas held in the period
between America's Cup events. I had secured a month's work
running the VIP hospitality programme at the first event in
Nice and, while it wasn't a permanent contract, I hoped that
if I did well it might lead to a job for the entire series. It
had been over six months since my last pay cheque; I needed

to start earning money if I was going to have a chance at following through on the promises I had just made in Uganda.

But I wasn't prepared for how much my sense of normal had shifted. I had thought that when I arrived back to 'normal' life I would feel immediately at home, back where I belonged. I hadn't anticipated the complete dislocation I would experience — the whole way I viewed the world had changed, and what once felt so normal now felt strange and unfamiliar. I heard a cork pop and looked down to see magnums of Moët & Chandon flowing like fountains, trays of exquisite canapés circling the room on the arms of tuxedo-clad waiters, and huge rounds of unpasteurised cheeses oozing their French perfection. I gripped the edge of the railing and closed my eyes.

That morning, after a two-day stopover in London, I had flown to Nice, where Dad was waiting for me at the airport. He was doing on-the-water commentary for the Louis Vuitton Trophy and had arrived the week before to get set up. *Sojourn* was safely moored in the Canary Islands and Mama would be arriving the following day.

Walking into the arrivals hall, I had looked around dumbfounded, unaccustomed to seeing so many white faces. It felt as if the world had been bleached, stripped of colour. Dad quickly spotted me and engulfed me in a warm hug, then hauled my dusty backpack into the car and drove me to my hotel.

He came with me up to my room, where I marvelled at the tower of fluffy pillows on the enormous bed, the crisp linen sheets and the luxuriously carpeted floor. There were no mosquito nets, no bars on the windows, no towels or scarves hanging from the roof. Just clean white walls, double-glazed windows framed by heavy curtains and an air-conditioning unit that kept the room at optimal temperature at all times. I gazed longingly at the bed, wanting to dive in and bury myself in a sea of Egyptian cotton, but there was no time — the regatta was starting the following day.

Not wanting to dirty the plush cream carpet, I dumped my pack on the tiled floor of the bathroom and had a quick shower, knowing that there'd be no time for that later — I would be going straight from work to that evening's press conference and opening cocktail party. I dressed in the uniform Dad had brought for me, then dug around inside my pack to find the bag containing the black dress and high heels I had bought in London in preparation for that evening. I stuffed them in my tote bag and followed Dad back to the car.

We drove straight down to the port, where the Louis Vuitton Trophy event village had been set up. Cranes were lifting the race boats out of the water after the day's training, and in the background the harbour presented a picture-postcard scene of the Côte d'Azur.

Up ahead were the offices where I was now due for a meeting, scheduled to bring me up to speed on that evening's press conference and cocktail party in the Opéra de Nice. Thanking Dad and telling him I'd see him later that night, I pulled out my notebook — a new one, not smudged with red earth like those I was used to — took a deep breath and walked into the meeting room. *I'll be fine*, I told myself, *I can do this*. It was my old America's Cup family and I'd always been capable of moving between worlds; this time it was just a bigger contrast — from a village in Uganda to another, very different, village in Nice.

But the fact was that I just couldn't do it. I'd underestimated

TOP Me as a baby, ashore in the Belep Islands in New Caledonia with my parents (standing), a French friend and some locals. MICHAEL POPE

BOTTOM At the 1995 Team New Zealand victory party in San Diego, with the children of commentator Peter Montgomery and sailing legend Sir Peter Blake. Clockwise from left: me, Kate Montgomery, Sarah-Jane Blake, Nick Blackman (my brother), James Blake and Johnny Montgomery. JO BLACKMAN

TOP The original thatched-roof classroom at KAASO and some of its very first students in 1999. COURTESY OF ST PAUL KAASO PRIMARY SCHOOL

BELOW LEFT The girls and their triple-decker bunks, hung with mosquito nets, inside Kiwi House in 2009. EMMA OUTTERIDGE

BELOW RIGHT Henry at KAASO in 2009, when I first met him. EMMA OUTTERIDGE

TOP LEFT With Brenda on the bridge at KAASO in 2009. CHERIE BROOME

TOP RIGHT With Cherie (centre) and Kirsty (right). We're dressed in *gomesi* (traditional Ugandan dress) for a 2009 function. IVAN KRUH

BOTTOM One of my early music sessions at KAASO in 2009. KIRSTY PELENUR

TOP Rehearsing *The Wizard of Mwanza* in 2009. Phionah is pictured front row centre, dressed in purple, with Stellah to her right in the yellow dress. CHERIE BROOME

BOTTOM The opening of Kiwi House in 2009. I'm pictured with Rose, Cherie and the KAASO girls who had just moved into Kiwi House. DOMINIC MUKWAYA

TOP Brenda leaving KAASO on the back of a *boda boda* in 2009. I didn't know if I'd ever see her again. EMMA OUTTERIDGE

BOTTOM Me and Cherie on our final day at KAASO in 2009, with Teacher Sarah (left), Dominic (centre) and Rose (far right). ENOCK WALUGEMBE

TOP My little friends at KAASO on our reunion in 2011. Brenda is pictured bottom right. EMMA OUTTERIDGE

BOTTOM LEFT With Kirsty (centre) and Cherie (right) at KAASO in 2012, preparing for Kirsty and Marcos's Ugandan wedding. DOMINIC MUKWAYA

BOTTOM RIGHT Visiting Henry at St Henry's College in 2012. EMMA OUTTERIDGE

TOP LEFT Me and Kirsty, dressed in our formal Louis Vuitton uniforms, at the official opening ceremony of the Louis Vuitton Cup on 4 July 2013. PAUL TODD

TOP RIGHT Me and Nathan just days after we got together in 2013, at the infamous Louis Vuitton Cup party in San Francisco. PAUL TODD

BOTTOM Sharing a moment with Nathan in the America's Cup village after racing in Bermuda. SANDER VAN DER BORCH

TOP With Henry and Stellah at KAASO in 2013. ROSE NANYANGE

BOTTOM Brenda proudly showing me her English exam paper on which she scored 87%. EMMA OUTTERIDGE

TOP LEFT KAASO children wishing their sponsors and supporters a Merry Christmas, 2013. EMMA OUTTERIDGE

TOP RIGHT Dropping Brenda off at her *jajja*'s (grandmother's) for the 2013 Christmas break. ROSE NANYANGE

BOTTOM Crossing the equator en route to the airport in 2013, with Dominic and Rose and their three youngest daughters, Rhona, Denise and Prima. STELLAH KYOMUKAMA

TOP Dominic outside KAASO. EMMA OUTTERIDGE

BOTTOM With the children in their after-school uniforms on the KAASO school field in 2014. HARRIET FLOWER

TOP LEFT Rose pictured with some of her children and KAASO students outside Kiwi House. EMMA OUTTERIDGE

TOP RIGHT Picking up Henry and David from St Henry's College in 2014. EMMA OUTTERIDGE

BOTTOM Damian and his *jajja* in 2014, pictured outside his *jajja*'s home. EMMA OUTTERIDGE

TOP Speech Day celebrations at KAASO in 2014. EMMA OUTTERIDGE

BOTTOM Brenda performing as part of KAASO's Speech Day. EMMA OUTTERIDGE

TOP The Kiwi Sponsorships Graduation Ceremony 2015. I'm pictured with Dominic, Henry, David and other graduates, cutting the celebration cake on the veranda of Kiwi House. COURTNEY LLOYD

BOTTOM With Henry on the steps of Kiwi House after his graduation. COURTNEY LLOYD

TOP With Rose and the 2015 Kiwi Sponsorships students in Freedom Square at KAASO. COURTNEY LLOYD

BOTTOM Brenda with her *jajja* outside her *jajja*'s house in 2015. EMMA OUTTERIDGE

TOP LEFT My brother, Nick, with Henry outside Henry's family home in 2015. EMMA OUTTERIDGE

TOP RIGHT Inside the KAASO classrooms, where students sit three to a desk. BEAU OUTTERIDGE

BOTTOM With Rose at a KAASO celebration. BEAU OUTTERIDGE

Walking the road to Kabira with KAASO students.
BEAU OUTTERIDGE

the toll that the past six months had taken on me. Just a few hours after that first briefing, I was standing frozen in my little black dress in the theatre box from where I had watched the press conference, and I was panicking. The formalities were long over; I knew I was supposed to be down there mingling with the guests — except I had forgotten what to say. The art of conversation in such a context was now lost to me. I suddenly felt too high up; I needed to get down from the galleries. Putting down my glass, I tried to coax my brain into switching to French as I made my way unsteadily down the marble staircase. I was vaguely aware of some kind of classical music playing amidst the clinking of glasses and the chatter of voices. The chandeliers cast an uneven light across my path and I wavered in my newly purchased high heels, the hard leather foreign to my rough village feet.

Engulfed by the crowd, I felt my panic continue to rise. A waiter in a white suit appeared and seemed to be asking me something, but the words just washed over me. His face blurred and I realised with horror that I was crying.

'*Non, merci,*' I mumbled and turned on my heel. I needed to get out. I was pushing my way through the sea of bodies when someone grabbed my arm. *Please let me go,* I begged silently.

'Come on Ems, let's go. Just you and me.'

Relief flooded through me — it was Dad. I nodded numbly, and let myself be led outside to where the cool autumn night brought the air rushing back into my lungs. We found a restaurant in the Marché aux Fleurs, and soon I was sitting at a table looking across at the most familiar face in the world, which was offering all the support and understanding I needed to get through the reverse culture shock and sense of dislocation I was feeling.

'It's so good to have you back, we've missed you,' he said. 'Jo will want to hear everything tomorrow, but I can't wait until then so you're just going to have to repeat your stories for her. Tell me about Uganda.'

And so I sat, pouring my heart out to my dad in Nice. He listened intently, his tears falling silently as I told him everything. Every story, every detail, all those things that couldn't be shared on the phone. I was so grateful to have him there to listen, and as I watched his face across the table, so full of love and care, I knew that he would help me through these next few weeks. But as one story flowed into another and I painted the picture of my rough, raw world in Uganda, so different from the polished, shining one I now found myself in, fear began to seep into my bones at the realisation that I would have to give up one for the other. I just didn't see how I could continue to go to the village and then slot back into my sailing life, or be here on the glittering French Riviera while still holding the dusty paths of Uganda in my heart. It seemed impossible not to have to choose between the two, and even though Dad reassured me that I would find a way, the thought of having to decide made me feel sick.

The days that followed were a blur. It was November and snow fell on the Alps, a spectacular, albeit freezing, backdrop to the sailing as icy winds whipped down from the mountains. I escorted guests from the VIP lounge on to a waiting superyacht from which we watched the racing, at times motoring around the headland to Villefranche-sur-Mer for long lunches when dramatic afternoon wind-shifts halted proceedings. Racing usually ran late, and I would stand up the bow of the superyacht in my thick jacket, buffeted by the winds as the sun sank behind the race boats, watching the horizon swallow the light, my thoughts straying back to Uganda.

Back ashore at my desk, I had set my screensaver to be a slideshow of photos from KAASO. I would find myself sitting there, staring at the photos while tears flooded down my cheeks, and eventually I had to take them down. I had said I was up for this job; now I had to follow through. So I battled on, struggling through tasks that once came easily, constantly questioning everything — why had I gone to Uganda in the first place, why had I left, and what was I doing here now?

In between the various evening functions I caught up with old friends and tried to articulate what I had seen and experienced in Uganda, but every time I felt my words fall short. As much as people wanted to hear my stories, it was still too soon and I was finding it difficult to speak of one world in the context of another that was so different. In the end, I realised that to survive these few weeks, I simply needed to shut my mind off from trying to bridge such a colossal gap, and just run on autopilot. Thankfully, in spite of my initial meltdown at the opening cocktail party and the occasional tearful moments at my desk, I did a good enough job for my boss, Christine, to offer me work for the rest of the Louis Vuitton Trophy series, running the VIP programme for the following year at ports around the world.

Matt and I had kept in touch throughout my time in Uganda, and after my month working in Nice he organised a surprise trip to Barcelona. The two of us spent several glorious days getting to know each other all over again, wandering the cobbled streets and ducking into little restaurants and cafes. Matt spoiled me, wanting to make up for all the food and wine I had missed over the past six months. But while I knew that he only meant the best, every time I opened a menu and converted the prices from euros into Ugandan shillings I burst into tears, thinking about how much maize that translated to. Trying to calm this neurotic girl stuck between two worlds, Matt would deliberately steer the conversation towards Uganda, hoping that sharing my stories would help bring me back from my slump. As the days went by, I slowly opened up, and by the end of our time in Barcelona nothing could stop my flow of stories.

During my final weeks at KAASO, Matt had heard a lot about Henry and my family's sponsorship of him. On my last night in the village, Matt rang me, telling me that not only would he sponsor one of the children on Rose's list, but he also had a friend, a fellow superyacht captain, who was interested in helping out, and together the two of them would sponsor a second child. I knew how much my journey had meant to Matt, who had always dreamed of doing something similar, but he had a difficult family situation which meant that he needed to work hard to support not only his parents but also their new spouses and his step-siblings back in Australia. He didn't have the freedom I had to just take off and follow his dreams without looking back, but knowing he could help with sponsorships meant a lot to him. And to me.

After Barcelona I said goodbye to Matt, with a promise to meet again soon, and flew to the Canary Islands where my parents were waiting on *Sojourn*. It had always been Dad's dream to cross the Atlantic as a family, and now his dream was about to come true; well, almost — he had three out of four family members on board. Nick, a professional sailor, had the most important regatta of his year about to take place in Malaysia so was unable to join us, which meant that Dad would have to settle for just me and Mama as his crew. The forecast looked light, but when we set sail across the Atlantic in early December — the best time of year to do the crossing — our boat was stocked with enough food to take us around the world and back three times.

We ended up breaking records for the longest Atlantic crossing in history, rolling on a windless sea for 24 days. Time was measured by the rising of the moon and the setting of the sun as the days rolled slowly by. Flying fish shot across the ocean's surface as if launched by underwater cannons, skittering over the waves until their tiny wings gave out and they plunged back into the deep blue.

At night, phosphorescence often glowed brilliantly in our wake; sitting up on watch, though, I was fixated by the darkness of the churning water deep below. We were carefully harnessed to the boat after dark, but that didn't stop my overactive imagination from dwelling on the impossible horror of falling overboard. I watched moonlit sunrises, spellbound as the world grew lighter and the sun prepared to make its appearance, a hazy glow where the sky met the sea and a sense of anticipation hanging in the air. To think that this incredible phenomenon happened every morning but most days of our lives we missed it. Days passed slowly, with nothing on the horizon but an endless stretch of blue infinity and the allure of what lay beyond.

I may have been out of Africa, but I was still far from home comforts: sailing across the Atlantic meant we had limited power and diesel. We had to conserve water, take difficult showers on rolling seas, hand-wash clothes in buckets, and face constant uncertainty and changing weather. When your world is continually rocking, even the simplest task becomes a challenge. The boat would buck and kick like a rodeo horse, throwing us around at random, so we always had to be alert, ready to hold on when a stray wave hit. I would often clamber up to the bow to sit wedged between the forestay and the anchor winch, scanning the horizon for any sign of life. We had seen dolphins every day for the first few days, but now, hundreds of miles out at sea, there was nothing but the three of us and the salty water lapping against the boat's fibreglass hull.

The long hours of solitude, however, were perfect for contemplation. I had the whole world to myself in the middle of a great ocean. Some nights the clouds would swallow the moon and I would be engulfed by darkness, falling thickly like a blanket across the sky. Other nights, the sky would be alive with stars, a brilliant canopy overhead.

One night on watch, not long after we passed the halfway point of 1500 nautical miles, I was lying in the cockpit looking up at a sky alive with movement as shooting stars tumbled through the darkness. It took my breath away. This exploding spectacle felt like an incredible gift — alone out at sea, it seemed like this was a private show for my eyes only. But as I gazed up in awe at the dancing sea of lights, my thoughts kept going back to Uganda. I was still trying to process everything I'd experienced, trying to consider how to adjust to life out of the village. I'd often wondered how people reconciled such different worlds, how they went from one to another with such seeming ease, without appearing to carry the weight of their previous experiences with them. I was unable to leave

Africa behind; it was staying with me long after the dust had washed off my feet.

As another trail of light blazed across the night sky, I thought of the children, my little twinkling stars, and wondered if they could see this same sky from the village. The sails were slowly flapping, another calm night, and I was reminded of a Katherine Mansfield quote I had once read, part of a letter she wrote to Ida Baker in 1922:

> *How hard it is to escape from places. However carefully one goes they hold you — you leave little bits of yourself fluttering on the fences — like rags and shreds of your very life.*

And suddenly I realised that this was exactly how I felt about Uganda. It wasn't something I could just process, file away and move on from — it was something that was now incorporated into my very being, a deep-rooted awareness that would live inside me forever. Unless I was going to move back to the village and live there permanently, I had to accept that life would go on and I would need to move with the ebb and flow of the tides, but I knew that a part of me would always be there, fluttering on that fence.

As *Sojourn* continued to crawl across the Atlantic at a snail's pace, I began to get impatient. Before leaving Uganda I had put together a document about sponsorship, complete with photos and bios of six children I hoped to find sponsors for —

the 'top six' on Rose's list. In my final group email I shared
Henry's story and attached my sponsorship document in the
hope that it might inspire others to come forward. And it did.
Cherie and her family agreed to sponsor a child, as did my
aunts from New Zealand who had been following my journey
closely over the past six months, supporting me with words of
encouragement as well as monetary donations towards Kiwi
House. Along with Henry and Matt's two sponsorships, that
meant that almost all of the children were covered — which
was wonderful, but I was still eager to have the final two
children accounted for before the school term started. Mid-
Atlantic, however, this was not an easy task.

Finally reaching the island of Barbados, we celebrated our
arrival and took our first shaky steps on land, re-living the
moment the three of us had shared 26 years earlier in the Bay
of Islands after sailing from New Caledonia. Ashore and back
in the world of communications, I found an internet cafe and
emailed Rose to share the good news that, including Henry,
five of the top seven children on her sponsorship list were
now covered. She wrote back thanking me for my work, but
telling me that there were in fact six student sponsorships
sorted. I was confused; was she including Kirsty's sponsorship
of Ambrose in her count? I wrote back, gently explaining
that there had been a misunderstanding and unfortunately
the sixth student, Teddy, did not have a sponsor but I would
keep looking.

After our trip was over, I flew back to New Zealand to
start work on the next Louis Vuitton Trophy event, and it
was there that the mystery was solved. I was at a celebration
party in honour of my brother's sailing team which had
been victorious in Malaysia, winning the overall World

Match Racing Tour for 2009. The party was being held in the ballroom of the Royal New Zealand Yacht Squadron and the room was packed when I entered. Making my way to the window, I stood gazing up at the Auckland harbour bridge towering overhead, its lights mirrored on the water in the still of the night. Waiters circled the room with trays of canapés, and for a minute I was transported back to that night at the Opéra de Nice. I could feel that old familiar sense of being overwhelmed threatening to consume me, and had to force myself to turn and face the room.

Fortunately, I found myself looking into the smiling eyes of Don Macalister, a close friend of my parents, who, along with his wife Gendy, had been a huge supporter of my trip to KAASO. Before my departure they had provided me with medical supplies, not only enough to cover the potential needs of the girls and me, but also enough to help stock the school sick bay. Don was an oral surgeon and he and Gendy were no strangers to helping those in need. Five years earlier they had filled their 45-foot cruising yacht with medical and dental supplies and sailed through the Pacific Islands, offering free dental treatment in villages on remote islands scattered throughout coral reefs.

They had enjoyed reading about my experiences in Uganda, commenting on how my emails had opened their eyes to a part of the world they had never been to, making them realise how incredibly fortunate they were. They had also shared my experiences and photos with their young grandchildren, pointing out how happy the children in Uganda were — even if, by our standards, they had very little — and helping their grandchildren build an appreciation for everything they had.

Don and Gendy had also contributed generously to Kiwi

House, and now their support was being extended even further: they were the mystery sponsors of Teddy. I had forgotten that in my sponsorship drive I had given out Rose's email address. Not wanting to bother me mid-Atlantic, Don and Gendy had simply liaised directly with Rose about their sponsorship of Teddy.

'Well, that makes sense,' I said, laughing as I explained to Don that I had thought I was going mad when Rose had said we already had six sponsors. 'Thank you so much for all your support, it really means the world to me — and to the children.'

'It's our pleasure, Ems,' Don said. 'Reading those emails you sent each week really struck a chord with us. We felt like we were there with you, living every joy, every heartache, right alongside you. Anything we can do to help out, we will — and I really mean that.'

'Thanks, Don, I appreciate it so much. It's such a relief to know that some of these children are going to make it to secondary school. It was so overwhelming when Rose first brought me her list of potential sponsor students — there were 18 names! But seven children really, really needed help, and now we have six out of those seven covered. School goes back next week, and I'm so happy to know that almost all of them will be able to attend.'

We were interrupted by speeches as Nick and his sailing team took to the stage. I clapped loudly, proud of my brother and all he had achieved. When the speeches were over, I went to go and give him a hug, but Don stopped me for a moment.

'Sorry, Ems, I just wanted to check — did you say you had found sponsors for *six* out of the seven children? What about the seventh?'

I knew that he hadn't intended to make me feel bad, but Don's question reminded me that there was still a child who would not make it if I didn't do more, try harder. I couldn't help feeling a little deflated. But I didn't feel that it was my place to *ask* people for their support — I needed them to come to me. Six years was too big a commitment for sponsors to make half-heartedly out of a sense of obligation. So I reminded myself of Rose's words and dutifully repeated them to Don, explaining that I could only do what I could do and I had to be happy with that. I forced a smile so that my face wouldn't betray my feelings of inadequacy.

Don nodded slowly. 'Yes, absolutely, of course. Well, amazing work, thanks for getting us involved. Gendy and I are really happy to be part of this.'

I thanked him again and went to find Nick amidst the buoyant crowd.

Early the next morning, I received a phone call. 'Ems? Hi, it's Don. You've got your seventh.'

'My seventh . . .?'

'Sponsor — the final one you were looking for. I couldn't stop thinking about it last night, so I called some old friends of mine and Gendy's. I've been telling them about your stories and they'd love to help. I'll send you through their details. All seven kids covered now. I think it's better that way.'

And so the 'Kiwi Sponsorships' began. Grinning from ear to ear, I thanked Don profusely. In Uganda I had felt like I was merely a small pebble in an ocean of need. I had hoped that through my writing I might be able to raise some awareness of KAASO and get people thinking about a world beyond their own. Now that I was out of the village, I could feel the ripples from my pebble spreading out across this huge sea of support, reverberating across the globe. I hung up the phone feeling excited that my steps were gathering momentum as others fell into stride with me.

As it turned out, Don and Gendy weren't the only ones feeling the ripples. Annie, our family friend whose mother had died of malaria in Vanuatu, was taking big steps too. Following our Atlantic crossing, my parents had continued to sail towards New Zealand, and a year later I joined them on the boat in Vanuatu in between working on Louis Vuitton Trophy events. Life was good. I loved my job travelling the world to the different regattas, and whenever I had time off I would visit Matt on the superyacht he worked on in Turkey. I arrived in Vanuatu excited to see my parents and ready for a month of island-hopping, only to find that we had acquired a deeper purpose to our cruising.

Having learned that we would be sailing close to Emae, the island of her early childhood, Annie had asked if we would go ashore on this tiny landmass of 32 square kilometres, with its population of just over 700, to try to find her mother's grave. Annie had been back once, many years earlier, when her now 33-year-old son was just a baby, but it had been a difficult trip and she was nervous about returning. We happily agreed to her request, making our way slowly through the archipelago of Vanuatu until we arrived at Emae.

We anchored off a long, sandy beach, then went ashore in the dinghy. We had been in touch with a local man named Robert who had volunteered to be our guide, and he met us on the beach with an entourage of young boys, each carrying a machete and a sling-shot — which could only have been for show as there were no obvious threats on this peaceful island. The boys reminded me of some of the older children at KAASO and I tried to hide a smile, touched by how seriously they took their escort duties. Together, we walked inland along a jungle path and eventually stopped at a large, leafy mango tree under which Annie's mother, Alice, had been put to rest. I was moved to see that the grave had been carefully cleaned and laid with tropical flowers in honour of our visit. After paying our respects, we left Alice to her resting place and our troupe of local guides showed us around the rest of the small island, taking us to visit the local school and walking us through the tiny villages scattered throughout the lush tropical bush.

Annie was incredibly grateful for our pilgrimage on her behalf, and was so inspired by the stories from our visit that soon afterwards she decided to go back herself. With her husband Tom, their two sons and their daughter-in-law, they flew to Vanuatu and chartered a yacht to sail to Emae. Thus a family was reunited with a grandmother they never knew who had died on an island far from home more than 60 years earlier, and a connection was re-established between a Kiwi family and the people of a remote Pacific island. Since that first visit, Annie and her family have been back several times, and are now active in supporting the local school and wider community on the island Annie once called home.

I loved hearing the updates from their journeys back to Emae, and as the ripples flowed outwards from Annie's stories, I knew it was time for me to continue my own journey.

In July 2011, just over a year and a half after I'd left KAASO,

I fulfilled my vow to return — and this time, I brought my parents with me. I was paying half of Henry's school fees and was now in a position where I could also commit to paying Stellah's fees for the next six years. I felt proud of what I'd achieved. While other 28-year-olds were getting married and buying cars and houses, I was still a globe-trotting nomad who had left her heart in Uganda. I could think of nothing I'd rather put my savings towards than Henry's and Stellah's education.

Dominic picked us up at the airport and we made our way down to KAASO. The roads were as bad as I'd remembered, but the colours seemed, somehow, even more vibrant. Music blared, marabou storks circled, trucks piled to the heavens rolled past and *bodas* swerved suicidally, but such chaos felt strangely normal. There were the inevitable detours — cousins to visit, people to greet — but none of that bothered me; I just smiled and enjoyed the overpowering sense of belonging.

I looked across at Mama, sitting next to me in the back seat, as we bumped over the rutted roads; meanwhile, Dad rode in the passenger seat next to Dominic, who chatted animatedly, thrilled to finally meet his 'Kiwi parents'. I couldn't wipe the smile from my face. I was doing what I had promised: I was on my way back. My joy was tinged with sadness, however; I knew that Matt would have loved to be joining me but we had decided to go our separate ways. He had been a phenomenal support throughout my first trip to Uganda and since then we had shared some amazing adventures, but that chapter had come to a close. We parted as friends, and he promised me that no matter what, his support for Zakia and Caroline, his two sponsor students, would not stop.

As we continued south I willed the sun to stay in the

sky. I wanted my parents to see the vibrant scenes that lined the roadside and to be able to take in their surroundings on the way to the village in the light of day, but darkness fell suddenly. I reminded myself that what mattered most was that they were here, that I was finally able to share with them this place that meant so much to me. As we got closer, excitement coursed through my veins. I couldn't believe how familiar everything felt despite the fact that it had been so long since my last visit.

We turned off the main road, and at long last began the final part of our journey down the red dirt road. Dominic turned to me with a wide grin. 'Is Madam Emma ready to go back?'

'I sure am!'

'Oh, Daddy, the children will be *so* excited to meet you and Mama!' Dominic said, beaming over at Dad, his new best friend.

'But they'll all be asleep by now,' I said, trying to hide my disappointment. It was close to 10 p.m., so we'd have to wait until morning to see all the children.

'Don't worry, Ems,' Mama said, and squeezed my hand. 'There's plenty of time. I'm just so happy that we're actually here! This is it!'

'I know, it all feels like a dream,' I said, looking out at the glow of kerosene lanterns as we drove through the last village before Kabira. My heart was racing as my anticipation grew, but it was also undercut by a niggling fear. I bit my lip and turned to Mama. 'What if the children don't remember me? It's been so long. They might not even know who I am after all this time.'

She shook her head and assured me that they would;

but she *had* to say that — she was my mother. I frowned, unconvinced, and stared out the window into the darkness.

As we came over the hill, there, in the beam of the head-lights, I saw it. The dusty tin sign, the wooden fence, the banana palms, the rusty iron roof of the volunteer house. Dominic tooted as we pulled in, and never could I have prepared myself for what happened next. I heard them before I saw them — hundreds of children emerging from the darkness, racing towards us. Before I had a chance to react, the car door was flung open and little hands were grabbing me, dragging me out into the throng. They screamed and cheered and flung themselves at me with catapulting Ugandan hugs.

'Well be back! Well be back! Madam Emma is BACK!' they cried, using the Ugandan version of 'Welcome back'.

I looked over to see that my parents had also been swept away by the mob and were standing, overwhelmed, while hundreds of hysterical children hugged them in welcome. Mama caught my eye and called out over the crowd: 'I think they remember you, Ems!'

I laughed as I was engulfed by yet another excited hug. Through the darkness I saw a figure standing there smiling, taking in the scene. It was Rose. I fought my way through the mass of bodies and threw my arms around her.

'Well be back, Madam Emma. We have been waiting,' she said with a smile. Before I had time to reply, the children had burst into song and the air was filled with voices.

'*Wimoweh, wimoweh!*' They sang their little hearts out, launching from one song to the next while I tried to make out who was who in this sea of faces grinning in the night.

Someone had found my guitar in the back of the car, and thrust it into my hands. Leaning against the car, I began to play while the children cheered that their beloved *endingidi* was back. We sang every song I had ever taught them and I was blown away that they still remembered all the words. Even the children too young to have been at KAASO when I was here last knew the words; the other children must have taught them.

I had just started the third encore of 'Que sera, sera' when I felt something pressing against my legs. I looked down to see Brenda, her arms wrapped around me, her eyes glowing with delight.

And then the tears began to fall and would not stop. I was home.

The month that followed was, quite simply, extraordinary. When returning to a place that you love so much, there is always the fear that your memory of it will be greater than the reality, that over time you will have idealised it beyond what it was. But somehow, my return to KAASO exceeded my expectations in every way imaginable.

The library and computer lab were fully functioning, with a full-time librarian overseeing proceedings. The books that Cherie, Kirsty and I had brought with us in 2009 had been added to those from the makeshift 'office library', and other volunteers had slowly been growing the collection. An assortment of old laptops, gathered over the years, had been set up in the computer lab, and volunteers and teachers had been running computer classes with the children.

The sick bay was finally being used to treat children,

and the incidence of malaria had dropped dramatically due to school-wide mosquito spraying — and a full-time nurse who was able to recognise the symptoms early and stop the children suffering as much as they had been in 2009.

My parents and I piled into the back of Dominic's car and, together with him and Rose, drove around to visit each of the seven sponsor children at their secondary schools. We started with David, who was being sponsored by Cherie's family at a school just down the road from KAASO. From there we turned south to the agricultural farm school where my aunts' sponsor child, Munjera, was studying with Zakia, sponsored by Matt and his friend Shane. Don and Gendy's sponsor child, Teddy, was out on the school field watching a volleyball game when we arrived, and she came racing over to greet us, all four foot of her engulfing us in warm hugs. We bounced our way over atrocious roads through the back streets of Masaka to Caroline's dusty high school, sending her greetings from Matt, then carried on north to see Justine, whose sponsors were Don and Gendy's friends. Dominic's car only just made it up the steep dirt road to the top of the hill where Justine's secondary school was perched.

Each of the children, now teenagers, was shy to start with, formally greeting us and responding to all our questions with murmured answers of, 'Fine, thank you.' But they delighted at the letters and photos I had brought from their sponsors around the world, and their faces lit up as they learned about the faraway people who cared so much about them despite never having met them. In turn, the students showered us with thanks for our visit and asked us to pass on their huge appreciation to their sponsors for their generous support. I loved watching the interaction between the students and my parents, the stories they had been hearing about for so long being brought to life before their eyes.

We saved Henry for last. My parents had been writing to him for the past 18 months and receiving letters of gushing gratitude in response, and I knew that both sides were incredibly excited to meet each other. We pulled into the gates of St Henry's College and signed in with the gatekeeper. Driving up into the school, we were met with curious stares from the other students, wondering who these incoming *muzungus* could be. As we parked outside the main hall, the school came alive with movement as excited faces jostled for position to see what would happen next. There, in the midst of them all, with the biggest, most brilliant smile, was our Henry. He came running over and threw his arms around me.

'Eh, Madam Emma! You came back!'

'Of course I did, Henry,' I smiled. 'I couldn't miss seeing you all grown up at secondary school!'

He beamed proudly and turned his attention to my parents. 'Good afternoon, Mum and Dad. I am so happy to meet you at last! I humbly thank you for this great opportunity and I promise to perform better and better and to make you so proud!'

I could see my parents fighting to contain their emotions as they engulfed their honorary son in a warm hug. 'We are so happy to meet *you*!' Dad said, eyes shining. 'We've been hearing so much about you from Ems and just love getting all your letters. You have already made us so proud — we're just so happy that we can help.'

We stood in the school compound outside the office block while Henry continued to thank my parents over and over again and proudly showed us his report card, which confirmed that he was excelling in his studies and getting involved in all aspects of school life. We parted with big hugs and promises to keep in touch, and rolled slowly out of the school gates. I was staying in Uganda for a full month, but my parents' time at KAASO was up. Dominic and I waved them off in Kampala after a brief but incredibly fulfilling ten days.

Back at KAASO, it was with great joy that I fulfilled my vow to Stellah. Since my departure in 2009 she had been keeping our music-tree choir going, and it made me so happy to sit together again, singing the songs we had once sung and learning new ones I had brought with me. Now thirteen years old and in her final year of primary school, Stellah was still incredibly shy but had the kindest heart I'd ever known, and I watched in admiration as she patiently helped guide the younger children through the songs. After our session, I asked her to stay behind. Putting down my guitar, I explained to her that part of the reason I had come back to KAASO was to let her know that I would sponsor her through secondary school. She stared at me, dumb with shock, her eyes wide, the words not sinking in. I thought back to the similar moment I had shared with Henry, standing in the rain, recalling his equally stunned face and his inability to comprehend the enormity of my words.

I smiled and gently repeated myself. 'I'm serious, Stellah. I'm going to sponsor you. You can continue your studies next year.'

'Oh Madam Emma!' she cried, launching herself at me in a fierce hug. I pulled her thin body close and slowly exhaled, savouring the moment I had waited so long for. I felt like I had finally completed something that had been suspended within me for a long time.

Despite my joy, not everything among my friends at KAASO was rosy. While I was thrilled to see Brenda healthy and full of life, I soon learned that her mother, whom I had met on Visiting Day, had died not long after I left KAASO in 2009. Her father, young and unreliable and unwilling to accept the responsibility of a child, was left to care for her but he often didn't bother to come and pick her up for the holidays; Brenda usually remained at KAASO under Dominic and Rose's care. I hoped, naïvely, that Brenda was too young to fully understand her father's betrayal, but as I watched her going about her business at school, now eight-and-a-half years old, I realised that she was old enough to feel the full weight of his failure.

Bigger issues were also affecting the school. In the last week I was there, drastically rising food prices and overwhelming inflation forced KAASO to finish the term early. Unable to continue feeding the children, the school had no choice but to send its students home to their families. Parents and caregivers flooded into the school grounds to pick up their children, but I soon realised with despair that the children far outnumbered the adults; by the end of the day, there were still over a hundred little faces, looking around bewilderedly, wondering why no one had come for them.

I asked Rose why so many had ignored the school's request to pick up their children. She just sighed, and reminded me that parents faced the same issues of rising food prices that KAASO did. Families that were unable to support their own children simply left them at school — out of sight, out of mind. It reminded me of that heart-breaking Visiting Day when I'd watched children wait at the school gates for relatives who never came — except that this was not simply a missed visit; this was a dire situation in which KAASO literally had no food to sustain the remaining children. Eventually, the school population dwindled until only a few children remained, Brenda among them.

I spent my final days at KAASO attempting to distract these 'forgotten' children from the fact that no one had come for them, playing games and singing songs until my voice was hoarse.

On one of my last nights in Uganda, I went up KAASO hill, which had been one of our favourite spots back in 2009, and sat looking out across the valley, a patchwork of green. In spite of my happiness at being back, there was guilt weighing on my mind. Soon I would be going back to my other world — a world of food and wine and running water and electricity and home comforts. I would be jumping on and off planes, travelling the world, seeing things the children here couldn't even begin to imagine, and it fell heavily on my conscience. The fact that in the year and a half since leaving KAASO I'd been able to go from being an unemployed volunteer to someone who earned a decent income, saving enough money to pay half of Henry's fees and all of Stellah's, demonstrated the mobility of the society I lived in. Although I was thrilled to be helping them both, I was still keenly aware that it was just a lucky accident of birth that gave me the power to do so.

Amidst all the need I saw in the village, it was hard to feel that I was ever doing enough, but I tried to quell the feelings of inadequacy that threatened to overtake me by repeating Rose's mantra to myself — *you must act with your head not your heart, and not get swept away by every story. You can't do everything, but you can do something*. I reminded myself that my luxury of having a choice didn't need to be a burden; if I used my fortunate position to help others as best I could, then I shouldn't have to feel guilty.

In a world where everything happens slowly, my month in the village passed all too quickly, and suddenly it was time for me to be rocketed back to my other reality. The Louis Vuitton Trophy series had come to an end and the next America's Cup cycle was starting up. I was shortly due to move to Paris to work full-time with Christine in the Louis Vuitton head office, flying to the various America's Cup World Series events from my Parisian base before moving to San Francisco, the venue for the 34th America's Cup, the following year.

As I said my goodbyes to everyone I knew and loved in the village, I began to wonder how I could sustain these expectations I had created. Would I really be able to keep coming back to Uganda once I started full-time work rather than just the contract event work of the past eighteen months? The irony was that even though I was now in a financial position whereby I could commit to my two sponsorships, with that privilege came time pressures. How would I get enough time off to keep returning to this place I loved so much? It was so far away in every sense imaginable — geographically, psychologically, physically. I knew that I didn't want to live in the village forever, but I desperately didn't want to lose my connections there either. How could I juggle two such different realities?

As my plane soared over Lake Victoria, I pressed my face to the window with a sinking sense of dread. I had left with no promises this time; no whispered words to signal my return. I knew that as much as I loved KAASO, I had a job now — a serious job that would require all my time and energy. The truth was that I honestly didn't know when I'd be back.

CHAPTER
ELEVEN

It was early January 2012 and I was in the Bay of Islands for a final trip home before moving to Paris. It was so nice to be there and to have our family back together — my brother and his English girlfriend, Grace, now lived in London and had joined us to celebrate our first Christmas as a family of five.

Summer in the Bay of Islands was always full of sailing, and the bay filled with boats of all sizes as the Bay of Islands Sailing Week got under way. As usual, we had a cast of thousands coming and going from my parents' house on the beach: friends, family, sailors and stragglers. One night, at one of the many barbecues on our deck, we had a group of sailors over, including Simon Gundry, an old family friend and round-the-world yachtsman.

'So, Uganda. How was that?' he asked at the dinner table. He was a man of few words, but those he did speak counted. If he was asking, it meant that he was genuinely interested.

I looked to my parents to answer. It made me so proud to

hear them talking passionately about our experiences together, and I watched Simon's outwardly tough exterior soften as he listened, spellbound, to their stories, hanging off every word.

The following morning, I walked out on to the veranda with a cup of tea and found Simon sitting with Mama, leafing through my photo book. For Christmas that year, Mama and I had made photo books for each other, documenting our time together at KAASO, and Mama loved showing them to the many visitors who wandered through the door, bringing her stories to life with the bright images. Simon said nothing, just nodded to me and then gazed at the little faces beaming up from the pages in his calloused hands.

We sat in silence for a moment, and when he looked up again there were tears in his eyes. With his bushy moustache and solid frame he looked as gruff as they came, but he had an enormous heart. He had six children of his own, and he worked hard and did well out of the concrete business he had established in Auckland.

'I'd like to sponsor one of your kids,' he said.

I stared at him in disbelief, the sleep barely gone from my eyes. A minute passed, and Mama motioned to me to thank him.

The words suddenly sank in and I jumped to life. 'Oh, wow! That's amazing! Thank you so much, Simon. I really, really appreciate it.'

He shook his head and stared down at the page, where a little girl from my P1 class looked up at him. 'Kids need someone to love them. Can't have them dropping out of school like that. Your mum told me how it all works. I'm in.'

He swallowed the last of his coffee, patted me on the back and turned to leave. 'Well, I'd better be off. Let me know how much you need,' he called over his shoulder and walked down the stairs.

Mama was unable to contain her excitement and gave me a big hug, in the process spilling my untouched tea, which I was still holding. 'Isn't that great, Ems? You know how much he loves kids, and when he heard about what you were doing he said he wanted to help. What's that now — nine children? I'm so proud of you,' she said, kissing my cheek before going inside to empty the dishwasher from last night's festivities.

'Ten,' I murmured, looking out to sea, still unable to believe it. Two months ago I had been working on an America's Cup World Series event in San Diego. I was sitting in the media centre one day with Mélanie, a good family friend and the wife of Bruno Troublé, a French sailor who had been instrumental in creating the Louis Vuitton Cup back in 1983. As was usual for me now, the conversation turned to Uganda. Once, in Nice, I had struggled to speak about KAASO without the tears forming, but now I found I was unable to stop talking. As I poured out my stories to Mélanie, the race commentary blaring in the background, she suddenly grabbed my hand and, just as Simon had done, told me she would sponsor a child. That made nine — the original seven students plus Stellah.

Simon drove away, giving me a wave as he left. As I watched him go, I felt so grateful to be surrounded by such an amazing community of people who were so willing to help. The waves crashed on the beach in front of my parents' house and the bay began to fill with boats. I thought of all the oceans Simon had crossed, and the itinerant lifestyle Bruno and Mélanie had led thanks to their involvement in the America's Cup. There was something about the fluidity of life in the sailing world that seemed to make helping people on the other side of the world not such an outrageous prospect.

Ten children sponsored. I grinned. The Kiwi Sponsorships were growing. It was going to be a good day.

I went inside to help Mama. After a string of large dinners over the past couple of weeks, she had decided it was time for a quiet night. 'Let's just have the five of us tonight. We can have a simple dinner and finally get an early night.'

I nodded in agreement; I had work to do. I had to contact Rose to share the good news that she had another child to find for Simon's sponsorship. She and I had come up with a simple system for our sponsorships: I would notify her of any new sponsors, and she would come back to me with the child at KAASO who most needed support. I didn't want to create any expectations by having lists of children to be sponsored each year, as it was hugely important to me that sponsors came to me and not vice versa. I understood how big a commitment it was, and I needed to know that it was *their* idea, not mine. Simon's sponsorship had come at the perfect time — the new Ugandan school year was just about to start, so it meant that another child could start secondary school along with Juliet, Mélanie and Bruno's new sponsor child.

That afternoon Dad went into the local town of Russell to catch up with some old sailing friends, and he phoned Mama on his way home: he had invited a few mates for dinner. I rolled my eyes when Mama told me, but she just laughed — this was typical Blackman style. Grace and I set the table for sixteen.

Dad came back with Simon and a bunch of other people I didn't know. The Global Ocean Race, a double-handed round-the-world yacht race, was taking place at the time and the boats were currently stopped over in Wellington. In one of the crews was a friend of Simon's who had come up to the Bay of Islands for a break during the stopover; the rest of the group seemed to be part of his entourage.

Among them was a British man in his mid-sixties named Mark Blomfield, whose role I couldn't quite work out — he seemed to be somehow involved in the race but it didn't look like he was part of the crew. It turned out that Simon had just met him that evening in Russell and, in typical Simon fashion, had insisted that Mark come with him to dinner at our place, assuring him that the Blackman door was always open. Mark thanked Mama profusely for having him over, apologising for barging in on our family like this. He seemed terribly proper, but there was a spark in his eyes that intrigued me and I went over to introduce myself.

'Lovely to meet you, Emma,' Mark said, with a warm smile. 'Your father tells me you're moving to Paris to work for Louis Vuitton soon? How exciting. And then on to San Francisco, is it?'

'Yes, I'll be based out of Paris but travelling to the various America's Cup World Series events before moving to San Francisco. I'm really looking forward to it,' I said, and I was — but I failed to mention how terrified I was of being based in the Louis Vuitton head office, wondering what I would wear and whether I would ever fit in among a bunch of European fashion gurus. 'What brings you to New Zealand?' I asked.

Mark, ever modest, didn't tell me that he was the European sales manager of a private jet company that was funding one of the Global Ocean Race teams. Instead, he simply said that he was here for some sailing. Before I had a chance to ask more, Mama was calling me to help with the dinner.

'Well, all the very best in your travels,' Mark said. 'I am sure you will do a marvellous job.'

I thanked him and went inside to find Mama.

After dinner I went to speak to Simon, promising to let him know who his sponsor child was as soon as I heard back from Rose, and thanking him once again for his support. Simon just grinned. 'You're the one doing all the hard work. I'm just happy to help.'

While everyone else sat out under the stars finishing the last of the wine, I noticed Mark inside standing at the coffee table, flicking through our photo books. I went inside and he looked up at me, embarrassed.

'Oh I'm terribly sorry, I didn't mean to pry. I just couldn't help noticing these books. Is this you?' he asked, pointing to a photo of a girl attempting to carry a jerry can of water on her head, surrounded by children walking back from the pond.

I smiled. 'Yes, it is. That was on my last trip back to Uganda with Mama and Dad in July. It was amazing.'

'Your last trip? You've been before? Is this a regular thing? What do you do over there?' Mark was full of questions, his face alight.

'Yes, I first went out to Uganda in 2009 and spent six months volunteering at the primary school you see in those photos — it's called KAASO, and it was set up by those two — Dominic and Rose,' I said, pointing them out as Mark slowly turned the pages. 'It started as a school for orphans with just twelve children but today there are over 600 children. It's an incredible place. The Rakai District where the school is located is where HIV/AIDS first hit hardest in Uganda and so many people were wiped out, mostly parents of— Oh, that's Henry,' I interrupted myself, distracted by his beaming face smiling up at me from the page. 'He's the boy I sponsor with my parents. I organise sponsorships for children leaving KAASO to help get them through secondary school — I've got ten in total now,' I added proudly. 'They're such amazing children, it's a real pleasure to help them. Actually, that was the best part of my last trip back, visiting all the sponsor students at their schools and seeing how much they'd grown since I last saw them in 2009.'

As I spoke about the sponsorships and the development of KAASO over the past ten years, sharing stories of both the successes and the hardships faced by the school, Mark asked more and more questions. He explained that he and his wife, Jan, had recently returned from a trip to Rwanda and were deeply moved by the stories they heard and the extreme poverty they encountered.

The more I spoke, the more I realised that this was what I loved: sharing my stories, watching people get swept away by the passion in my voice. Mark was a perfect stranger; he hadn't received any of my group emails, but the deep concern in his eyes made me feel that I needed to tell him everything, to fill him in on all I'd seen and experienced. As Mark told me in turn of his time in Rwanda, it only encouraged me to share more; I knew he understood what I was talking about.

Slowly it began to dawn on me that I had become a bridge between these two worlds — my community at KAASO and my sailing community around the world — and all those fears I'd had when I first arrived in Nice about having to give up one world for the other melted away. I realised that people *were* interested, they *did* give a damn. Even if they were sailors used to spending their lives at sea, there was something about this landlocked African village that struck a chord with them, and I began to understand that *this* was my purpose. I didn't need to live permanently in the village; I needed to be out here, in the world, meeting people and speaking from the heart on behalf of the community I loved so much.

Halfway through my stories, Mark motioned for me to stop. 'Sorry to interrupt, but I'd just like to give you this. It's my card, it's got all my contact details. You see, I'd like to sponsor a child,' he said. 'If you'd be so kind as to email me the bank information, I'll transfer you the money. I'd really love to help.'

Two sponsors in one week? I was over the moon; I felt like jumping for joy. 'Thank you so much, Mark. That's wonderful, really! Wow, thank you . . .' I said, smiling. But as I stood staring into the face of this man I barely knew, a dark thought crossed my mind. *Oh God, I hope he doesn't feel like I'm telling him all these stories to guilt-trip him into feeling obliged to help?* I immediately began to backtrack. 'Thanks, but you really don't have to . . . I'm sorry, I get so carried away talking about KAASO, I've talked your ear off, you probably felt backed into a corner. Look, thanks so much for your kind offer but let's not rush into this — it's a huge commitment. Why don't you just talk to your wife and have a think about it?' I was floundering, falling over my words. I felt terrible — had all my sponsors felt pressured into getting involved?

'Nonsense, I wouldn't have offered if I didn't want to do it, and Jan will be delighted to help. We're sponsoring a child and that's that. Now, tell me more,' he said. 'How exactly do the sponsorships work?'

His expression clearly spelled out that he was serious about wanting to help, so I took a deep breath and continued. I explained that it was a six-year commitment, that the children attended boarding schools around the country, and that Rose helped manage the sponsorships by receiving the funds I transferred and going to each school to pay the children's fees and checking up on them whenever she could. The more questions Mark asked, the more I felt convinced that he had chosen to sponsor a child of his own free will.

'The best part is the hope in these children's eyes,' I said. 'They've had nothing, no one to support them, and all of a sudden they feel like they *matter* — that there is someone out there who believes in them. It's incredible the effect it has on them.'

Mark gently took his business card out of my hands and reached into his shirt pocket. I watched it happen in slow motion, terrified that he might be retracting his offer. Had I gone too far? Instead, he took a pen from his pocket and, on the back of his card, wrote 'x2'.

'I'd like to sponsor *two* children, please.'

I almost kissed him.

I flew to Paris still buzzing from my summer of sponsorship success. While the Ugandan school year got under way, I launched myself into work. I was living in a hotel room in the Latin Quarter on the Left Bank, and walked to work each morning over the Pont Neuf — freezing in February when icy winds whipped through the city, and glorious in August when little sandy beaches popped up along the banks of the Seine. Work was frenzied, with an intense travel schedule; I spent more time out of Paris than in it, working remotely from Christine's house in the South of France, from hotel rooms around Italy, and on trans-Atlantic flights between Boston and Paris. We were preparing a host of different events: the Louis Vuitton Classic, a classic car rally from Monaco to Venice; the America's Cup World Series events in Naples and Venice; and a black-tie dinner for the America's Cup Hall of Fame Induction Ceremony in Newport, Rhode Island.

Mark kept in regular contact in between his own busy travel schedule, emailing me frequently with questions about KAASO and Charles and Anthony, the two boys that Rose had chosen for him to sponsor. Mark was so encouraging of everything I did that it felt like I had my own private mentor, cheering me on from across the globe.

Mark was not the only one supporting my Ugandan endeavours. When Cherie and Kirsty emailed me to say that they were hoping to organise a Kiwi Girls reunion at KAASO that European summer, I was torn. I had only been working for a few months, certainly not long enough to have accrued leave for a three-week trip to Uganda. But when I approached Christine with the idea, she not only supported it — she encouraged it. We both knew that I would be working more than my fair share over the coming year, and my proposed Ugandan trip fell during a brief bit of down-time between events. She approved my leave without question.

When I told Mark that I would soon be heading back to Uganda, he was ecstatic. He and Jan were enjoying a break at their holiday house in Mallorca, and when I added that I would be celebrating my twenty-ninth birthday the following week with friends in Ibiza, I was thrilled but unsurprised when he flew over in a helicopter to meet me. Over a glass of wine at Ibiza airport, we talked about Uganda before my flight back to Paris. He had brought with him letters and pocket money for Charles and Anthony, and I promised to deliver them and update him on the boys' progress.

Back at the office in Paris, Christine had another surprise for me. She had been in touch with the head of the Louis Vuitton IT department, telling him about my upcoming trip to KAASO and the computer lab I had helped to create for the school. The following week, twelve two-year-old laptops arrived at my desk, cleared and ready for me to take to KAASO. I managed to fit half of them in my suitcase, and Christine had one of my colleagues send the rest to Uganda by DHL. I felt overwhelmed by the support I had around me in what I had thought would be such a daunting environment. As Christine slipped a wad of euros into my hand 'to help the children however you can', I understood once again that people cared more than I realised.

On the fourth of July, I flew out of Newport, Rhode Island, after a week of America's Cup sailing and rooftop cocktail functions. The Hall of Fame dinner had been a great success and I was ready to be reunited with my Kiwi Girls.

Since leaving KAASO, Cherie, inspired by the dedication to education she had witnessed in Uganda, had decided to go back to university in Auckland and complete her studies. She was now halfway through her degree in Development Studies and was enjoying learning the theories behind so much of what we had seen in Uganda.

Kirsty had spent the past three years living with Marcos in Cambridge, UK, and was now coordinating the scholarships and alumni programme for the Gates Cambridge Scholarship, an organisation dedicated to building 'a global network of future leaders committed to improving the lives of others'.

Marcos and Kirsty had recently got engaged, and Kirsty had emailed Dominic and Rose to share the good news, suggesting that maybe we could have a small engagement celebration as Marcos would also be coming to KAASO.

What followed was a full-blown Ugandan wedding.

Pulling in through the school gates at KAASO with Dominic, I found the girls and Marcos already there — they had arrived the week before me. Wedding preparations were in full swing. Rose had had a beautiful Ugandan wedding *gomesi* (traditional Ugandan dress) made for Kirsty, as well as bridesmaid dresses for me and Cherie. A *kanzu* (what looks like a white nightgown worn over a suit) was waiting for Marcos. A cow was to be slaughtered — much to the horror of Kirsty and Marcos, both vegetarians — and a feast was being prepared.

Dominic and Marcos sat and discussed budgets, and we all slowly began to realise just how much this wedding meant to the school and the community. At KAASO the previous year with my parents, listening to Dominic and Rose call them Mummy and Daddy, I had come to understand that we were seen as part of their family. Now, Kirsty and Marcos's wedding celebrations made me realise that we Kiwi Girls were also considered part of their family. Everyone from the surrounding villages wanted to ensure that Kirsty and Marcos had a proper celebration and felt the full weight of the community's respect and appreciation for their support of KAASO.

The wedding day dawned hot and sticky, the dry season in full force. Excitement was tangible throughout the school as children swept the compound and lined up ready for the wedding procession from Dominic and Rose's house to the makeshift school hall. The children cheered and waved branches as we walked down the dusty path, our bodies dripping in the sweltering heat. There was no formal ceremony, but Dominic and Rose gave heartfelt speeches, Brenda, Immy and the other choir members did a performance they had prepared for the bride and groom, and there was dancing and feasting throughout the day. Later that night, once the children had gone to bed, the whole village was invited into the front compound and a local DJ provided music over a crackly speaker. One of the teachers stood up and made an announcement in Luganda, and everyone began to form a line. We were confused at first, but then the realisation dawned; we watched, mortified, at the scene unfolding before us.

'No, they're not . . . ?' Kirsty's eyes were wide.

The entire village had lined up before the bride and groom and, one by one, people came forward to kneel before them and deliver gifts. Wedding presents. When the subject had come up earlier, Kirsty and Marcos had explicitly said to Dominic and Rose that they absolutely did *not* need wedding presents — but this was a tradition and the people clearly believed that it must be upheld. And so we sat as men and women, old and young, came forward to present their gifts — baskets of avocados, bottles of soda, parcels of peanuts, bundles of fruit wrapped in banana leaves, and any other offerings they could spare. As embarrassed as Kirsty and Marcos were by the pile of gifts that soon towered before them, it was an incredible display of how much we meant to the people here. We felt well and truly embraced as part of the community, accepted among them despite our foreignness.

The next day, wedding celebrations over, it was time to

start the sponsor visits. We started with Charles and Anthony, now attending Sacred Heart Kiteredde just down the road from KAASO. It was the same high school attended by David, who Cherie and her family were sponsoring. Charles and Anthony were thrilled by Mark's letters and the pocket money he had sent them, and they shyly asked about their sponsor: where he was from, how I knew him. Our visit took place in the school library and I found a globe, which I used to point out where we had met — way down *there* in New Zealand — and where Mark lived — way up *there* in the UK. Cherie was happily reunited with David after three years, and he gratefully thanked her for all her support.

I had another wonderful catch-up with Henry, and with all the other sponsor children. They were doing so well. I loved seeing how much they had grown over the past year, slowly turning from the children I had first met into fine young adults. It was frustrating, however, to have so little time with them. At each school we had to go through the arduous process of signing in at various posts and offices throughout the school and explaining in detail the purpose of our visit, even though I had done the exact same thing the year before and hoped that they might remember me. I only had an hour to spend at each school before 'visiting hours' were over. The children were always happy to see me but also rather formal, standing stiffly in front of their group of peers who inevitably gathered around, curious to witness our catch-ups. I longed to have more time with them, to hear every detail of their lives at boarding school, but all too soon a teacher would come and take them back to class.

Stellah had grown much taller in the year since I'd seen her, and she came running towards me. 'Madam Emma, I did not know you were coming!' she cried, breathless as I hugged her.

'They didn't tell you?' I asked, but then realised that was hardly surprising. As Rose had told me back in 2009, so few people followed through on their promises to return that it was probably better to be surprised by a visitor than to be forever waiting for someone who never showed up. I took her hands in mine and looked her in the eyes. 'I'll always come back for you, Stellah.'

The words came out before I had a chance to think too much about them, but somehow I knew them to be true. I hugged her tightly goodbye and left before she could ask exactly when my next visit might be.

Back at KAASO, I did as much guitar playing as I could, sitting under the music tree with Immy and Brenda and our motley choir that fluctuated day to day from anywhere between five and 95 members. With the girls and Marcos, I met with Dominic and Rose to get an update on the school's progress and to go through the priority list. We were thrilled to learn that KAASO had recently been registered. Up until then, KAASO had not 'officially' been a school in the eyes of the Ugandan government, so the children had travelled on the back of the open school truck to go and sit their exams at Kamuganja, the government school. Now that KAASO was registered, they would no longer have to travel across the country. It was a huge step forward for the school, and we congratulated Dominic and Rose on their success.

I returned to Paris dusty, dirty and exhausted. My fingers were raw from guitar playing, my skin was scorched from the relentless equatorial sun and my face was aching from smiling, but I felt immensely satisfied. In spite of the demands of my full-time job, I'd managed to make it back to Uganda within a year and I hoped that this would be a trend I could continue.

Back in the hotel room that had come to be my home, I sat looking out over the rooftops of Paris — old brick buildings and spired domes piercing the skyline, the Eiffel Tower glittering in the night. I had emailed reports to each of the sponsors, detailing my visits to their sponsor children and sharing photos of the children's smiling faces, which I'd taken after some gentle coaxing — reminding them you had to *smile* in photos, not *frown* as was usually the case in Uganda. Mark responded immediately to my stories of Charles and Anthony and I felt warmed as I read his glowing words. I was forever grateful that the sponsors seemed to get as much joy as I did from these visits.

But as satisfying as the sponsorship programme was, KAASO was also facing a great challenge: they had run out of space to house the children. Now that KAASO was officially registered, the school had to comply with government regulations — and the triple-decker bunks in the current dorms were considered illegal. The authorities that granted the school's registration had demanded that all bunks be reduced to double-deckers, which meant that a new dormitory had to be built. If government officials returned to find that this requirement had not been met, they could close the school down immediately.

It was now almost midnight. I was absolutely shattered and had an early-morning flight to San Francisco the next day, but there was something I had to do and I knew I wouldn't sleep until it was done. I took a deep breath and began to write. I outlined the problems KAASO faced, emphasising how far the school had come from those early days of twelve children in a single thatched hut to now, a fully registered school overflowing with children eager to enrol. I outlined the budget for a new dormitory — US$8000 — and broke down the ways in which people could contribute, as I had done for Kiwi House. I finished my email by thanking my ever-growing list of readers for their continued support.

'And I'm not just talking financial,' I wrote. 'Every email, every word of encouragement, every conversation I have had with you all fills me with hope and inspiration that people really do care. I can vouch with all my heart that KAASO is a worthwhile project, that Dominic and Rose work tirelessly and selflessly to give these children a chance — and they do so always with a smile.

'As I take in my final views of Paris, I wonder, as I do so often, how it is one can move between two such disparate worlds. For me, it comes down to the people. In each of my two worlds I'm surrounded by genuine people with hearts of gold which means that no matter where I am, I feel at home.' I pushed send, then tumbled onto the soft sheets of my hotel bed, falling into a deep sleep.

The next morning, I awoke early as the sun crept in through the open curtains, zipped up my suitcase and left my Parisian hotel room for the last time. The streets of Saint Germain were peaceful in the early-morning light, and the world felt unusually still as my taxi rolled down ancient roads, so quiet after the chaotic streets of Kampala. The tourist crowds had not yet started bustling through the narrow laneways, and the locals were not yet awake. Only the pigeons were about, foraging for crumbs among the cobblestones. I boarded my flight and quickly checked for emails on my Blackberry before take-off, still trying to catch up on all the work emails I'd received over the past few weeks.

One message jumped out at me, entitled URGENT. It was from Mark, in response to my fund-raising email. He wanted to know how many people I had approached, and how much I expected to receive from them. He agreed that yes, it was an incredibly high priority and yes, we should aim to get construction going as soon as possible and proceed non-stop until completion. Could I send through the bank details so that he could deposit £1000 immediately to get the fund-raiser started? 'Awaiting your thoughts,' he signed off.

As the plane doors closed I scrawled a quick reply of thanks, telling him I'd be in touch once I landed. I smiled all the way to San Francisco.

From the window of the plane, I looked down on the winding maze of Paris sprawled below me, thinking about Mark. To have such phenomenal support was not new to me; I had experienced it before from family and friends when I was first in Uganda, but with Mark it was different. Until only a few months ago, he hadn't even known me. He didn't know my family, my history, my background, he hadn't followed my stories over the past three years. He came from nowhere, out of the blue, and yet he trusted me so much. That trust meant the world to me.

I couldn't help feeling that some higher power had brought Mark into my life, that our paths were meant to cross that night at my parents' home in the Bay of Islands. There was a reason we had met. It wasn't only the support and encouragement he offered — it was also the fact that he never made me feel like a fraud for moving between two such contrasting worlds, or made me feel that it had to be one or the other: continue working for Louis Vuitton, or help the children in Uganda.

In fact, he himself was an example of someone who earned

a lot of money doing what he loved but was also committed to using his resources for good. Yes, he was an executive at a private jet company — but he used a good portion of the money he earned to support the things he believed in. Not only was he funding Charles and Anthony's education, but he had also helped build a dental clinic in Zanzibar, paid a Maasai warrior's university fees in Kenya and contributed to local projects on his recent trip to Rwanda.

Mark was slowly showing me that the 'corporate' world I had always been wary of and 'doing good' didn't have to be diametrically opposed, as I had once thought. On the contrary, he would advocate that you could do *more* by moving in influential circles and using your position to raise awareness of the causes you so passionately believed in. I decided to take his philosophy on board.

I settled easily into my new life in San Francisco, quickly falling in love with the quirky, eclectic ways of this foggy city. I moved into a beautiful house in Pacific Heights with Christine, and we operated out of the America's Cup offices on the Embarcadero, driving through the city's steep and crooked streets to get to work each day.

Mark continued to assist with the dormitory fund-raiser from afar, checking in every few days to see how progress was going. Donations were coming in bit by bit, and it was a buzz to receive each new message of support. However, I was now the Event Manager for the Louis Vuitton Cup and my job was incredibly busy. An America's Cup World Series event was starting almost immediately in San Francisco, and with a steady flow of guests arriving from around the world I found myself swamped by work and struggling to keep on top of the fund-raiser. Mark's encouragement never stopped; just when I needed inspiration, I would open my inbox to find another of his positive messages, motivating me to stay on track and reminding me to have faith that we would achieve our target.

One thing was concerning me, though, and I didn't know how to address it. From time to time, Mark would casually allude to some kind of sickness and I was concerned by how much time he seemed to be spending on hospital visits in between business trips around the world. I didn't want to pry, and he never elaborated further or seemed to slow down in spite of his illness — whatever it was — so I kept my worries to myself.

On the contrary, far from slowing down, Mark upped the ante, offering for the month of September to match dollar-for-dollar any donation towards the dormitory. In addition, he was also actively involved in helping the KAASO community in other ways. When he learned that Rose had an injured back and was having difficulty moving, he paid for her medical treatment in Kampala, insisting that she was the 'backbone' of KAASO and that without her, nothing would function; her treatment was imperative. On discovering that Anthony had had a skin condition since birth, he paid for his sponsor child to see a specialist to try to find a cure or at least some relief. He was relentless in his desire to help in any way possible.

In October I attended the Fort Lauderdale International Boat Show, bringing the Louis Vuitton Cup trophy with me in an attempt to entice wealthy superyacht owners to the Louis Vuitton and America's Cup events in San Francisco the following summer. On arrival in Florida I received an email from Dominic with photos of the progress being made on the dormitory — the walls were constructed, the roof was now on and the floors were soon to be cemented. I excitedly forwarded the photos on to Mark and eagerly awaited his reply. His response was slower than usual, arriving nine days later, but he enthusiastically congratulated me on how far the dormitory had come and, in his typically humble way, glossed over the fact that he'd had a 'hiccup' the previous week in Mallorca so was currently in hospital. But, he assured me, he was turning the corner and would soon be on the mend. 'Not a dull life!' he joked.

This worried me anew. I still didn't know exactly what this mysterious illness was, but Mark and I had developed such a close friendship over the past ten months that I decided to just come out and ask him. I did not like the reply I got. It was liver cancer 'with a few added complications'. He explained that he had found out just before flying to meet me in Ibiza four months earlier. 'Last week I was very sick indeed, but I am leaving hospital today after a very quick recovery so that is something in my favour!' he wrote. 'However, to quite a degree now I am having my wings clipped re travel and will stay in my house in London — more relaxing.' He went on to ask about Rose's back and Anthony's skin condition, always more concerned about others than about himself. I wrote back saying how sorry I was to hear, and urging him to rest and look after himself.

Back in San Francisco, the fund-raiser continued to steam ahead. Cherie and Kirsty were also helping to solicit donations from their networks, and thanks to Mark's dollar-for-dollar campaign we had almost reached our target. I wrote to him several times, thanking him for his unfailing support and letting him know that we had all but done it, but he had gone unusually quiet. Work, however, had not, and the holiday season kept me busier than ever with even more events to organise than usual.

The week before Christmas, I flew back to New Zealand for a break. I was looking forward to spending time with my family and, in particular, my Gramps, who was now 90 years old. I arrived in Auckland on a sunny December day and was met by the smiling faces of my parents. I updated them on the dormitory's progress and excitedly showed them the pictures of construction, now not far from completion.

'And how's that amazing man, Mark?' Mama asked. 'He's been a huge help, hasn't he?'

I bit my lip. For the past two months I'd been emailing him constantly but hadn't had a single reply. 'I honestly don't know. I haven't heard from him since the end of October . . .' I struggled to keep my voice level. 'It's so unlike him, I'm actually really worried.'

'Oh Ems, I'm sure he'll be fine. You know how busy he is. He's probably just been flying around the world and back. You'll hear from him soon,' Mama reassured me.

But Christmas came and went, and I entered the New Year with still no word. Finally, on the second of January, I could take it no longer. I had to know. I had asked Simon if he had heard any news, but he had only met Mark that one night in the Bay of Islands and had not been in touch. Not knowing who else to ask, I did what people do these days. I googled him. But before I had finished typing his name, another word appeared, predicting the results of my search.

'No, no, no . . .'

The words blurred on the screen as I found what I had been dreading.

Mark's obituary.

He had died almost two months earlier, and I'd had no way of knowing. The obituary stated that he had died 'unexpectedly but peacefully at home, aged 66'. A service, which I had obviously missed, had been held in London in late November and it was requested that no flowers be sent but donations would be welcome to the Zanzibar Action Project, the organisation behind the dental clinic that Mark had funded the previous year.

I was devastated. I had known deep down that something terrible must have happened for him not to have replied to my emails, but that didn't stop me feeling as if the walls had come crashing down around me. I was lost; I had no way to contact his wife, Jan, whom I had heard much about but had never met. If only I could send her a message to let her know how deeply sorry I was, to tell her how much of a difference her husband had made, both to my life and to those at KAASO, but I had no way of reaching her. My complete isolation from her made the news even harder to bear.

The tears fell freely as I tried to comprehend how life could be so unfair. What a waste. What a complete and utter waste. How could the world be robbed of such good people? As I sat, sobbing, I was taken back to the horrific day in December 2001 when my family had learned that Sir Peter Blake, New Zealand's most famous sailor and one of our family's closest friends, had been shot dead by pirates during an environmental mission in the Amazon.

Peter had broken multiple world records sailing around the globe, including several trips with our friend Simon, and he had won and defended the America's Cup for New Zealand. From there, he had set his sights higher, taking on something greater than all his sailing achievements put together. Peter established Blakexpeditions, an environmental organisation, and set sail around the world on a 118-foot aluminium ice-breaker boat. As well as conducting environmental research with the support of the United Nations Environment Programme, he raised awareness of the importance of conserving our environment and looking after the world's oceans through his interactive website and daily log.

The day before Peter was killed, sitting at the mouth of the Amazon where they had just completed their latest expedition, he wrote in the Blakexpeditions log:

> Again I raise the question: Why are we here? . . .
> We want to restart people caring for the environment as it must be cared for . . .
> To win, you have to believe you can do it.
> You have to be passionate about it.
> You have to really 'want' the result — even if this means years of work.
> The hardest part of any big project is to begin.
> We have begun — we are under way — we have a passion.
> We want to make a difference.

Like Peter, Mark wanted to make a difference. He had invested his faith, energy, time and money into me and my work at KAASO, and together we had begun, we were under way, we had a passion and we wanted to make a difference. The stories of these two great men, both now lost, washed over me and my tears fell heavily. What could justify such a gross waste? Why was it that inspiring people were brought into my life only to be taken away all too soon? Peter had been my childhood hero; our families had shared countless holidays together, and his absence had left a deep hole in my life. Now Mark, whom I had only known a year, but who in that time had been my biggest supporter, my loudest cheerleader and my faraway friend, was gone.

I didn't know how I was going to carry on without him. I had come to rely on his support, his endless optimism. In just a few days I was due to fly back to resume work in San Francisco and I didn't know how I'd face it. I also didn't know what I was going to do about Charles and Anthony, the two boys Mark had been sponsoring. He had paid for their first year of secondary school, but there were still five years left to go and I had no idea how I was going to manage. I'd made a promise to Rose to follow through on my commitments — part of my sponsorship programme was a 'guarantee' that I would find a way to see the children through their six years no matter what. But I hadn't anticipated this. In the short term I knew that I could borrow money in time for the new school year, but in the long run it was a problem I'd have to address.

I cried until my tears ran dry, and then made a resolve.

Mark had been brought into my life for a reason. He was the embodiment of the Rakai District Chairman's words all those years ago: 'When God has given you plenty, it is also good to remember that there are others who are not so lucky.' Mark had shown me that if people knew what was going on, they *would* care; and although nothing could bring him back, his legacy would live on inside of me and at KAASO. I would make sure of that. Just as Peter had made a difference to so many people in New Zealand and around the world, I would do all I could to make a difference at KAASO and within my network of loyal supporters. I would justify the unshakable trust and faith that Mark had had in me. I would carry on the work we had started together and I would do all I could to make Mark proud.

CHAPTER
TWELVE

I t was a clear January afternoon when I landed in San Francisco. I had said my goodbyes to family and friends, knowing that I would not be back in New Zealand for at least twelve months. It was the year of the 34th America's Cup and the event was fast approaching. I hit the ground running.

Our Louis Vuitton Cup team was expanding and I was thrilled with our latest addition. While still in Paris, Christine had told me we would need someone to help run the hospitality in our VIP lounge. They had to be well presented, personable, highly organised and hard-working, plus someone I could work closely with for the next nine months.

I didn't hesitate to recommend Kirsty. She had been in Cambridge for three and a half years since leaving KAASO, as Marcos had been invited to do his PhD upon completion of his Master's. She was enjoying her work at the Gates Cambridge Scholarship but was ready for a change. Marcos was about to start writing his thesis — which he could do from anywhere — so Kirsty jumped at the opportunity, and she and Marcos moved to San Francisco. It was amazing to be reunited with my fellow *muzungu* in such an unlikely setting, and I loved having Kirsty back in my daily life again.

With just under six months to go before the racing started, there was a lot to do. We would be hosting hundreds of guests over the event period and every last detail had to be perfect — from the moment they were met at the airport, to the welcome gift on their bed, to their chauffeur-driven cars, to the canapés in the VIP lounge, to the décor of the boat that would take them out to watch the races on San Francisco Bay. We were a high-end luxury company and it was this attention to even the minutest details that made us what we were.

One of our tasks was to design and oversee the construction of a 150-square-foot VIP lounge at the end of Pier 27 on the Embarcadero. Everything was custom-built, from the New-York-designed teak-topped bar, to the white leather couches, to the slatted oak coffee tables, to the suspended display cabinets soon to be filled with the Louis Vuitton Cup collection. It was a time-consuming process and I struggled to get my head around the fact that the entire structure — which, in addition to our VIP lounge, would house Club 72 (the official hospitality lounge of the America's Cup) and team lounges for Artemis Racing and Oracle Team USA — was temporary. Two days after the event finished, the entire building would be dismantled, all our hard work undone.

Meanwhile, in Uganda, construction of a different kind was taking place. While our temporary structure was being assembled in San Francisco, in the village of Kabira a new dormitory was going up — one that would be there for many years to come. Mud bricks were being laid, iron sheets nailed to roofing poles and barred windows installed. Eight months after I had sent out my first fund-raising email, the dormitory was completed. Dominic emailed me a report of the official opening ceremony and I pored over the photos he attached. I grinned to see dozens of boys lined up along the concrete veranda in their red school socks, waiting to be invited inside their new home, while speeches were made and ribbons were cut. I thought back to the opening of Kiwi House and the immense pride I had felt at seeing our ambitious project through to completion. I remember standing on the veranda of Kiwi House and feeling the full weight of the community's gratitude.

Dominic went on to say that it had not just been a simple dormitory opening. My eyes filled as I read his words, explaining that the whole community had gathered together to hold a memorial service to acknowledge the man who had been so instrumental in bringing this dream to life. Mark's vision and perseverance were recognised and his name would live on forever at KAASO, on Mark House, the dormitory that now stands proudly behind Freedom Square. Tears slid down my face and I once again wished that I had a way of contacting Jan, to share with her these beautiful photos of what her husband had helped to create. I had tried every avenue to reach her but had only been met with a string of dead ends.

I turned my attention back to my work. On San Francisco Bay the sailing teams were practising in earnest and I was right in the thick of it. Standing in my hi-visibility vest and hard hat at the top of a ladder on the construction site of the lounge, I would watch the boats flying around the Bay. More than ever before, the boats were something to behold. This America's Cup had seen a major break from the style of past boats. The 82-foot monohulls of the previous twenty years had been replaced by 72-foot catamarans with 130-foot wing sails that towered like giant aeroplane wings over the trampolines that joined the two hulls. These new boats didn't sail *in* the water — they foiled *on top* of it, and seeing them literally flying around the choppy waters of the Bay was spectacular.

Changing to these new boats was a controversial decision, with some people fully behind it while others feared that the technology had gone too far. As the teams tried to perfect their foiling manoeuvres, there was a simmering fear among the America's Cup community that perhaps this was taking things *too* close to the edge, that someone might get hurt in this new generation of boats that went twice the speed of the wind. On the infamously breezy waters of San Francisco Bay, that was a frightening prospect. But the rules had been set and the design parameters prescribed by Oracle Team USA, the defender — one of the America's Cup's unique and long-standing traditions — and the show would go on.

One day, while walking from our offices at Pier 23 to the lounge construction site next door, Kirsty excitedly told me about an email she had received. In between juggling her work duties, Kirsty was also acting as the Volunteer Coordinator for KAASO. Cherie had taken on the role for the first two years after leaving Uganda, but as her university studies intensified it became harder and harder to keep on top of her busy workload and Kirsty happily took over. Now,

Kirsty told me about a letter from the National Educator Program in the United States that Dominic had forwarded to her. They had invited Dominic to speak at an educational conference in Long Beach, California. Not only that, but they were also asking him to attend their International Leadership Fellows Institute in Tampa, Florida, three weeks later. It was an incredible recognition of his commitment to education, and since all of his transport, lodging, food and tuition would be covered, Dominic was coming to the US!

That evening, Kirsty wrote back to Dominic saying we were delighted to hear his good news and to let us know if we could help in any way as the Kiwi Girls were with him 100 per cent. Dominic's response quickly brought us back down to earth — it was only his *domestic* transport that would be covered, and he would have to make his own way from Uganda to the United States. Off the back of such a major fund-raiser for Mark House I didn't feel comfortable hitting up my network of supporters again so soon. Instead, Kirsty sent an email appeal to all the past volunteers of KAASO, explaining the remarkable opportunity that Dominic had been presented with and asking them to help contribute towards the $2000 cost of his flights and visa. The response was not as good as we'd hoped for, but we were unwilling to give up. Then, a fortuitous conversation at a dinner party changed everything.

Several months before, Christine and I had organised a black-tie celebration dinner in honour of the London Olympic medallists who were also involved in America's Cup teams. I was sitting next to Iain Percy, three-time medallist from the UK and a sailor for Artemis Racing, the Swedish America's Cup team. He asked me how I was and what I had been up to since I last saw him in Newport, and looked more than a little surprised when I told him I'd been in Uganda. He was intrigued, and asked endless questions about KAASO and the various projects, fund-raisers and sponsorships I organised there, in turn telling me that his father and sister had both done medical volunteer work in East Africa. He had also read a lot of African literature and we swapped book recommendations. As usual, the irony was not lost on me that all this was taking place over a four-course meal in the Presidential Suite of the St Regis Hotel. However, it seemed that this was just the way things happened in my life nowadays, and I reminded myself that Mark would have told me to use such situations to my advantage rather than being ashamed of them.

At the end of dinner, Iain said he'd love to help support KAASO, and asked me to let him know when the next project came up. Now, four months later — just after we had heard the news about Dominic — Christine and I were hosting a dinner at our house for some of our friends in the America's Cup family and Iain was among them. He and I got chatting, and I told him the amazing news that Dominic had been invited to the United States to participate in two different educational conferences.

'Wow, that's great news!' Iain said with a wide smile. 'When does he come?'

I sighed. 'Well, it's still only an idea. All his course costs, food and accommodation are covered but his flights are not ... so Kirsty and I have been trying to raise funds through the volunteer network, but it's a slow process.'

'Do you think it would be a worthwhile trip? Would he get a lot out of it?' Iain asked, suddenly serious.

'Absolutely,' I said, 'it would be phenomenal. For all that

Dominic has seen and done, he has still never left East Africa. For him to be out in the world, meeting people and sharing the KAASO story would be hugely valuable — not only for him but for the whole KAASO community.' I went on to explain that the volunteer network wasn't currently as active as we'd like it to be and so a lot had fallen on the three of us Kiwi Girls to help fund projects at KAASO. Through Dominic meeting more people around the world and drumming up support with his contagious enthusiasm, we could extend our network of supporters, which would be a huge help.

'Well, count me in. I said I wanted to help, and I meant it. Flick me through the bank details and I'll send some money your way. Nice work,' he said with a smile.

Having learned from Mark that people only gave when they genuinely wanted to, I accepted Iain's offer, thanked him, and sent through the bank details as requested. Three days later, $1000 showed up in the account.

Even though I'd experienced similar generosity before, it still never ceased to amaze me. Here was someone who spent his entire life on the sea, an acclaimed sailor who had never been to my landlocked village in Uganda but who gave openly and generously when he heard my stories. I was sure that his connection with Africa via his father and sister helped, but there was something more than that — the kind of 'no borders' existence I had grown up with seemed to make it easier for people in the sailing world to relate to my experiences in Uganda, even if it was a completely different world to their own. It was a mentality — a worldliness, an openness to change, a sense of ease with ever-shifting horizons — that simplified things for my sailing friends.

While some people wondered how I could possibly move

between Louis Vuitton and the America's Cup and a village in Uganda, my friends in the sailing community were used to bouncing from place to place, filling their passports with stamps as often as other people filled their cars with petrol, learning to adapt to different weather conditions in unknown places, working out how to go about their daily lives in countries where they spoke not a word of the language. I felt incredibly grateful to be part of such an incredible community.

But it wasn't only my sailing friends who were offering support. Judy Johnson, a friend of Mama's back in the Bay of Islands, had also heard about Dominic's trip from my parents and wanted to help. Judy owned an educational book publishing business in Sydney and had already sent over several boxes of books and resource materials to help stock the KAASO library. When I explained the opportunity that Dominic had before him, she wrote back saying that she would love to help such an amazing man and would gladly put in the remaining $1000. And just like that, Dominic was on his way to the US. Kirsty got to work arranging his visas, his schedule and his trip.

Meanwhile, work was becoming increasingly frantic. In addition to my duties in San Francisco I was also helping organise a major superyacht event in London, and as Dominic's trip approached, so did my own to London. However, the week before flying out, I awoke to an email that knocked the wind out of me.

It was from Mark.

I stared at my screen, unable to bring myself to open it. A tiny glimmer of hope flickered through my mind, but it was quickly replaced by confusion, hurt and the cold feeling that it must be some cruel mistake.

I clicked on the message and exhaled deeply. It was from Jan, Mark's wife. She was wading her way through his emails with the painful job of informing his far-flung friends around the world of his death. It was surreal to read her words, and I felt grief surge through me all over again as she told me of that terrible day in November. She went on to say that she was aware of Mark's sponsorships of Charles and Anthony and would continue the support that Mark had started. I felt a weight lift from my shoulders; I had borrowed money from Simon and my parents to cover the boys' school fees, hoping that one day I would hear from Jan and be able to repay the loans. It was a huge relief to have this resolved.

Jan thanked me for all I did, and signed off saying that if I was ever in London I should give her a call as she'd love to meet me because Mark had spoken so fondly of me. I immediately wrote back, explaining that as fate would have it, I was actually coming to London the following week and would love to meet her.

I felt both excited and deflated. Seeing Mark's name in my inbox after so long brought memories flooding back of the amazing connection we had once shared, and the loss of him hit me all over again. But at the same time, I was relieved to have finally made contact with Jan and felt incredibly lucky that my itinerant lifestyle was enabling me to meet her so soon after hearing from her.

On the morning of my flight I was at home alone. Christine was already in Europe and would be meeting me in

London the following day. While waiting for my taxi I made a coffee and wrote to Jan, telling her once again how much I was looking forward to meeting her. The ring of my phone startled me in the silent house, and I looked down at the screen — Mama. Dad was once again working for Team New Zealand, so my parents were also living in San Francisco. We caught up regularly and Mama was no doubt ringing to wish me a safe trip and say goodbye.

I answered the phone and could tell immediately by her voice that something was horribly wrong.

'Mama, what's going on? Is everything okay?'

I heard her take a deep, ragged breath. 'Yes Ems, we're fine. It's Gramps. He's . . . he's gone. Dad's just booking our flights home now.'

'No . . .' I stared out the window, tears rolling soundlessly down my face. It had been so hard saying goodbye to Gramps when I left New Zealand just a few months before. He was 90 years old and there had been a feeling throughout our family that this would be our last Christmas all together. All of Dad's family had gathered in Dunedin (in the South Island of New Zealand), where my Gramps lived, including my aunts who were sponsoring a student named Munjera through the Kiwi Sponsorships. I smiled when I saw the photos I had sent them proudly displayed in frames around their houses, and they plied me with questions about Munjera's daily life, her family, her school and her aspirations.

On my final morning in Dunedin I had sat with Gramps in the conservatory of his cosy brick house, the sun streaming in through the glass. Although it was a warm summer's day, Gramps sat, as usual, in his button-up shirt, trousers, shoes and socks. While my family were all beach-loving sailors, I had never seen Gramps take his shoes off — never mind come swimming in the sea. That day, the rest of the family was out and it was just the two of us, sitting companionably in faded floral armchairs.

Gramps asked me how I was enjoying San Francisco and then went on to share stories of the time he had spent there during World War II. He had joined the Air Force and left New Zealand on a ship bound for the war in Europe. Their first stop was Canada to receive his pilot training, but by the time the training was complete the war in Europe had ended and so he was redirected to the war in the Pacific. He was transported to San Francisco to await his ship south, docking in on Angel Island and then spending several wonderful weeks in the foggy city. It was an incredibly exciting time for Gramps, his first overseas adventure, and his eyes were alight as he talked about walking with his fellow soldiers through the crooked streets in their uniforms and the overwhelming hospitality they received from civilians everywhere. New Zealand soldiers were popular in the United States, and Gramps and his fellow pilots were welcomed as family wherever they went. I smiled, trying to picture him as a young man all those years ago, striding proudly through the streets of San Francisco in his Air Force uniform.

Sitting chatting in the sun, the afternoon slowly slipped away and when I saw my parents' car starting up the quiet cul-de-sac on which Gramps lived, I knew we would soon be leaving.

'It's been a really special time, Gramps. I'm so happy I could make it home to spend Christmas with you.' I looked over at him, dwarfed by the chair he sat in, wondering how he had suddenly become so small. I tried to find the words to say goodbye, but I didn't trust myself to speak.

He turned to me slowly, his piercing blue eyes looking right through me behind his thick glasses. 'Emma, there's something I want to say.' He held my gaze with a look I'd never seen before, and something passed between us, an understanding. 'I want to tell you how proud I am of you. For all that you do for those children. It's really . . .' his voice wavered and I fought to control my own tears, wanting to etch this moment forever in my mind. 'Something. It's really something. You didn't just talk about it, you went and did it, and I know it wasn't always easy. But I want you to remember that I am so very proud of you.'

I went over to him and wrapped my arms around him, shocked by how frail he had become. 'Thank you, Gramps. Really, it means so much to me. I'm so glad I could make you proud.'

I could hear my parents in the other room, wheeling their suitcases over the linoleum floors. I kissed Gramps on the cheek, told him I loved him and quickly left before he could see the tears flooding down my face. I somehow knew that it was the last time I would ever see him — and now, as I sat at my kitchen bench in San Francisco, I was facing the fact that I had been right.

On the phone, Mama was asking me if I was still there. 'Yes, yes, I'm here. Oh poor Daddy-o, he must be . . . Mama, I have to come home with you. I need to cancel my flight to London. I, I—' I began to sob; Gramps was my last surviving grandparent and the world felt suddenly empty without him.

'Ems, it's okay,' she gently calmed me. 'I've spoken about it with Dad and he said that you need to continue with your trip. You've worked so hard on this event and you should be there. Besides, Nicko is in London and this way the two of you can be together. You had such a special time over Christmas with Gramps, you don't need to see him now. Hold on to those memories.'

I rode wordlessly in the taxi to the airport, grateful that the driver was tactfully ignoring my blotched face and puffy eyes. I thought back on that night in the Bay of Islands, more than seven years ago now, when Gramps had pushed me to follow my heart and do something to address the issues I felt so passionately about. To know that I had finally done that and made him proud was a great relief, but it still didn't stop the dull ache inside me.

I arrived in London in a daze and was grateful to be met by my brother's familiar face. Together we wrote a speech to be read out at Gramps's funeral on our behalf, and then Nick escorted me to the superyacht event. It was taking place at the Mall Galleries just off Trafalgar Square and the gallery had been transformed with sailing images and video projections. Wealthy superyacht owners and international media strutted down the red carpet as the America's Cup and Louis Vuitton Cup trophies glittered over the room of bustling bodies. Lady Pippa Blake, Peter Blake's widow, had come up from her home on the south coast of England and she and Christine kept a watchful eye on me. It was a relief to have familiar faces around to help me feel not quite so far from home.

On my last day in London, I met up with Jan in a tea-room in Sloane Square. Over a triple-tiered cake stand laden with cucumber sandwiches and cream scones, we shared stories of Mark. I told her how Mark and I had met in the Bay of Islands and of my surprise when he had offered to sponsor not one, but two children. As I described the overwhelming support I received from him in the year that followed, Jan smiled and took a sip of her tea, her eyes shining. 'Ah, Mark. He could never do things by halves — always one to launch headlong into things. It was all or nothing with him. And I loved him for it.'

She told me about their travels together, the adventures they had shared, and Mark's huge heart and his desire to help all those he encountered along the way. 'But he wasn't a fool about it,' she made sure to say. 'He wouldn't just help any old person. No, they had to prove that they really *wanted* it, whatever "it" might be. They had to be passionate and they had to be hard-working. Mark had the ability to spot that in people and he responded accordingly. So if you had his support, oh my, you really had it.'

I nodded in agreement. I had certainly experienced that.

I showed her photos of Mark House and told her about the memorial service held in his honour at KAASO. I had also printed photos of Charles and Anthony, and I watched as she held them in her delicate hands and carefully examined them. 'Ah yes, Mark loved these boys. And he loved what you're doing. Well, most importantly, he loved *how* you're doing it. No fuss, no fanfare, just direct support from sponsor to child. Marvellous system you have — well done.' I tried to smile, feeling emotion well up within me yet again. Her praise meant so much and made me feel closer to Mark again.

Jan and I parted with a promise to keep in touch, and she assured me that her support for the boys would continue as Mark had agreed for the full six years; the money would be transferred that week. I thanked her, glad to know that Mark's memory would live on in Jan and relieved to know my loans would soon be repaid.

Back in San Francisco, things were heating up; summer was approaching and momentum was beginning to gather. The countdown to the first race was on and the teams were busy training. However, less than two months before the first race, tragedy struck Artemis Racing, the Swedish team, during a training incident on San Francisco Bay. Andrew 'Bart' Simpson, one of their crew members, was trapped within the wreckage of the boat and his heart-breaking death sent shock waves through the America's Cup family. Everyone was reeling in disbelief; it could have been their husband, their father, their best friend.

It was an incredibly difficult time for our tight-knit community as everyone grappled with the tragedy and further questions of safety were raised. This was the pinnacle of sailing: the boats *were* being pushed to the limit and with that came risk, but it just seemed unthinkable that someone from our America's Cup family could be lost right before our eyes on San Francisco Bay. This wasn't an offshore round-the-world race where sailors were battling 10-metre swells in the Southern Ocean. It was round-the-buoys racing off a Californian city front. It wasn't meant to be like this.

An investigation committee was established to look into the safety aspects of the boats, eventually determining that each crew member should undergo extensive dive training and be equipped with full body armour, oxygen tanks and knives for cutting themselves free should the need arise. It was frightening to think that such measures were necessary, and critics of this new era pounced on the danger factor. They pointed out that people had been cautioning against this new level of technology, which had swept away our sport so that now the boats flew like rocket ships. Yes, it was spectacular — but had we gone too far? The older America's Cup generation had always preferred the more traditional monohulls, but this new era had brought younger sailors into the game and the jury was out as to where the future of the sport lay.

Understandably, Artemis Racing was hugely shaken and there was some doubt as to whether the team would continue. However, showing unbelievable strength and determination, the team members banded together and, in honour of their lost teammate, miraculously got their second boat ready against all odds to make the start line just in time.

At the helm of the boat was a determined young 27-year-old by the name of Nathan Outteridge. We had first met at a rooftop cocktail party at the America's Cup World Series event in Newport, Rhode Island, the previous year and a friendship had quickly formed. Nathan had also been at the celebration dinner following the London Olympics, having won a gold medal in the 49er class with his teammate Iain 'Goobs' Jensen. In the months that followed we saw a lot of each other, as Nathan had also moved to San Francisco and was living down the road from me in North Beach.

Nathan had been driving the boat during the incident, and the tragedy fell heavily on him. We kept in regular contact in those tough early days, exchanging messages and meeting up frequently. As hard as it was to deal with the accident, Nathan was also incredibly keen for the team to move forward, knowing how important it was for everyone's spirit not to simply give up. I admired him deeply and would find that whenever we went out as a group, Nathan and I would end up drawn together, spending the whole night talking only to each other. It soon became clear that there was something there beyond just a friendship. On 26 June, a year to the day after our first meeting in Newport, we went out on our first official date at Tony's Pizza in North Beach. The conversation flowed as easily as the wine, and as I sat looking at him across the table, his face so open and warm, a sailor with a deep understanding of the world and wise beyond his years, but with a cheeky grin that drove me wild, I knew I had found the love of my life.

From then on, we were inseparable. I had never been happier, and everyone who saw us would laugh that it had taken us so long to see what they had all been watching blossom over the past year. For the first time in my life, I understood the concept of 'walking on air'; it felt like my feet did not touch the ground for months. I practically moved into the apartment Nathan shared with his brother Beau, who was also working for Artemis Racing as a videographer, and we became like a little family. My parents adored Nathan, too. Only a week after we got together, Nathan's parents happened to be over visiting from Australia. Overnight, it felt like our two families had known each other forever. I survived on almost no sleep, attending nightly evening functions with Nathan at my side and then coming home and staying up talking through the night. There was always so much to say; it felt like we had to make up for every moment of the past 27 years we had spent without each other.

In early July, the Louis Vuitton Cup began amidst a fanfare of confetti, bands and exploding fireworks. There were dozens of international media reporters flying in from around the world, and it was an insanely hectic time for me as I ran around trying to meet all their demands. I took our invited media guests out on superyachts, escorted them on wine-tasting excursions in the Napa Valley, set up base tours so that they could meet the teams, and arranged countless dinners and cocktail parties over the three days of the opening celebrations.

Just before racing started, we hosted the Louis Vuitton Cup party, an event to rival all others, famed for being in a secret location — which meant that 800 guests would have to be picked up and transported without knowing their final destination. Perched atop a hill overlooking the Golden Gate Bridge, the Legion of Honour was a replica of the eighteenth-century palace with the same name in Paris. Entering between grand pillars, guests sipped cocktails beneath the starlit skies of San Francisco on a rare clear summer's night, then joined in the dancing in the interior galleries of the museum. Nathan and I danced the night away, and as we swirled around the dance floor the world felt whole again.

The official opening ceremony of the 34th America's Cup took place on 4 July 2013. Following the ceremony, our Louis Vuitton Cup team hosted a three-course dinner at a New Zealand restaurant on the Embarcadero, and after the meal our guests were transported by golf cart to our newly opened VIP lounge, the first of many events that would take place within its walls. With sweeping views across the Bay, we stood on the balcony to watch the San Francisco fireworks display while magnums of Moët popped around us. I circled the room, chatting to our guests, always keeping a watchful eye on Christine to ensure that she was happy with how things were running. As the last guests left, Christine gathered our team to share a celebratory glass of champagne together. We had done it. The lounge was open, our first weekend was off to a great start and all the press were giving glowing reports so far. I clinked my glass against Kirsty's and quickly drank my champagne. It was almost midnight and, as wonderful as this was, there was someone waiting for me.

The Embarcadero was gridlocked, so I went on foot. I ran through North Beach and up the hill to Taylor Street, weaving through the crowds in my 'formal' uniform — a white shift dress with a Louis Vuitton Cup bandana and navy Louis Vuitton high heels. Nathan and Beau were with Goobs and his girlfriend, Claire, out on the balcony of their apartment, watching as the night sky continued to explode with fireworks across the Bay. I ran into Nathan's waiting arms and then sat with my head on his shoulder as Beau played the guitar, his sweet voice ringing out into the night. I couldn't have been happier — life was perfect.

But as I looked up at the twinkling sky, the stars and the fireworks flickering through the night, I suddenly thought of Dominic. My heart dropped. He had arrived five days earlier in Long Beach, California, and today was the closing day of his conference — meaning that he had already made his speech. I hadn't even called him to see how it had gone. In the midst of cocktail parties, VIPs and superyachts, I had forgotten about him. I felt terrible.

A few days earlier, Kirsty had received an email from Dominic confirming his safe arrival — and commenting on how tall all the buildings were. She had forwarded it on to me but I hadn't had time to reply. No, I hadn't *made* time to reply. Dominic had asked whether either of us might go and see him while he was in Long Beach — less than a one-hour flight away from

San Francisco — but it was the busiest weekend of the whole event and there was no way we could leave, even for just a day. He wrote back saying that he understood, but I wondered how *I* would feel to be in a village an hour from KAASO and for Dominic to be 'too busy' to come and see me. I thought of Mark, juggling a private jet company, a family and multiple philanthropic projects as well as an aggressive illness. He had never gone more than two or three days without checking in on me, and here I was unable to call Dominic when we were in the same country. The guilt weighed heavily on my mind.

The next day, I sent Dominic a quick email, promising to write more soon; but now that the event had started, it steamrollered ahead and life got even busier. The racing got under way and I went out each day on the VIP boat with a dozen exclusive guests, explaining the racing while they watched, awe-struck as the 72-foot catamarans flew past, launched out of the water by their foils. Artemis Racing's accident had given them little chance of winning but the team still gave it all they had, and I felt incredibly proud of Nathan, Iain and the rest of the team. They were eliminated in the semi-finals while Luna Rossa, the Italian team, progressed through to the Louis Vuitton Cup finals to race against Emirates Team New Zealand.

I couldn't help but get excited as New Zealand confidently took the victory, winning the Louis Vuitton Cup and moving through to the America's Cup finals to compete against the defender, Oracle Team USA. Perhaps, I thought, this could be it. It had been eighteen years since New Zealand had first won the America's Cup against the Americans, and ten years since we'd lost to the Swiss. It felt like our time had come again.

Things, however, did not go to plan. In a first-to-nine

series, Oracle began the match on minus two points after a rule infringement during the America's Cup World Series. The racing got off to a good start for Kiwi fans. Dad had been with Team New Zealand for 25 years now and, fortunately for me, as part of the Louis Vuitton Cup team I was able to support 'our' winner, the challenger who had won the Louis Vuitton Cup — Emirates Team New Zealand. We took the first few races off Oracle with relative ease and, although Oracle won a few sporadic races, by the end of the first week of racing we were up 8–1. All we needed was one more race win and the Cup would be ours. I was on cloud nine.

With Artemis Racing now officially out of the competition, Nathan's job was over for this cycle and he flew out with Goobs to Marseille in the South of France to resume their Olympic campaigning, their first Olympic event since London 2012. At the airport Nathan wiped away my tears, reminding me that I was going to be so busy celebrating the New Zealand victory that I wouldn't even have time to miss him. I waved off his plane, then went to work the following morning wondering if this would be the day that New Zealand won the America's Cup and we would all be heading home.

One of the unique aspects of the America's Cup is that whoever wins the Cup makes the rules. The winner determines where the next event will be, when it will take place, for how long, in what boats and under what conditions. New Zealand winning the Cup would mean that we would all be moving back to Auckland and the idea was immensely appealing; it had been six years since I had lived in New Zealand and I was excited to bring Nathan there and set up a life together in Auckland.

But nothing is over until it's over. Oracle took one race

off the Kiwis and then another, closing the score to 8–3, but we were all still quietly confident. We only needed *one more point*; it seemed impossible to fail. Every night I would speak to Nathan in Marseille, and every night he would remind me to be patient, promising me that tomorrow would be our day. Every day he was proven wrong. The score slowly closed until, four days after the event was meant to have finished, the buildings dismantled and the containers packed, the score had come to an unbelievable 8–8. With the momentum of a flooded dam bursting its banks, the Americans took the last race to win the 34th America's Cup 9–8. It would go down in the record books as the greatest comeback in sailing history — and I had to hand it to them: it showed nerves of steel to pull off such an extraordinary achievement. Nathan arrived back in San Francisco to find me exhausted, disappointed and incredibly flat.

It felt as if everything was lost — Valencia all over again. My job was ending, I had to move out of my apartment, my visa was soon to expire, and we had lost the Cup. *Again*. I also felt like I had let Dominic down. We had only managed to speak twice during the seven weeks he had been in the United States and I knew I should have done more to support him during his trip. Where had my resolve gone? I had vowed to do all I could to honour Mark's legacy, but I had not kept that promise. I had not done him proud. Sure, we had opened the dormitory in his name and it had been with great pleasure that I'd met Jan, but what else had I done? I'd found the funds to fly Dominic to the United States, but Kirsty had done most of the work and I'd struggled to even keep in touch with Dominic during his trip, which I had learned had been lonely and overwhelming for him at times. I felt like I was just scraping the surface of my commitment to KAASO, that everything was flapping on the fence and I was doing nothing properly.

The one thing I did have going for me now was that I had Nathan, my rock. He was endlessly supportive and encouraging and reminded me of all I had done this past year.

'Em, you're being too hard on yourself,' he said. 'What you've achieved this year in spite of working crazy hours is just amazing! KAASO has a new dormitory, Dominic came to the US and there are twelve kids at secondary school thanks to you. Isn't that enough?'

I knew it sounded like a lot, but deep down I felt it wasn't. I'd been swept away by my glamorous sailing world, which I loved, but I needed to get grounded once more in my KAASO world. I needed to get my hands dirty and my feet dusty. I needed to pull out my long skirts and notebooks streaked with red earth. I needed to do justice — real justice — to Mark's legacy and to go deeper. And I couldn't do that here.

It was time to go back to the village.

PART FOUR

EQUILIBRIUM

What counts in life is not the mere fact
that we have lived. It is what difference we
have made to the lives of others that will
determine the significance of the life we lead.

**— NELSON MANDELA, IN HIS
ADDRESS DURING THE 90TH
BIRTHDAY CELEBRATION
OF WALTER SISULU**

CHAPTER
THIRTEEN

stepped off the plane in Entebbe to Dominic's waiting
smile. It felt so right to be back, and I knew immediately
that this was exactly where I was supposed to be. It had
been hard leaving Nathan; we had been inseparable for
months and I would miss him terribly during our six weeks
apart, but we knew that it was the best thing for both of us.
He had to get back into his Olympic campaign and was also
in the midst of negotiations for the next America's Cup; I
needed to go and reconnect to KAASO, to spend some *real*
time in the village again.

On the drive down to Kabira, Dominic told me about his
trip to the United States. I wouldn't have thought it possible
for him to be even more motivated, more inspired and more
determined than when I had last seen him, but his time in the
US had opened his eyes to a whole new world and he was
buzzing from his newfound connections.

He brushed aside my apologies for not being in touch
more, reminding me how busy I was. I cringed; there was no

one on the planet busier than Dominic, but he still had so much respect for me and *my* time. I wondered if he had any idea what I had been so 'busy' doing — he knew I worked on sailing events, but was VIP hospitality really so important that I couldn't take the time to drop him a line every now and then? However, I knew that if I hadn't been working so hard, I wouldn't have been able to afford to come back here, not to mention the people I was reaching in my sailing world who were helping to support KAASO. Somehow I think Dominic understood that even before I did, and, in his usual cheerful way, he simply grinned, thanked me yet again for raising the funds for his airfares, and shared his stories.

His educational presentation in Long Beach had been well received, 'touching everybody in the conference' and securing many offers of support. He described in great detail the rooms on board the *Queen Mary*, where the conference participants were staying, with the very soft beds, the TVs and in-room wireless networks. He ate at his first buffet, which he animatedly described as 'a room with various types of food — and you can have as much as you want!' In Florida, he swam in the ocean for the first time in his life and, staying at the home of one of the National Educator Program directors, learned to wash dishes and clothes 'with machines'.

Beyond Dominic's observations of the differences between life in the village and in the United States, the trip also gave him the opportunity to make more connections for KAASO and he eagerly told me of his new friends from China, Croatia, Afghanistan and the US. I could picture him, with his contagious enthusiasm, charming people everywhere he went, further extending the community of support for KAASO as Kirsty and I had hoped he might do.

'At the end of it all,' he said, 'it was the most wonderful experience, but I will say — I was ready to come home to Uganda! I tried all those strange foods — what do you call them? Hamburgers? They are okay, but eh! I missed my *matooke*. It was also very hard for me to contact Rose and I was waiting so much to see her again. Everyone back here is very interested in hearing my stories, and they cannot believe when I show them the photos of these houses in America. It was all so different . . . I enjoyed — but I am happy to be home now.'

I smiled, thinking back to the days when I felt so guilty leaving KAASO, knowing that no one in the village would get to experience the home comforts I was going back to. Dominic's trip made me realise more than ever that 'home comforts' are relative — all the things I'd missed during my time at KAASO were those things Dominic found unusual in the United States, and vice versa. As comfortable as I felt in the village now, I knew it would never be my home; but I had finally learned to be okay with that. And, in the same way, as much as Dominic had enjoyed his time in the US, he was not about to start applying for a green card anytime soon.

We turned off the main road just before Kyotera and the dusty red earth stretched before us. We would soon be back at KAASO. My heart began to beat faster; it had been almost a year and a half since I was last there. I couldn't wait for the cacophony of sound, the flying hugs and the tangle of limbs that awaited me. I was not disappointed. The children were all lined up at the school gates, Brenda standing in front, leading the singing. She was almost eleven years old now and she had grown so tall, her thin frame stretching skywards. The children sang and danced as we drove in, and before I knew it my two suitcases full of supplies had been whisked from the car and lined up neatly in my bedroom, next to my freshly made bed. I thought of the little water fairies waiting on us back in 2009. Some things never changed.

Rose, Teacher Sarah, Susan and all the staff were there to greet me; Rose laughed as I stumbled over the little bodies clinging to my legs, trying to embrace her through the crowd.

'Well be back, Madam Emma. We are all so happy to see you!'

The children took me by the hand down to Mark House, where they proudly showed off their new dormitory. I was impressed: every bed was neatly made and mosquito nets hung over each set of bunks. I smiled as I followed them around and, as they each showed me which bed they slept in, my thoughts turned to Mark. I wished he could be here to share in this moment — he would have loved it — but I felt him watching over us as the boys excitedly led me through the maze of bunks. I snapped away photos to email to Jan, while the children stood beaming at their new home, posing for my pictures.

As on each of my earlier trips to Uganda, I planned to visit all of the sponsor children, but this time things were different. Previously, I had arrived during term time so had travelled to each child's secondary school for my one-hour catch-up during designated visiting hours. However, as it was now November, the end of the school year, the secondary students were in the midst of their final exams and visiting hours were non-existent. We would have to wait until the exams were over and the children went home. I didn't mind. I had plenty of time, and I was happy to work in with their schedules. It also meant that if my visits were to the children's homes, I could spend longer with each of them. I decided to try to make the most of my extended catch-ups, learning as much as I could about the children's backgrounds and their family histories so that I could share the stories with their sponsors. What I didn't realise was that by travelling to each of the children's home villages, I would come to understand what I had never really grasped before: the full extent to which these sponsorships were changing the lives of the children, their families and their communities.

We started with David. Rose and I jumped on the back of a *boda* and rode over dirt roads for about 20 minutes towards David's home village of Kyanika. Cherie and her family had been sponsoring David since the start of 2010. Along with Henry, he was one of the original sponsor students, and I'd visited him at his school on every trip I'd made to Uganda. David was open and friendly and we'd spent a lot of time together over the years; I'd cheered him on at soccer matches, helped him with his studies, caught up on stories about his friends at school and heard about his favourite subjects — biology, chemistry and mathematics. I felt like I knew him well. But as our *boda* pulled up outside the crumbling mud hut that housed what remained of David's family, I realised how little I actually knew about his life.

I had been to dozens of mud huts before, but this was one of the saddest I'd seen; I struggled to hide my shock that this was where my smiling young friend came from. The walls were crudely made from mud caked against a rough wooden framework, and the rusted tin roof was held in place by large rocks — cheaper than nails — and sagged heavily in the middle.

David came out to greet us, immaculately dressed in a

pale pink collared shirt and long black trousers, and warmly welcomed us inside. As the wooden front door swung closed behind us, my eyes struggled to adjust to the dim light. David's mother was waiting inside and she motioned for us to sit on one of the colourfully woven flax mats that covered the dirt floor.

A shadow fell over the room and I looked up to see David's grandfather standing in the doorway. His face was weathered by years in the fields, deep crevasses running across his skin. His milky eyes betrayed his failing eyesight, but he stood tall, exuding poise in spite of the torn *kanzu*, the traditional dress of Ugandan men, hanging off his frail frame. David introduced me, and he nodded with a slow smile of recognition, then eased himself onto a lone plank of wood that rested on two bricks, serving as a bench seat.

Sitting inside the cool, damp walls, I learned that David's father had walked out on the family when David was still young, leaving his mother to bring up her five children alone. Her own father, sitting here with us, had taken the family in, even though he was struggling to make ends meet through subsistence farming. While David and I chatted about his dreams of becoming a doctor one day, across the room I could see his grandfather listening intently to our conversation, not understanding a word but in awe of his grandson who was able to converse so fluently in a foreign tongue.

It was clear that life had not been easy for David's family. However, it struck me that despite their poverty, their difficult circumstances and their lack of anything beyond the bare essentials needed to survive, their spirits were high, their dignity intact.

Our *boda* returned to collect us, and as Rose and I went to leave, David's mother produced overflowing bags of tomatoes and avocados from their garden, as well as a live chicken. To receive a chicken as a gift of thanks was a huge honour, and the significance was not lost on me. I thanked David's mother profusely as Rose tactfully picked up the chicken, aware of my ongoing fear of birds.

Our *boda* fully loaded, we pulled away from the hut. I looked back and saw the little family standing on the side of the dirt road, watching us go. It dawned on me that were it not for his sponsorship, David would likely have become an illiterate subsistence farmer like his grandfather. Instead he was the shining star of the family — a student at secondary school, studying towards his dream of becoming a doctor. The pride this brought his family was huge, and while it was clear that all their hopes lay on David's shoulders, he took it all in his stride, flashing his wide grin and waving as we turned out of sight. I felt so grateful to play my small part in helping his dream come true.

Over dinner that night, I told Dominic about our visit to David, explaining that Rose and I would be going to visit Zakia the following day.

'On a *boda*? Isn't her village somehow far away?' Dominic asked.

I had no idea and looked to Rose, who shrugged with a smile. 'It is somehow very far, but what can we do?'

'Well, if you don't need the car tomorrow, Dominic, I could drive?' I offered.

They stared at me in disbelief. 'You drive?'

'Of course,' I smiled. I watched their stunned faces; it hadn't occurred to them that I might possess such a skill, which at that time was incredibly rare among women in Uganda.

So the next day, Rose and I set off in Dominic's car on the first of many 'girls' road trips' across Uganda. In the back seat sat Zakia's twelve-year-old stepbrother, who would be our guide in helping find their home village, which Rose had never been to. We left in the cool early morning, eager to get under way. Two and a half hours later, we had driven down roads that wouldn't pass as footpaths, crossed dry, rocky paddocks, made our way through herds of long-horned cattle and even traversed a lake. When the track we were following disappeared completely into a thick forest, Zakia's stepbrother looked sadly down at his hands and we concluded that we were officially lost. Rose called out to a man wheeling his bike, laden with crates of tomatoes, and asked for directions. He pointed one way and then another and, with a nod, set off on his way. Right. Eventually Rose managed to get hold of one of Zakia's uncles, who came on a motorbike to find us and expertly guided us through the hills.

When we finally pulled up outside Zakia's home, her entire extended family was waiting for us. The house was much more substantial than David's, with plastered walls and a nailed-down roof, but it housed over a dozen family members. They each greeted me by name, and as we followed them inside I could hear the younger children giggling as they whispered, 'Madam Emma, Madam Emma!' It surprised me that they all knew my name, but I supposed that *muzungu* visitors were rare in these parts.

The women of the family had prepared a veritable feast in honour of our visit. I watched as a multitude of dishes appeared, and then realised with horror that it was *all* for me and Rose; everyone else had disappeared behind a thin lace curtain inside the house. Kneeling on woven mats that covered the concrete floor, we ate as much as we could but there was still so much left over. Once our hosts were certain that we had satisfied our appetites, they reappeared and I was relieved to find that the food we had not eaten was being fed to the little waiting mouths behind the curtain.

Rose helped translate my questions about Zakia's family, which I wanted to relay to Matt and his friend Shane, Zakia's sponsors. I learned that her mother had died of HIV/AIDS when Zakia was just three years old, and her father was also HIV-positive. Fortunately, her stepmother, now sitting smiling before us, was an incredibly kind woman who had welcomed Zakia and her siblings into the family, insisting that they attend KAASO with her own children — a rare act of generosity from stepmother to stepchild in Uganda.

I had brought a letter and a map from Matt to show Zakia and her family where he was from — Australia — and where he was currently living — Turkey. I tried to explain that he lived on a very big boat called a 'superyacht' and it was his job to drive the boat around for the owner, but, not surprisingly, I was met with looks of confusion. Matt had marked out that season's trip around the Mediterranean, and Zakia traced his journey with her finger along the line he had drawn from Turkey to Greece to France. I wondered what she pictured when she tried to imagine Matt on this thing called a 'superyacht'. It was so far removed from her own reality, but, as globalisation continued its far-reaching spread, these young students were learning more about and becoming increasingly connected to the big wide world. It was important to me to be completely honest in letting them know the truth about their sponsors and what they did for a living.

While lunch had already seemed like a huge gift of thanks,

that was only the beginning. Pouring out from behind the lace curtain, Zakia's family members showered me with gifts — woven bags and baskets, packages of eggs, beans, tomatoes, avocados and giant bunches of *matooke*, all carefully wrapped in banana leaves. Their gratitude was immense and I felt truly humbled by their thanks — and overwhelmed by the mountain of gifts piled before me.

Although it was hard to ignore the voice in my head screaming 'It's too much! Please keep this food to feed your family', I had come to understand the importance of *accepting* as well as *giving*, so I knew to receive the gifts graciously. These beautifully wrapped parcels were the only way the family had to repay the huge gift they had been given: Zakia's education. For me to turn these gifts away would be to say, 'Look, you can't even afford to educate your children, so keep this food because you clearly need it.' An unimaginable insult. The parcels that lay before me were what enabled Zakia's family to keep their dignity intact. Even if the eggs and beans never made it to Matt and Shane, the mats and baskets would and the story of this visit would be shared in intricate detail.

The next morning, Teacher Sarah asked if she could join me and Rose for the day, curious to see what took place on our 'visits'. We gladly agreed, and her contagious laughter filled the car during our long journey to the village where Teddy, Don and Gendy's sponsor child, lived. Teddy's mother had died seven years earlier of 'headache', and her father lived in another town two hours away where he had found work as a security guard, earning the equivalent of US$35 a month. Teddy now lived with her stepmother and step-siblings. They spent the morning graciously hosting us; then, just as lunch was being served, Teddy's father came flying into the village on the back of a *boda*. He worked long hours and never got a day off, but when he heard that I had come to visit, he begged his boss to let today be his one day off for the year.

Now, as we sat in their small sitting room eating together, he grinned at me as Rose translated his words: 'Madam Emma coming to my very house in this small village. Eh! I have never even dreamed about it but now this day has come!' He walked me around the village, proudly introducing me to everyone he knew. I was met with such warmth, such familiarity, and it suddenly struck me that the reception I was getting was not just because of the support I had brought to their community, but because they felt they already knew me. It hadn't occurred to me that while I was out in the world sharing stories about KAASO and the sponsor students, back here in the children's home villages, their families were talking about *us* — the sponsors and I were household names to them.

I thought back to the recognition on David's grandfather's face when I was introduced to him, to Zakia's little siblings whispering my name as I entered their house, and now Teddy's father introducing me to his entire village like a long-lost relative. The excitement my visits caused wasn't because I was a *muzungu*; it was because I was considered part of the family. The emotion of that realisation flooded through me. As I walked slowly on, struggling to compose myself, I felt a warm hand engulfing mine, giving it a gentle squeeze. Teacher Sarah had come to walk alongside me.

'Madam Emma, I've understood it today,' she said solemnly. It was the first time I'd ever seen her serious. 'How much it means for you to visit these homes in these small villages. You are showing them that you really care — you are not one of those "big" people who just send money but will never come down these bad roads to see for themselves. The people here, they feel honoured you are in their homes. Just today, I've realised how much that means.'

I nodded, not trusting myself to speak for fear of bursting into tears. I had realised the same thing. And it meant the world to me.

Before long, the term at KAASO ended and parents, friends and neighbours poured into the school grounds, some on foot, some on *bodas*, a rare few by car, to pick up their children and take them home. The school population plummeted overnight from over 600 children to less than 100, and then slowly emptied out until only a few students remained. Brenda was among those left behind.

Each day, she would appear soundlessly at my door, a shy smile on her face.

'Madam Emma, please can I read a book?'

I had brought with me a small library of books that I kept in my room to read with the children during my time at KAASO, after which they would all be gifted to the main library. I would sit, watching in awe as Brenda hungrily ploughed her way through my collection, reading aloud to me, turning page after page to find out whether Cinderella would be reunited with the prince. It never ceased to amaze me; back in 2009 she had been bottom of my P1 English class and I would often sit with her after class, trying to explain the lessons in a language that was far beyond her. Now, she came to me daily with stories to tell and laughter to share. One day she arrived at my door, proudly clutching a piece of paper, much in the same way she had held her mother's gold coin in the handkerchief on Visiting Day.

'What's that, Brenda?' I asked, knowing that she was dying to show me.

She turned the page around. It was her end-of-year English exam, just back from her teacher. And there was '87%' written in red pen across the top.

'English is my best subject now, Madam Emma,' she told me, and I squeezed her tight, my heart bursting.

But for all these wonderful moments we shared, there was something not quite right. There was a spark missing in Brenda, and I couldn't quite work it out. On her eleventh birthday, it all became clear. I had wrapped a small gift for her, knowing that while birthdays were not really celebrated among the children, she was one of the few left at KAASO and I wanted to do something special for her. Brenda unwrapped the parcel and looked up at me when she saw it — *Cinderella*. 'For me?' she asked. I nodded and she smiled back, but it was only a half-smile.

'Is everything okay, Brenda?' I asked, sitting down on my bedroom floor next to her.

With her eyes fixed on the image of Cinderella, dancing in the arms of the prince, she fiddled with the pages nervously, then whispered that her father had died a few weeks earlier.

First her mother and now her father. How could life be so cruel to someone so young? I took her in my arms and told her how sorry I was, but she just looked up at me with a sad smile that seemed to say, 'That's life.'

Our visits to the sponsor children continued, and over the next few weeks Rose and I travelled hundreds of kilometres over dusty, bumpy roads, met armies of relatives, drank countless cups of tea, and were gifted with multiple squawking chickens, taking me back to my very first day in Uganda four years earlier with the chicken that had hit me in the face as it escaped from the boot of Dominic's car.

It was an intensely emotional time, but I had to keep going; there were still more visits to make — including two that I knew would be very difficult. With handwritten letters tucked carefully into my diary, Rose and I set out on a two-hour drive followed by a half-hour trek, which brought us to a little house on a hill where Charles, one of Mark and Jan's two sponsor children, lived with his grandmother and his young orphaned cousins and siblings. Charles's father had died of HIV/AIDS in 2010 and his mother was long-gone — no one knew whether she was dead or alive. His extended family had travelled a long way to be there for my visit, and they literally fell on me in a flood of tears, thanking me profusely for helping their late brother's son. Three years after his death, their grief was still so raw within the stark concrete walls of their family home.

I felt terrible bringing more heartache into their already difficult life, but I needed them to know the truth. Gently, I sat down and explained that Mark had died the previous November. The family was distraught, but it was clear that their anguish wasn't because of worry about whether Charles's sponsorship would continue; it was because they considered Mark a part of their family. Nonetheless, it was a huge relief to hand over Jan's letter, confirming that she would continue what her husband had started. I watched as Charles carefully translated the letter while his family murmured their words of condolence, promising to pray for Jan and for Mark's memory. A similar scene played out in the home of Mark's other sponsor child, Anthony. While it was hard to re-live the loss of Mark all over again, I was grateful to leave knowing that both boys would still be provided for.

There was one family that I had visited on every trip to Uganda, and now it felt like coming home to walk through that blue wooden door and be engulfed by the warm arms and raucous laughter of Henry's mother, Noeline. In spite of the hardships she had endured, she was always upbeat and positive and would shriek with delight when she saw me, and then insist on preparing a feast as enormous as her smile so that Rose and I could enjoy the fruits of her labour from the gardens. Henry would rush around waiting on us, flashing his cheeky grin, while Merisha, his little half-sister, sang songs to us that she had learned in nursery school, and Ronald, his three-year-old half-brother, crawled into my lap, half thrilled and half terrified by my presence.

It was dark when we arrived back at KAASO after the visit to Henry. Brenda was waiting for me, and we read stories together until it was time for her to go to bed and me to go for dinner. Dominic arrived late and, ladling spoonfuls of steaming beans onto his *matooke*, announced the news that was quickly spreading across the world: Nelson Mandela had died. I still marvelled at the spread of information here. From the early days when Dominic thought you checked emails at the post office through to today with mobile phones and even TVs popping up in various villages, the world was becoming increasingly connected no matter where you were.

We spent the rest of the night talking about Nelson Mandela and all he had managed to achieve against such great odds. It seemed somehow appropriate to be hearing the news here, on the African continent. Halfway through our conversation, I realised that Dominic and Rose were discussing Mandela's passing without any great sadness. He had been 95 years old, an impressive life span for anyone, and while he had suffered greatly and lived through incredibly difficult times, he had also shaped a generation and his legacy would echo through the rest of time. That was not something to lament.

When I got back to my room that night, I tumbled into bed, exhausted. In the darkness, I heard something drop, and pulled back my mosquito net to find a letter lying on the ground. I picked it up and, tucked safely beneath my net, read it by torchlight. It said:

Dear Madam Emma,

Hope you are cool and good. Thanks for coming back to KAASO and loving us. Thanks so much for being there for us. I appreciate your endeavours and all that you have done to make life be life and not something else.

I personally appreciate you for the change you've brought in my life. I'm grateful for all you have done to move me forward and bringing a smile to my face. It is only of now that I can realise my dreams being unfolded before me, and my future brightening.

Thanks for the love and care you have always shown me. I'm grateful for everything you do and I promise that I will never let you down and I will always be there for you.

I love you.
Your Kiwi son,
Henry Rogers Ssemunywa xxoxox

My eyes shone, and in that moment I truly understood, for the first time in four years, the full extent of what these sponsorships were achieving. I thought of all the conversations at cocktail parties that had translated into offers of support, that turned into bank transfers, that became wads of shillings that Rose withdrew in Kyotera and then transported across the country, bumping her way over pot-holed roads to pay school fees to various bursars.

I knew all that, of course — but it was what happened next, the actual *education* part, that I hadn't fully thought about. The hours upon hours of lessons the children were having, the ideas and concepts they were being taught, the attitudes they were adopting, their growing determination to succeed, and the pride that all this brought their families. But it was even *more* than that — these sponsorships brought hope. Hope of a better life, hope of a future, hope for parents that their children could be educated and really make something of themselves. Nelson Mandela's rousing words rang in my ears: 'Education is the most powerful weapon which you can use to change the world.'

Looking down in the torchlight at Henry's letter, I realised that this was just what we were doing. Henry's sponsorship wasn't changing the whole world, but it was certainly changing *his* world. And the value of that could not be underestimated.

I thought about the first letter he came to me with and the disappointment my initial answer had brought him. By agreeing to sponsor him in the end, my family and I had given him the opportunity to have the bright future he deserved in a world where receiving a high-quality education was the key to everything. I knew how much he appreciated the chance to continue his studies, but I don't think I had ever truly understood the full extent of his gratitude until that moment.

By going into the villages of the sponsor students, deeper and further than I had gone before, I was seeing with my own eyes the transformation that was taking place in these children, their families and their community. It was truly humbling — and I vowed to continue the work I was doing.

My final sponsor visit was complicated. Having just finished her first year of secondary school, Stellah had come back to KAASO for the holidays. We had enjoyed many happy afternoons under the music tree together, but when the idea of visiting her home village came up, Stellah froze. I knew that her father was not a kind man, and that her mother had been driven away to work as a maid in Kampala, where she earned barely enough to scrape by. When I asked Stellah whether she would be going back to her home village for the holidays, she shook her head vehemently. As I slowly coaxed the story out of her, I began to understand why.

Three years ago, she told me, her father had decided to get rid of the burden of Stellah, her brother and her sister. While they were away at school, their father took all of their possessions and set fire to them. Fortunately the children were not there during this fit of rage so they escaped physically unscathed, but the emotional damage ran deep. When I spoke to Rose about Stellah's situation, she said that she kept Stellah at KAASO during the holidays for safety.

'This is one visit we will have to miss, as it is not wise for us to take you there. If Stellah's father sees that she is supported by a *muzungu*, I fear this will make her situation worse. Her father does not even know she is at secondary school — he does not care — but it is best this way. We will take Stellah to Kampala when you leave — her grandmother's house is nearby and she can stay there for Christmas.'

I bit back my tears, unable to comprehend the horror that Stellah had lived through. No wonder she loved to lose herself in music. It was probably her way of distracting herself from her cruel reality. *An accident of birth.* What had Stellah done to deserve such a fate?

Life at KAASO was full of such highs and lows, such contrasts of beauty and cruelty, simple joys set against thundering injustices. It was a place where I felt like I lived a lifetime in a single week. It took so much energy just to get through each day — my mind exhausted from trying to understand, to take everything in, to solve all the problems in this corner of the world, and, in the absence of any solutions, to work out how best to deal with them. It was often overwhelming.

In my final days in Uganda, I had a near-death experience which encapsulated these paradoxes, contrasts and challenges. I was driving Dominic's car up to Masaka when I was startled by a commotion in the bushes on the side of the road. I looked over, and suddenly a flash of white appeared and a crested crane came flapping magnificently across my path. Crested cranes are the national birds of Uganda and are spectacularly beautiful with their golden crowns arching heavenwards. I was mesmerised by this rare sighting when, all of a sudden,

I looked up to see that a truck had crossed onto my side of the road and was hurtling straight for me. I swerved off the road into the ditch and, in doing so, I ran over a dog. The dog, it turned out, was already dead, but the incident was no less disturbing. In those few seconds I felt like my life in Uganda had been summed up — one minute you are awestruck by profound beauty, the next you find yourself staring death in the face as the raw truth of life smacks into you.

My time at KAASO ended with a Christmas party for the sponsor students. Everyone rose at dawn and got to work. Sacks were laid across the school's courtyard, giant cauldron-like pots were lined up, fires were lit and the *matooke*-peeling began. The boys slaughtered chickens, and we decorated the school hall with flowers, leaves and Christmas decorations that I had brought over with me. Henry and I chopped down a Christmas tree — a branch from one of the trees in his mother's garden — and we decorated it with balloons, as was traditional in Uganda.

After our Christmas lunch we held our inaugural meeting of the newly formed 'Kiwi Sponsorships Committee'. Henry was elected as the Chairperson, Stellah the Deputy-Chairperson, David the 'Mobiliser' and Juliet was to be the Secretary. The purpose of the committee was to help bond the sponsor students together and to enable the younger ones to learn from the older ones. Henry and his classmates were finishing their fourth year of secondary school, while Stellah's year had just completed Senior One; it was helpful for the different age groups to interact and pool their knowledge, allowing them to all work together towards a successful future.

Before the meeting drew to a close, Rose stood to make a final address. She shared the extraordinary story of Dominic, one of 27 children whose mother had died just after he was born. His father's other wives did nothing to help him and he was essentially left on his own to make his way in life, with only his elderly grandmother as support. Dominic put himself through school, working on the Headmaster's gardens, digging on people's farms, doing any odd job he could find to help keep himself in school.

'Director did not have anyone to pay his fees, he had to make it on his own. You are those lucky few who do not have to worry about school fees. You have a great opportunity before you, but do not take it for granted. You must "do a Dominic" — by that, I mean that you must work hard to make something of yourself, to demonstrate to those sponsors that their investment in you was worthwhile. After this long journey, you must come out as *something*.'

It was incredibly moving to hear Rose speak so passionately about her talented husband, and I watched the students' faces held captivated by their Headmistress's words.

After one final music session, it was time to say goodbye to my little friends. Henry came running over and threw his arms around me with a radiant smile. 'Madam Emma, don't be sad. We will meet!' I grinned in spite of myself. He knew me so well, understanding how emotional I got each time we said goodbye, so I did my best to hide my tears as I hugged him before wedging myself into the back seat of Dominic's car. The car was crammed to bursting — both Dominic and Rose were coming to Kampala to visit Rose's family, bringing their own children as well as Brenda and Stellah who we would drop at their respective grandmothers' houses on the way.

As we began our long journey north, I could feel that old familiar ache in my heart. The longer I stayed in Uganda, the deeper I went, the more I cared and the harder it became to leave. I was so looking forward to seeing Nathan again — he would be waiting for me at Sydney airport in Australia — but that didn't make it any easier to leave my village home.

I had no idea what the following year would bring for me, and the thought scared me. I knew Nathan wanted to talk through 'our future', which was less about *if* we would be together but *how* we would be together. While I was in the village, he had purposely been holding off running through his travel schedule for the coming year with me, which I knew meant that it wasn't going to be easy. He would be juggling an Olympic campaign with his duties as skipper for Artemis Racing — both full-time jobs and both pulling him in different directions, from Sydney to Rio to San Francisco. I had always lived my life from event to event without the certainty of a continuing job, but this was different. I now had someone else to factor into my life and I wasn't quite sure how I was going to manage it.

One thing that had become crystal-clear over the past month, however, was that KAASO had become an integral part of me. Not in a one-off-six-months kind of way, or even a six-year-sponsorship kind of way. But in an ingrained-in-my-very-core-for-the-rest-of-my-life kind of way. Just as coming to Uganda for the first time had required me to have faith that I would find my direction, leaving now to start an unknown life with Nathan was requiring that same kind of faith. It was time to start a new adventure.

I knew that I would find a way; I just wasn't sure how yet. But sitting in the back seat with Stellah's warm body pressed next to mine and Brenda's little hand in my lap, I realised that I just needed to do as people here did. *Let life be*. Laugh, sing a song, let it all wash over you, and keep moving forward. There would always be a school, a family, a village and a community on the other side of the world waiting to welcome me with open arms. What more did I need beyond the knowledge that I would forever return to this place that I loved wildly even if it would endlessly confuse me and make my heart break?

CHAPTER
FOURTEEN

S ummer was in full swing when I arrived in Sydney the week before Christmas. It was bliss to be reunited with Nathan, and we chatted non-stop on the two-hour drive north to Wangi Wangi, his home town in Lake Macquarie. Nathan had a small house on the lakefront just down the road from his parents' place and, knowing that his family was as close as mine, I assumed that we'd head straight up to their house after my much-needed shower.

'Yes, they're dying to see you, so we'll go up and say hi soon. But first, I really need to run through this with you,' he said, motioning for me to join him at his laptop where he had pulled up his calendar for the following year, 2014.

'Really? We have do that right now?' I laughed, still dripping from my shower. 'I've barely washed the dust off my feet.'

'I know, I'm sorry. I don't mean to rush you but I've been holding off on confirming this for a month now and the guys at Artemis really need to know my movements.'

'By today?' I asked.

'By yesterday, actually.'

'Alrighty then . . .' I took a seat next to him, wondering how hard it could be to work out a simple calendar.

Very, very hard, it turned out.

The year started out easily enough, with trips between New Zealand and Australia for various regattas in January and February, but got steadily more complicated as both the Olympic season and the America's Cup training and racing started in full force. There was an Artemis team-building camp in California, followed by Olympic training back in Australia, then a flight to Munich to pick up a car and drive to a regatta in the south of France before driving the Olympic boat back through the Swiss Alps where it would be stored. That would be followed by a trip to Brittany on the Atlantic coast to test-drive a new foiling boat before heading back to San Francisco for more Artemis training. From there, things got even crazier. Spain, Finland, England, Brazil, Sweden, New Zealand, back to Spain and on to Bermuda, with trips to San Francisco and Lake Macquarie interspersed throughout.

I took a deep breath. Where did I possibly fit into this? *Let life be*, I reminded myself. Trying to stay positive, I smiled and said, as lightly as I could manage, 'Well it's simple, really. I'll just colour-code all the different places on your calendar and whichever colour is the most prominent is where you'll be most often, so I'll base myself there. I can get a job there and you can come visit me in your spare time.'

It was clear that there was no 'spare' time factored into this calendar, but Nathan just nodded and let me do my thing. He could no doubt see exactly where this was heading, but he knew me better than to interrupt me once I'd set my mind to something. I set each country a different colour and shaded every regatta and training session accordingly. When I was done I studied the spreadsheet, trying to work out which colour cropped up the most, thus determining where my new life would be — but no answer presented itself. The page was a psychedelic rainbow of colours. The colour changed every week or two, and very few colours recurred for any length of time. I burst into tears.

'There's no room for me,' I sobbed. 'I don't fit into your life! This is impossible.' I was still slightly delirious from over 30 hours of travel, and my Ugandan resolve to just go with the flow had quickly evaporated. 'I'm never going to see you . . .'

Nathan took me in his arms. 'Hey, Em, come here. It's okay. We'll make it work. It'll be fine, I promise.'

'But how?' I cried. 'Look at this — it's crazy! If I base myself in any of these places I'll only see you once or twice a year.' I hadn't waited 30 years to meet my soulmate only to live a world apart. Neither of us wanted that, but there just didn't seem to be any other way.

'I know. Look, I've had a lot of time to think about this since you've been away,' Nathan began slowly, choosing his words carefully. 'And I've come up with a solution.'

I stared at him dubiously as he wiped away a tear that was clinging stubbornly to my chin.

'You travel with me,' he said. I sat, waiting to hear more, but that seemed to be it — his magical solution.

'What do you mean, I *travel with you*? Everywhere? I just fly around the world with you? You'll be sailing every day — what will *I* do?' The questions came out thick and fast, with the most worrying one hanging unspoken in the air: What would people think of me? I had no intention of being *that* girl who just followed her boyfriend around the world. I was far too independent for that.

'Think about it for a sec, Em,' Nathan said patiently. 'We travel together, we get to explore the world and visit amazing places, and we'll create so many incredible memories that we will look back on for the rest of our life. And wherever we go, you can keep doing your work for KAASO. You'll meet so many new people on the road and you can tell them all about KAASO and, knowing you, they'll probably all be lining up to sponsor your kids after half an hour of chatting to you. Look, you're always saying you don't have enough time for all your different projects in Uganda. This is your chance.'

In my mind the wheels were starting to spin, and I began to picture a life where I actually had time for the things I felt so passionately about. Time to keep in touch, time to follow through, time to go back to Uganda for regular visits. I could start up that KAASO blog I had been talking about, I could get better organised with my sponsorship programme, and I could do things thoroughly rather than just scraping the surface. But then reality kicked in — what would I do for a job? I didn't mean something to pass my time — I'd have more than enough 'work' to keep me busy — I meant to earn *money*, that vital substance needed for survival. I had savings from my time in San Francisco, but not enough to travel the world for a year. Before I had a chance to speak, Nathan read my mind.

'I will support you Em — financially. All my flights and accommodation are covered anyway, and I can use my air miles for a lot of your flights. And before you go giving me that look, I can assure you this is a two-way thing — these next few years are going to be seriously busy and I need your support. We're a team, we work best together. I've spent hours studying this calendar and I just don't see any other way. Em, I'm asking you to trust me, to at least give it a go. Please, come with me.'

I sat staring into his eyes that were so full of love and care and concern and hope. I was about to say that I needed time to think about it, to wrap my mind around everything, when a little voice in my head spoke up. *Em, the love of your life just asked you to travel the world with him. He is promising to support you not just financially but also emotionally. He has a huge journey ahead and he wants you to be there with him every step of the way. Do you really need to think about it?* Opportunities like this don't present themselves often, and I had been taught that when they did, to throw caution to the wind and grasp them with both hands. When had I ever been one to take the sensible option?

I leaned forward and kissed him.

'I take it that's a yes?' he asked with a grin.

'Yes,' I said.

And so our magical mystery tour began. We changed continents every couple of weeks, catching more planes, trains, taxis, buses and ferries than I'd thought possible. I had to be incredibly organised, sorting out the never-ending logistics needed to maintain our ridiculous lifestyle, booking flights, renting apartments, reserving hotel rooms and figuring out local ground transportation around the world. My French and Spanish proved incredibly helpful, and Nathan marvelled as I navigated my way through cultures, currencies and international cell-phone companies, while my exasperated brother tried to keep up with my ever-changing string of local phone numbers.

Meanwhile, my sponsorship programme in Uganda was thriving thanks to the time I was now able to put into it. On my last trip to KAASO, once our sponsor visits had been completed I had sat down with Rose to do an overview of all the existing sponsorships, including those beyond the scope of my Kiwi Sponsorships programme. I learned that Brenda was being sponsored by a past volunteer at KAASO, which was a relief to me — she had been on my mind ever since I'd learned about the death of her father, and I had planned to speak to Rose about sponsoring her had she not already had a sponsor.

Unfortunately, there were many stories of well-intentioned sponsors who had taken on students but, over time, had been unable to continue and had dropped their support, not realising how difficult a position this left the students in back in Uganda. While this was disappointing to hear, I understood — it was a long commitment and the fees were expensive. People got busy with their own lives and KAASO would fade into the background, the urgency of need forgotten. Eventually, Rose and I decided that the best way to streamline things would be for me to incorporate all of the existing sponsorships into the Kiwi Sponsorships, including the 'dropped' children whom I hoped to find new sponsors for. Rose was relieved to have the system simplified and I was buzzing with purpose.

From around the world I emailed the various sponsors, sharing the stories of my visits to their children's home villages and attaching the photos and videos I had taken of the children and their families. In my group email update, I included a small piece on the 'dropped' students, asking if anyone knew of someone who might be interested in helping.

I was blown away by the response. Don and Gendy wrote

back immediately offering to support one of these students, in addition to their sponsorship of Teddy. Not only that, but the stories they had been sharing with their own children and grandchildren about my trips to Uganda had really resonated, and now their daughter, Sarah, and her husband, Matt, wanted to get involved in sponsoring a child. Jono Macbeth, a sailor from Oracle Team USA's winning crew and now the Sailing Team Manager for the new British America's Cup team, and his wife, Teressa, wrote a beautiful message saying that they were firm believers in providing opportunities to those less fortunate than others, and was there a child they could sponsor? Simon readily agreed to take on a second child, and Janine Smith, the manager of the sailing holidays company I had worked for in the Greek Islands, who had been following my stories over the years, also offered to sponsor a child. I couldn't believe the momentum that had gathered in such a short time — within just a few months, the Kiwi Sponsorships had gone from twelve to 21 children.

This whole sponsorship programme had started in the hope that enabling children to get a good education would equip them with the tools to make their own way in the world, and to become role models in their own communities, just as Dominic and Rose were in theirs. I believed passionately that if the children were given a chance to make something of themselves, they would — all they needed was a start, an education. The initial trigger had been one boy — Henry — who had impressed me with his determination and his unwillingness to give up on his dream. Now, it seemed, others were starting to see what I had caught a glimpse of in that hopeful young face five years earlier. It felt like everything was falling into place.

On a spring morning in 2014, I arrived in San Francisco to an email from Henry, sharing with me his exam results. He was proud to announce that he had been fourth in his year, and then went on to say:

> For the good news I have to tell you is that as I was preparing to return to school, something happened and this is . . . I GOT A SCHOLARSHIP FOR MY HIGH SCHOOL AT ST HENRY'S COLLEGE!
>
> And this was due to my conduct and hard work for the past four years at school. The scholarship is from The University Of St Thomas in the United States Of America. And what is so exciting about this is that if I perform well at the end I MAY study my University course there in the USA.
>
> All these opportunities have come my way because of your support for me at St Henry's College.
>
> Thank you so much and send all my regards to the Kiwi family!
>
> BIG UP AND KEEP SMILING
>
> Love Henry — Kiwi Son xoxo

I was speechless. His final two years of fees for secondary schooling at St Henry's would be covered, and there was a chance that he might even get a scholarship for college in the US. It was beyond my wildest dreams. Even though it was 5 a.m. in New Zealand, I had to ring my parents to share the good news. They were sleepily over the moon, assuring me that they would send congratulatory messages to Henry once the sun came up. I forwarded the email on to Nathan, who was out sailing on San Francisco Bay, then went and celebrated with a coffee and a diary-writing session in North Beach.

Buoyed by Henry's incredible news, I finally set about creating the blog I had been talking about for so long, pulling together all my stories from the past five years at KAASO and illustrating them with photos. The idea was that my blog would help me share my stories more easily with those I met along the way, and might even reach a new audience of people who stumbled across it online. *I Left My Heart In Uganda* was launched in early May, and on the first day I had over a thousand people visit my site. I couldn't believe it. All the time I had been painstakingly uploading posts, backdating my stories since my first trip to Uganda, and wondering if anyone would ever read them, it now seemed that yes, they would. Travelling as the girlfriend of an incredibly busy sailor could be a lonely business at times, but this massive response made me feel less alone; I felt connected to a community of people that cared.

Not only did my blog launch bring me a sense of encouragement, but it continued to build my network of support. Another America's Cup sailor, Glenn Ashby, and his wife, Mel, who were old friends of Nathan's from their time together competing for Australia at the Beijing Olympics, wrote to me saying that they had seen my blog launch and were interested in sponsorship. They had been looking into some of the bigger, more commercial child-sponsorship programmes, but so many had large administrative costs and they wondered if they might be able to sponsor more meaningfully through me instead.

I wrote back saying that I'd be delighted to have them as sponsors, assuring them that any money they gave would go directly to their sponsor child — no admin fees, no staffing costs, just a straight bank transfer from me to Rose. I also let them know that they would have a close, ongoing personal relationship with their sponsor child, something that was very important to me. I knew of some child-sponsorship programmes that suddenly re-allocated new children to sponsors as their organisation shifted regions, leaving the sponsors wondering what had become of the other child they had previously been supporting. This had happened to Don and Gendy, which is what had led them to sponsor Teddy through me; I had loved watching over the years as their relationship with Teddy deepened, to the extent that now she was considered part of their family.

Glenn and Mel's email came at the perfect time: just that morning I had received an email from Rose, asking for help. It was incredibly rare for Rose to reach out to me so directly, and I knew that if she had, the situation must be serious. She was asking for assistance on behalf of Violah, a fourteen-year-old girl who had been a school dependent at KAASO for the past eight years. Violah's mother had abandoned her when she was two years old and her father had dropped dead on Christmas Day three years later, leaving Violah in the care of her elderly grandmother, Betty. Five of Betty's twelve children had passed away and she was doing her best to support her household of orphaned grandchildren, but her health was declining and the burden was becoming too great. 'When the prospect of a sponsor was discussed with Betty,' Rose wrote, 'she was overcome with tears of joy and gratitude. We are seeking a sponsor who can secure Violah's secondary education, giving her the opportunity for a bright and successful future.'

When I shared Violah's story with Glenn and Mel, they instantly agreed to help. 'A big reason for us wanting to sponsor a child is because of our girls. We want them to understand the simplicity of life. We feel as though we are the lucky ones to be able to be involved in Violah's life. Thank you for providing us this opportunity.' I sent photos of Violah, and she quickly became a source of fascination for Glenn and Mel's young daughters, who asked endless questions about the Ugandan girl smiling at them from their fridge door. Why did Violah's mother leave and why did her father die, and what did their house look like and why did the children shave their heads and could they draw pictures for Violah, *please*? I was so happy to be able to bridge another gap between my two worlds. The pleasure these sponsorships brought not only to those sponsored but also to those *sponsoring* was evident. I no longer felt guilty about asking for money from those who came to me genuinely wanting to help.

I was on a high: children were being sponsored, sponsors were feeling fulfilled, Rose's burden was being eased, I was spreading the KAASO story, and people were responding with offers of support. The District Chairman's words from all those years ago rang again in my ears: 'I request that you become our ambassadors in your country and around the world. Wherever you go, speak to your communities and please, attract some assistance for us.' I had done just that, and it felt good. I should have been satisfied. However, there was a niggling voice in the back of my head that I had been fighting to ignore ever since I first agreed to travel with Nathan. It was the voice of judgement, the voice of other people's opinions, that asked, 'So, Emma, what do you *do?* I mean, for a job?' I wasn't working, I wasn't earning my own money, my boyfriend was supporting me — and I was embarrassed by that position of privilege. As much as I had always shied away from the 'normal' path, it still felt wrong not to be working; and even though Nathan assured me constantly that what I was doing was incredibly valuable, not only to him but also to the sponsors and the children in Uganda, I hated to think what people were saying behind my back. Every time I arrived at another event with Nathan, the voices in my head sniggered, 'Ah yeah, here comes Em again. Just following Nath around the world.'

The frustrating part was that my lack of paid work wasn't from lack of trying. I had hit up every contact, every lead I had in the sailing world, seeing whether there was a way I might be able to work remotely or on a part-time basis, but everyone had come back with the same answer: it was all or nothing. As much as I toyed with the idea of accepting one of these full-time offers, I knew that if I committed to taking a job across the world with my own manic travel schedule, Nathan and I would never, ever see each other. So I bit back my tears as I replied, thanking people for the opportunity but regretfully declining. Another brick wall hit in my search for the impossible — a job that would fit in with the lifestyle of an elite athlete travelling 365 days a year.

It never occurred to me that it wasn't actually possible to find a normal job within such an abnormal world, and that I was simply adding my name to a list of many people before me who'd had to give up their own full-time working careers to be at the side of their other half living a life less ordinary. I rang Mama, knowing that she had travelled the world with Dad for years; maybe she would have some advice for me.

'Ah, Ems.' I could hear the smile in her voice, which seemed to imply that she had been waiting for this call for some time now. 'Welcome to my world. You have no idea how many times your dad helped me through my own identity crises over the years. I lost several jobs along the way so that we could be a family together and so that we could take the amazing opportunities presented to us. It's certainly not easy, but you're doing the right thing. Sorry, but no one in our family was ever destined to be normal.'

Her words helped immensely, and an email from Dominic soon afterwards re-ignited my sense of purpose. He had been invited back to Florida to complete the final stage of the two-part leadership and educational fellowship he had begun the previous year. This time I knew to ask about money, and learned that — as a testament to the impact Dominic had had on the National Educator Program — they were once again offering to support all his in-country costs but, yet again, their budget could not stretch to international flights.

Since his last trip, Dominic had formed a partnership with an American school, which had donated over twenty laptops to the KAASO computer lab. He had also built relationships with local community leaders in the US who had been helping with school fund-raisers for KAASO. The conference he attended had introduced the idea of 'Career

Academies' — projects within schools that equipped students with practical skills while they continued their studies. KAASO had established a poultry project and expanded their piggery, now run by young students under the watchful guidance of teachers. The flow-on effect from Dominic's trip to the United States was immense, and I knew I had to find a way to help him get back for the final section of the course.

Dominic had always had a way with words, and I was still smiling at his quirky turns of phrase when Nathan came home, salty after a day's training on San Francisco Bay.

'What's so funny?' he asked, as he walked in the door.

I told him about Dominic's request, then read him the last line of the email aloud: 'I feel that if I continue with this course, it will give me a great chance to change KAASO, Uganda and The World.'

'The World? That's a big call,' Nathan said with a grin.

'Yes, it sure is,' I said. 'It's so Dominic. I just wish I had another $2000 in the KAASO fund-raising account. There have been so many new sponsors coming on board — which is amazing — but I don't want to overstretch my network. The last thing I want is for people to start feeling like every email I send is a request for money.' I turned to face Nathan. 'Anyway, how was your day? Pretty breezy out there, right?'

Nathan gave me a run-through of his day's training, then went to have a shower. I was still sitting, re-reading Dominic's email and trying to work out what to do, when Nathan came out. He slipped his arms around me, reading over my shoulder. 'Still trying to solve the problems of The World?'

'Something like that,' I said, distracted.

'I'd like to help,' he said.

'Mmm.' I kept reading, his words not registering.

'Em, I said I'd like to help. You know you only need to ask. I agree that it's incredibly important for Dominic to finish what he started. I'd like to pay for his flights.'

I swung around to face him. 'Seriously?' Nathan already helped me with my sponsorships and was always so supportive of my trips back to Uganda; it never occurred to me to ask him for direct help for KAASO.

I threw my arms around him. 'Thank you, thank you, thank you!' I cried, so grateful for his endless support. I kissed him, and he smiled his cheeky grin as I set to work. There wasn't much time before Dominic was due to fly out and I had a lot to organise.

As the preparations for Dominic's trip began to take shape, I stopped off in New Zealand to visit family and friends on the way to meet up with Nathan, who had gone back to Australia for an Olympic training camp. It was wonderful to see Cherie, who had recently graduated with her degree in Development Studies and was now working in Auckland with families from refugee backgrounds. She took me to an evening food market, set up by former refugee women who erected stalls and cooked up their national dishes from around the world, selling their meals to crowds of hungry market-goers. My taste buds were tingling as we walked from one stall to the next, the night filled with the mingling smells of exotic spices as bubbling dishes simmered and splattered in giant pots. Everywhere we went, women came running over to embrace Cherie, engulfing her in their warm arms, wooden spoons waving through the air.

'This girl — she is an angel!' they would tell me again and again. 'Cherie, she do so much for us. We say THANK YOU!'

I smiled as children came running out from behind their mothers' long dresses to come and see Cherie, who pretended to chase them; they squealed with delight as they ran for cover. I thought about the different paths Cherie and I had taken since leaving KAASO almost five years earlier. After finishing her Bachelor's degree in Auckland, Cherie had worked with New Zealand Refugee Services before getting involved with a not-for-profit that ran the WISE Collective (Women — Inspired — Strong — Empowered and Enterprising), a project which helped women from refugee backgrounds develop the skills and resources required to help generate income to support their own families. The not-for-profit also established Safari Multicultural Playgroups for children of refugee backgrounds, benefiting not only the children but also their mothers. The playgroups gave women the chance to interact with other mothers, as well as offering free adult English classes — empowering women who were often isolated at home while their husbands went to work.

Cherie had made the conscious decision to stay in New Zealand, to invest in her local community and to help those who had made long and dangerous journeys to reach our far-flung corner of the globe. In choosing to work for a non-profit, she was committing to a life where money would be tight and trips back to KAASO difficult, but she would be surrounded by that same love and gratitude I felt at KAASO, right here in her own backyard.

I felt so happy for Cherie that she had found her purpose here among this vibrant, colourful community of extraordinary women. Their wide smiles that erupted into contagious laughter made me think of Teacher Sarah — and suddenly I felt incredibly lonely. Bone-achingly, tear-stingingly, finding-it-hard-to-breathe lonely. Standing there in the night markets, watching Cherie in her element among these women who visibly adored her, I realised how much I missed that sense of community, of feeling like I belonged. The work I did for KAASO was immensely satisfying, but it was mostly remote and I missed that daily interaction, missed being part of a team, missed walking into my old office in San Francisco with a task list as long as my arm and racing through the day to get things done. I missed the high I got from being incredibly busy but somehow managing to achieve everything with a big push — and with an amazing group of people around me.

I had given up all of that to travel with Nathan, and while he always reminded me that *we* were a team and could do things together, he worked long, fourteen-hour days, leaving me alone in cities where I knew no one with hours to mull everything over. While our relationship was as strong as it had ever been, I began to feel my own sense of self slipping away.

Over a plate of Congolese stew, I tried to explain to Cherie my feelings about my lack of identity, my worry that everyone was judging me for doing nothing, not earning my own keep but just following Nathan around the world. Who had I become? Cherie listened, shaking her head before interrupting my melancholic monologue. 'Ems, are you crazy? You do so much for KAASO, it's incredible! You are using this opportunity of travelling with Nath to do so much good. I'm in awe of your dedication to KAASO, and I know so many people feel the same way. Yes, I have a great community here, but you have that at KAASO — not to mention all your sailing friends around the world. Don't forget that I feel guilty that I can't get back to Uganda like you can. You help keep me connected to David and everyone at KAASO, and I'm so grateful for that. The grass is always greener and you know that. You do more than you realise.'

As we left the marketplace, Cherie's words rolled around in my mind and I slowly realised that she was right. This sense of community that she felt here was what I felt at KAASO. And suddenly it struck me that KAASO had become part of my identity. The sense of self-worth, of satisfaction, of belonging, of 'this is who I was born to be' that I once felt in my role with Louis Vuitton, I now felt in Uganda, flying down rutted roads on the back of a *boda* with Rose. And who was to say that working in an office was a more meaningful, more *valid* way to spend your day than trying to help a village community? Sure, my 'job' didn't pay me a wage, but it certainly gave me all the fulfilment and satisfaction I needed, and my 'work' benefited a lot of people.

I understood acutely how lucky I was to be supported by Nathan but, if Mark were here, I knew he would tell me to stop fussing over what other people thought and just get on with the work I was doing. He would remind me that I could reach far more people with the means to support KAASO by continuing on the path I had chosen, and there was nothing to be ashamed of. It wasn't like I was using my position of privilege to buy diamond rings and Dom Pérignon.

At the end of July, Dominic took off for the US, and this time I felt satisfied to have organised most of the logistics and planning myself. I kept in touch with him every day that he was away, speaking to him several times on the phone as well as with his hosts from the National Educator Program. They told me how thrilled they all were to see Dominic again and how much of an impression he was making on everyone at the course.

Each of the participants was to give a presentation, updating the others on the programmes they had implemented over the past year since they had first met, and the organisers told me that they were intentionally saving Dominic's presentation for last. As anticipated, it was a showstopper: everyone was blown away by how much Dominic and Rose had achieved in just a year. The poultry project had taken off, the piggery had expanded, the children were helping in the school gardens, and the vision for future projects was expansive. Dominic graduated from the International Leadership Fellows to a standing ovation; I watched the video the organisers sent me of Dominic, dressed immaculately in his suit and shined shoes, beaming with pride while the room exploded with applause. I knew that I had not let him down this time.

With Dominic's trip complete, it was time to start planning my annual return to KAASO. I pulled out my notebooks, turned a fresh page, and began to get sorted. Nathan's brother, Beau, had always voiced an interest in joining me on one of my visits to Uganda, and when he heard about my plans for my upcoming trip he immediately offered to come with me. It was a bit of a sore spot between Nathan and me that Nathan was unable to come to KAASO — but it would not have been appropriate, given his Olympic and America's Cup commitments, to take off to a landlocked village when he was supposed to be training on the water every day. He promised to come with me as soon as both events were over — in 2017 — but in the meantime I was happy to have Beau join me.

Given Beau's background in photography and videography,

we decided to use our trip to make a short film series about KAASO. From across the globe, we emailed ideas back and forward, brainstorming themes and interview topics, hoping to further spread awareness of the KAASO community and to widen its web of supporters and volunteers. We studied short films on different NGO websites, trying to work out how best to tell the various aspects of the KAASO story. Beau kept joking about putting a Go-Pro on a child and doing a 'day in the life' segment. I just laughed, and told him that all he'd get would be the curious faces of other children trying to work out what the hell was strapped to this poor kid's head.

But while Beau and I were mapping out storyboards, something huge was brewing across the continent — a plague that would threaten to destroy lives, families and communities. Oblivious, I pushed on with our plans to head back to the village I loved so much, believing that nothing could stop us. But the world was about to get in the way.

CHAPTER
FIFTEEN

I first heard about it from Mama. Nathan's Olympic World Championships in Spain had just finished and we were on a short escape together down in the coastal town of Tarifa, the same place where I had first laid eyes on the African continent while living in Valencia. Nathan and I had just sat down to breakfast when Mama rang. She asked how things were going, and I told her how much Nathan and I were loving having a moment away from the world before heading to San Francisco. While it would be busy there, I was excited to have more than a month in one place — a luxury in our itinerant world — during which time I could get sorted for Uganda.

'Yes, well that's actually what I'm calling about, Ems. I don't want to worry you, but I wanted to check you're keeping up with the news. You have heard about the Ebola outbreak, haven't you?'

I took a sip of my tea and smiled. 'Yes, Mama. I have heard about Ebola in *West* Africa and it's awful. But, just to remind you, that's an entire continent away from Uganda over in *East* Africa.'

'I know, Ems, but I just wanted to make sure that you were aware of what's going on and that you are keeping an eye on things over there. I don't know if you fully understand, but this is really serious — people are dying in the thousands and there's no cure. It's not something you should be ignoring, okay? You know I'm only saying this because I love you.' Mama's voice was shaking.

In hindsight, I should have listened to the fear in her voice and done my research so that I could honestly reassure her I was monitoring the situation. Instead, I brushed her off.

'Mama, seriously, I'm fine. Ebola is on the other side of the continent and I'm going back to Uganda as planned. You don't need to worry. Look, I'd better go. Chat soon. Love you, bye.' I hung up and deliberately avoided Nathan's gaze, knowing that he was staring at me with eyebrows raised.

'Em, that was a bit harsh,' he said. 'You know she's just worried about her little girl.'

I suddenly felt irritable. 'Well I'm not a little girl, okay? I'm 31 years old and it's ridiculous to be worried about something that's not happening anywhere near where I'm going. I don't want to talk about it,' I said. 'There's nothing to talk about.'

But there was plenty to talk about. This was just the beginning of the conversation about Ebola, and as the first case reached Texas in the US, it wasn't only my mother who was beginning to panic. I read with scepticism what I considered to be hysterical news articles — the world media blowing things out of proportion. Paranoid groups were getting together to stock up as if the world was ending, encouraging others to buy 'Ebola suits' and prepare for months of being housebound. While the tragedy unfolding across West Africa broke my heart, the media's reaction to individual cases in the West sickened me — people only cared if the threat was in *their* backyard. So what about the Africans?

Two days before my flight to Uganda, my phone rang. This time it was Dad. I swallowed hard. That meant things were serious.

In his painfully logical way, Dad slowly presented his argument. While he understood that the Ebola outbreak in West Africa was still a long way from Uganda, no one could predict with any certainty which way this epidemic was going to go, so why put myself unnecessarily at risk? 'Look, Ems, there's no reason you have to go *now*. KAASO will always be there and Dominic and Rose will always welcome you with open arms — whether it's next week, next month or next year. We're not telling you that you *can't* go, we're just asking you to reconsider — and to actually put some thought into it this time.' He paused and I could hear the emotion in his voice. 'Think what it would do to us, to Nathan, to Nick, if anything happened to you. We couldn't . . .' he caught himself. 'We're just asking you to think about this — seriously. Please, Ems.'

I couldn't speak. Tears streamed down my face and I felt as if I'd been kicked in the guts. Even though my parents were supposedly only asking me to *think* about it, the fact that it was Daddy-o, the one I could never *not* listen to because he was somehow always right, meant that the decision had already been made. I told him I'd think about it anyway, hung up, and then cried as if the world was ending.

I felt embarrassed to have the luxury of choice — to be able to decide whether or not I would travel to a 'dangerous' continent. *Bad luck to all those unfortunate Africans stuck in Africa, the* muzungu *would wait until the world said it was safe to resume travel.* I pictured Dominic and Rose explaining to all my little friends at KAASO that Madam Emma thought it was too dangerous to come and see them. It killed me.

That night, I ranted furiously to Nathan. 'Don't they know how far it is from East to West Africa? Africa's not a country, it's a whole bloody continent, 30 million square kilometres, triple the size of Europe with 54 countries. Do you think if there was an Ebola outbreak in Ukraine, people would stop going to London? No! Of course they'd still go to London because it's not "Africa" — but that's less than *half* the distance between Uganda and West Africa!'

Nathan just let me speak as I rode my high-horse of geographical statistics until eventually I wore myself out. 'Oh, Nath, I so badly want to go,' I whispered. I felt heartbroken that the only thing keeping me from losing my identity was about to be taken from me. While 2014 had been an amazing year in many ways, it had also been a challenging one as I grappled with my sense of self. I had given up my job, and at times felt myself disappearing into the shadows in my new supporting role. In Uganda, I had found a way to make a real difference and I couldn't bear the thought of stopping. 'What do you think I should do?'

'Em, I know how much going back to KAASO means to you — on so many levels — and it hurts me to see you like this. Would I stop you from going? No, I don't think that's up to me. I trust you to do what you believe is best. Would I be worried about you? Of course, I couldn't bear it if anything happened to you. But this is something you need to work out on your own and I will respect your decision either way.' I looked up at him, in awe of this person who understood me so well. However, he wasn't going to let me go blindly. 'You need to do your research, though, and show us you have weighed up all the options and understand the full story — then you know we'll all support you.'

I stayed up all night, glued to my computer, obsessively researching every fact I could about Ebola. I learned that in recent years there had been small outbreaks in Uganda, in 2007, 2011 and 2012 — and that I had actually been in Uganda during some of these. The worst had been the 2012 Ebola outbreak, which had killed seventeen people, but Uganda had been widely praised for its response, working together with the World Health Organization to quickly and effectively quell the outbreak. The president made public announcements on radio and TV, urging Ugandans to take precautions against the disease, much like the Ugandan government's widespread HIV/AIDS awareness campaign in the 1980s.

My friend John, who had shared his insights on volunteering years earlier, was actually now living in Uganda. He had gone to Kampala to do his Master's in Peace and Conflict Studies and ended up falling in love with a Ugandan woman, so had remained in Uganda after his studies. John and Mirriam still lived in Kampala, together with their young daughter, and I emailed John in the middle of the night explaining my dilemma and asking him what the situation was actually like over there. It was daytime in Kampala and he got straight back to me, assuring me that life continued 100 per cent as normal and adding a link to the World Health Organization site which showed no travel warnings for Uganda. 'The onus may actually be on not worrying your parents — I do not see an outbreak happening on the same scale as Ebola in West

Africa, but as you say, this cannot be guaranteed. Could you defer a couple of weeks?'

As always, John's words rang true. I realised that this wasn't actually about me — it was about my parents, who had loved me and cared for me my entire life. This was the first time they had ever asked me not to do something, and while they certainly weren't cautious types themselves, this was a different kind of unknown. On the phone to Dad earlier, I had pointed out that it wasn't exactly safe to set sail across the Atlantic Ocean on a 43-foot yacht and that most people would have considered that an incredibly dangerous undertaking, but he simply reminded me that that was something 'in his control'. It wasn't the time to bring up stray containers, rogue waves or curious whales, but I knew that at sea Dad felt that he was taking on risks he understood.

Me choosing to venture down a path strewed with potentially fatal, incurable diseases was far beyond the control of any of us, and the helplessness my parents felt in the face of that was too much. And it wasn't just my own family, it was also Nathan and Beau's — how could I promise their parents that Beau would be safe when I had no assurances? While I still believed that we would be absolutely fine, it wasn't a decision I could make in isolation. I knew that I had already caused my parents — Mama especially — great anguish over the past few weeks with my flippant attitude towards this deadly outbreak. And as much as it hurt to make the decision now, two days before my flight, I knew that I couldn't be responsible for any more pain. I agreed to postpone our trip.

My parents were immensely relieved and hugely appreciative of my decision, thanking me profusely and promising me that it was only because they loved me so much.

Beau was disappointed but unfazed — 'Hey, there's always next time!' — and his parents were understanding, respecting my decision and appreciating me putting family first. The call I was dreading most was to Dominic and Rose.

It took me over an hour to get through to Rose, and when I finally heard her voice, singing my name down the line, I fell apart. I couldn't bear to say the words. But Rose was, above all, a mother, and a very wise one at that, and although she was disappointed to hear that I would not be coming as planned, she understood that my tough decision had been made not for myself but for my family. She knew how much I needed her support right now.

'We will be looking forward to your arrival any day,' she reassured me. 'Whenever you come, we will be waiting. There is a proverb we have here in Uganda: "The elders sometimes do not see so well but still, they understand some things." We must honour them, even if it is hard. For our love for you and your family, we will respect your decision.'

I hadn't thought it possible to admire Rose any more, but in that moment I loved her more than I ever had. I agreed to abide by her proverb and to respect my parents' wishes. This was a time to act not in accordance with my own wants, but out of respect for others' needs. When it came down to it, I knew that I couldn't put my parents through that worry and assure them that everything would be alright, because I simply didn't know. I had every confidence that Ebola would not reach Uganda, but who was I to say? I was just a Kiwi girl who had left her heart in Uganda.

The month that followed brought a lot of soul-searching. Postponing my trip not only forced me to think about my identity; it also made me realise how much my attitude towards Africa had changed. Africa was no longer a concept, a symbol of my desire to do good, but a real and specific place full of people I cared deeply for. It frustrated me that the world still lumped all 54 African nations into one threatening basket. I had a network of friends in Kampala and a village community who I knew would do all they could to help me if I ever needed it. I felt as at home in the village now as I felt anywhere in the world.

What worried me most during those difficult weeks, though, was the underlying fear that my parents' sense of foreboding might actually be justified. What if Ebola actually did sweep across the African continent and engulf the village that I loved so much, cutting off my access to KAASO for months, even years? The idea that I might be prevented from returning to Uganda in future terrified me, but I also knew that the real danger would be to my KAASO family, and that having to combat Ebola on top of the challenges they already faced would be devastating for them.

I spent hours tracking Ebola's progress, living the highs as breakthroughs were made and the lows as more cases cropped up and the outbreak continued its malicious spread. I held my breath, hoping like hell that this devastating disease would soon be stamped out so that innocent people could return to their lives — and I could go back to my Ugandan home. I felt restless, impatient to return. Dad's words — that there was no hurry, that I could wait out the New Year and return the following year — provoked irrational anger within me. Why did I feel so strongly that I had to go *now*? Why such urgency?

I tried to voice my thoughts to Nathan but my words fell short.

'I can't even explain *why* it's so important to me to go back before the year is out, but I can't wait until next year and I don't know why. It might sound ridiculous, but that's just how I feel.'

I was too agitated to decipher the look Nathan gave me, but I knew that he understood me when he said gently, 'You're not being ridiculous. I know you need this, Em, and you need it now. So, sit and do what you do best — write up your thoughts and convince your parents why you should go back.'

And so, one month after I first agreed to postpone my trip, I sat and pieced together my case, demonstrating, belatedly, that I had put serious thought into it and now had a proper handle on what was happening. I showed how the situation was slowly improving and that I believed I would be safe.

As I wrote, I realised that this whole situation could have been avoided if I had simply listened to Mama's early concerns about Ebola, done my research and addressed each of her worries logically and rationally. Instead, I had brushed her aside, aggravating her fears and causing her many sleepless nights. But now I wrote from the head, not the heart, using links to articles as supporting evidence to back up my points. When I showed my email to Nathan, he smiled. 'It's perfect, Em. It's respectful, it's factual, it's rational — and for once you have managed to take the emotion out of it. You acknowledge the risks rather than dismissing them, and present a solid argument as to why it's safe enough for you to go. I'm convinced.'

Buoyed by Nathan's support, I sent the email to my parents and then paced our rented San Francisco apartment manically, wondering what their reaction would be. Thankfully, their reply came within an hour.

'You go to Uganda with our full support, love and

admiration for what you do for Rose, Dominic and "your children". Thank you so much for taking our concerns into consideration when coming to your decision to go — we really appreciate this. We love you heaps and are sure you will have a safe, productive and enjoyable trip to KAASO.'

I literally jumped for joy. Nathan laughed as I danced around the room. 'Just in time,' he said. I hugged him, unable to contain my excitement. It was the end of November and I was going back.

Unfortunately, Beau was unable to join me as he was now busy filming at various sailing events and his window of free time had gone. Although this meant I was going on my own, I was so happy to be returning that I didn't mind. 'Another time, for sure!' we agreed.

I got hold of Dominic to share the good news and he whooped with excitement. 'Oh, Madam Emma!' he cried. 'That is very good. We will be waiting!'

And they most certainly were. I stepped off the plane in Entebbe to find Dominic there to meet me as usual, although this time he had a surprise for me. Rose jumped out from behind him, beaming. She held out a bunch of colourful roses, then engulfed me in a warm hug. It was the first time Rose had ever met me off a flight; usually I had to wait to get to KAASO to see my dear friend, and I was thrilled to have the long drive south together to catch up on the year.

Darkness had blanketed the village by the time we pulled in through the school gates, but that didn't deter the 350-child choir that was waiting, singing their excited *wimowehs* at the top of their lungs, their voices ringing out through the village. To celebrate my return, my room in the volunteer house had been decorated with hand-drawn signs welcoming me home, flowers hung from my mosquito net and balloons suspended from the strings overhead. The children took me by the hand and led me into the dining room, which had been equally decorated from floor to ceiling with handmade 'welcome home' banners. It was incredible to be back.

In the weeks that followed, I experienced an outpouring of love like I'd never felt before. I had always felt warmly welcomed and appreciated at KAASO, but nothing like this. I slowly realised that all the time I had been so terrified that I might not make it back, everyone here had also feared the same thing. It was similar to when I understood that the children in the villages talked as much about their sponsors and me as I talked about them. What if I decided never to return again? It was entirely out of their control, and I thought about how helpless my little friends must have felt. Now, everywhere I went I was met with the same sentiment: 'Thank you for loving us.'

I first heard it one night sitting up late with Rose, trying to map out all of our sponsor visits to make sure none were missed. Teacher Sarah came inside to collect Jonah, her two-year-old son, who was sleeping on the couch. She wished us goodnight, then stopped in the doorway and turned to me.

'Madam Emma, thank you for loving us,' she said, Jonah's little face resting against her shoulder. 'Really, you are loving us so much and we are so grateful for all you are doing and those people back home — eh! They are loving us too!'

'How could we not love you?' I asked with a smile. Teacher Sarah roared with laughter, and went off to bed. I couldn't wipe away my smile for days. We were like a family reunited and I couldn't have been happier.

One week into my trip, we celebrated Speech Day, marking the end of the KAASO school year. It was a colourful day filled with singing, dancing and drumming, and I watched with pride as Brenda, now in P5 and the soloist in the choir, led the younger children through their movements. Their performance received rapturous applause from the crowd. As I stood cheering and clapping, Brenda looked over at me and gave me a radiant smile. I thought my heart might burst.

Once the celebrations were over, the children began to flood out through the school gates with their mattresses, metal suitcases and all their worldly belongings on their heads. It was overwhelming trying to farewell all the children at once, this mass exodus of over 600 little bodies who marched like ants out the front gate, spreading out across the country to spend the Christmas holidays with parents, grandparents and distant relatives.

I heard someone calling my name, and looked around to find that Brenda was leaving. 'Wait!' I said, and sprinted over. She explained that she was going to stay with a friend for the holidays. The girl's mother looked at me with a kind smile that assured me she would take care of my young friend, and I nodded in thanks. I bent down to hug Brenda, struggling to stop the flow of tears that had begun to spill down my cheeks. I brushed them away as I waved goodbye, this time knowing that we would meet again on my next visit.

The only consolation for all the departing KAASO children was that it signalled the return of the Kiwi Sponsorships children, who came 'home' to KAASO for the holidays. Every day I was met by another flying hug from a newly returned student from secondary school, some of them now eighteen and nineteen years old. I had always referred to the sponsor students as 'children' — but now, as they stood towering over me, I had to admit that they were growing up faster than I realised.

I made a special trip to Masaka to pick up Henry as well as David, who was now also studying at St Henry's College. Rose had suggested I go, knowing how much it would mean to Henry to introduce me to all his friends. As I drove in through the school gates, I was bowled over by the two handsome young men who met me in their crisp white shirts and school ties. They welcomed me with excited hugs and enormous grins, and then gave me a tour of their school, explaining that as they were going into their final year, they were now the 'elders', so it was up to them to set a good example and be role models for the younger students. It made me so proud to see these boys that I had met as hopeful young twelve-year-olds now making their way in the world and helping guide the next generation.

Over the next few weeks I met with each of the sponsor students, some in their home villages and others, whose homes I had already been to, at KAASO. I was impressed by their maturity as they explained to me that they understood that their sponsorships were not everlasting and it was up to them to make something of themselves given the incredible boost they had already been given in life. I helped them map out the next few years and listened to their hopes and dreams, hearing how they planned to make them come true. Many of them planned to branch off to vocational courses for their final two years so that they could enter the workforce with practical skills at the end of their sponsorships. I beamed with pride as I jotted down their stories to report back to their sponsors.

One afternoon I was catching up with Damian, who was being sponsored by Don and Gendy's daughter and her husband. He was explaining how he hoped to do a two-year plumbing course after Senior Four so that he could get a trade and one day become an entrepreneur and set up his own business. In the meantime, he explained, he wanted to start saving for his future by creating a tomato garden in the holidays, which he could harvest before going back to school in early March. Both of Damian's parents had died of unknown causes and he lived with his ageing grandmother, who also took care of half a dozen of her other orphaned grandchildren in a small mud-brick hut not far from KAASO. Damian's grandmother was willing to give him a plot of her land for the project, but he lacked the initial capital to get his tomatoes in the ground.

Sitting cross-legged on the floor of my room, the wheels were turning in my mind as I listened intently to this eighteen-year-old boy carefully explaining the process of creating a tomato garden, the materials required and the costs involved. I gave him a blank sheet of paper, and told him that if he could come back to me with a detailed budget and plan as to how he would achieve his goal, I would lend him the money. He stared at me in shock, waited until I clarified that I was serious, then thanked me profusely and disappeared. Two hours later he was back, budget in hand.

Under the supervision of Teacher Sarah, I gave Damian an initial deposit of US$30 and the project got under way. In the evenings I would walk down to his grandmother's house to find him slashing the land with a machete and preparing it for planting. He purchased seedlings and manure and worked tirelessly to get everything in good shape. It was a sizable plot — over half an acre — and he had his work cut out for him, but he persevered.

My final week at KAASO was a busy one. I finished the last of the sponsor visits, celebrated Stellah's seventeenth birthday with her, organised another Christmas party for the sponsor students, and held our annual Kiwi Sponsorships Committee meeting. As always, I was sad to be leaving, but I had demonstrated to everyone at KAASO that I would always return and I felt confident that it was a trend that would forever continue.

On my last evening at KAASO, I went down to Damian's tomato plot to say goodbye and was amazed by how far he had come in the one week since our first discussion. He had slashed two-thirds of the land, dug holes, filled them with manure, planted seedlings and carefully covered each one with a homemade banana-palm shade to protect them from the unforgiving Ugandan sunshine. I stood watching as he worked, but he stopped when he saw me and came bounding over, hoe in hand, to greet me. He looked radiant, and when I asked if he was enjoying himself, I thought his face might explode from smiling so much. He was in his element.

We went through his budget together and he showed me his careful calculations of each and every shilling I had given him so far, outlining how he planned to spend the rest. I handed over the balance of US$120 along with a 2015 year-planner and his eyes lit up.

'Madam Emma, thank you!' he cried. 'Really, I am appreciating all you are doing for me so much.'

'I look forward to my first bite of your tomatoes on my next visit,' I said with a smile. I hugged him goodbye, and let him get back to work before the sun set and it was too dark to see.

As I walked back up the path to KAASO, I watched the sky fill with the orange glow of sunset and thought about what incredible things could be achieved with a whole lot of determination and a little bit of capital. Damian's tomato project was like a microcosm of the entire sponsorship programme — a helping hand on to the first rung of the ladder was all these children needed to be racing their way towards the top. I smiled as I crossed the school field, feeling that Damian's tomato project had made every agonising minute of waiting to come back to Uganda worthwhile.

As my trip and 2014 both came to a close, I finally felt at peace. A hard year was ending, but my purpose had been revived and with that came the hope of a better year about to begin. And I suddenly realised that this was what Nathan had known all along — that look I had not been able to decipher before leaving, *this* was what it was about. He had understood, even before I did, that if I didn't come back to Uganda this year then I would have felt that the entire year had been about *his* dreams, not mine. My trips back to KAASO helped ground me in something that was entirely my own; they were integral to my sense of identity, making me feel like my own person, not just Nathan's other half. It amazed me that he could know me better than I knew myself, and suddenly I felt excited to get home to see him, to thank him. As the last of the rays of sunshine slipped behind the iron sheets of Kiwi House, I felt whole again.

CHAPTER SIXTEEN

At Sydney airport I launched myself into Nathan's waiting arms and thanked him for being my wonderful soulmate. He laughed and said, 'Hey, we're a team. That's what I'm here for.'

We chatted all the way on the drive up the coast to the lake, and I felt that life was as good as it could possibly get. But somehow, over the next few days, things just kept getting better. Alex, a friend from the America's Cup world whose husband, Grant Simmer, ran Oracle Team USA, had been moved by my emails from Uganda and wanted to know more about sponsorship. Within days, Mark, a fourteen-year-old boy whose father had abandoned him when he was little and whose mother was severely disabled, got the chance to have an education. A few days later, on Christmas Eve, Nathan and I were doing some last-minute Christmas shopping when I received a notification on my blog. Curious as to who would be writing to me on Christmas Eve, I opened it. It was from a woman named Pip Palmer who had heard about my blog through a mutual friend I had worked with in the Greek Islands seven years earlier. She had been following my stories avidly from the superyacht she worked on in Palma de Mallorca, and wanted to sponsor a child. She also wondered if it was possible to pay the six years up-front. I couldn't believe it! This was the first time that someone I'd never met had asked to sponsor a child, and the trust she had in me to transfer all the funds up-front blew me away. I raced to catch up with Nathan, who had walked on ahead, and share the good news.

Nathan just looked at me as I told him the story, and grinned his irresistible grin. 'Of course she wants to help, Em. How could she read your stories and *not* want to help?'

I squealed for joy and kissed him. A few new KAASO volunteers had also taken up sponsorships, and these two new ones meant that I now had 30 children being sponsored. It was the best Christmas present ever.

After Christmas, Nathan and I drove down to Sorrento on the Mornington Peninsula, just south of Melbourne, where he was competing in the Moth class — a one-man foiling boat that defies all laws of gravity. The regatta had drawn a bunch of our friends from the sailing world, including Glenn and Mel Ashby, Violah's sponsors, who lived nearby, and we spent New Year's Eve at their house. Sitting around a bonfire, I shared with them the story of my recent visit to Violah. They struggled to hold back their tears when I told them about Violah's grandmother Betty, who had broken down and wept with gratitude when I visited them in their little mud hut. She had taken my hand into the weathered folds of her own and laid bare her heartfelt thanks while Rose translated: 'I would be dead without your help. This burden, knowing I could not support my granddaughter, it was too much. But now I can die happy. Even if I die tomorrow, I am okay. I will be happy because Violah is supported, thanks to you.'

When I finished the story, Mel was the first to speak. 'Em, we're just so grateful to you for getting us involved,' she said. 'We are so lucky in our life here in Australia. I know we're not doing much, but we're just glad to be doing something.'

'You're doing more than you realise,' I said with a smile. It was these intimate moments with the sponsors — who were also my friends — that made the sponsorships so special to me. As I moved between worlds, I felt like I was bringing gifts from one to the other and it brought great joy to all of us.

The countdown to midnight approached, and we all went out onto the balcony to watch the fireworks. Nathan stood behind me with his arms wrapped around me.

'Here's to an amazing year,' he whispered as the countdown began. Fireworks exploded across the bay and I thought back to the similar scene we had watched together eighteen months earlier, on the fourth of July in San Francisco. It was incredible to think how much had happened since then.

Nathan and I resumed our life on the road, flying between San Francisco and Sydney every two weeks as we juggled Nathan's America's Cup commitments with his preparations for the Rio Olympics. On our last trip back to Australia before the European season commenced, Nathan suggested inviting my parents to come over to the lake from New Zealand. When our parents had all met in San Francisco, they had got on like a house on fire; it would be fun to have everyone together. I invited them to come, but Dad, incredibly busy at work, said he wasn't sure he would be able to make it. I was disappointed, but didn't push it.

Then, the week before we were due to fly to Australia,

I pulled up outside the Artemis base in San Francisco to pick Nathan up from work and found him standing outside, talking on the phone. He hung up when I arrived and jumped in the car with a wide smile.

'That was your dad,' he said.

'Oh yeah?' They often chatted about sailing and the America's Cup, so I was hardly surprised. 'Did you tell him to come to Wangi?' I asked. 'He'll probably come if he knows the invitation is from you.'

'I did actually,' Nathan said, not meeting my gaze.

He hummed all the way home. At the time, I thought nothing of it.

My parents arrived at the lake on a sunny Friday afternoon in late March. That morning, Nathan had woken up in a great mood, telling me how much he was looking forward to the coming days.

'It's going to be a weekend full of surprises!' he said with a grin.

'Oh, really? Sounds like fun!' I said, trying to hide my own smile. I had slowly begun to suspect that my parents' coming for the weekend might be something more than just a social visit. Ever since that first night at Tony's Pizza in North Beach, Nathan and I had both had an overwhelming sense that this was it — we had each found our match and we would be together forever. We had often talked about marriage, and it was very much something we both wanted, but I was old-fashioned and wanted the question to come from him. He knew me well enough, however, to know that if he proposed with a diamond ring then the answer would be a resounding 'no' — I had read too much about blood diamonds to believe that anyone could really know if a stone was 'conflict-free' and

I didn't like what they represented — a flashy status-symbol of wealth as a show of love. If Nathan was going to propose, he knew he'd have to think outside the box for an alternative to the traditional engagement ring for his unconventional girl.

However, I didn't want to get my hopes up so I pushed my excitement to the back of my mind as we sat with my parents that first night, enjoying happy hour out on the veranda, watching the twilight sailing taking place on the lake in front of us. Nathan's parents, Tony and Jasmine, joined us for dinner and we worked our way through several bottles of wine, our families hitting it off as always. Nathan, sitting across the table from me, spent most of the night grinning like a Cheshire cat, which made me feel that my suspicions might not be unfounded. I began to wonder when the big moment might be. But he said nothing, simply laughed and whispered across the table that we could probably go to bed now and our parents wouldn't even notice, they got on so well.

Around midnight, the wine continuing to flow, Mama suggested that it might be time for a cup of tea. I was disappointed; the night would soon be winding down, the moment gone. I realised I had been crazy to think that Nathan might propose at the dinner table in front of both sets of parents. I went with Mama into the kitchen to boil the kettle, but Nathan jumped up and followed us.

'Let's have champagne!' he said, coming up behind me.

My heart stopped and I turned to face him. 'Now?' I asked.

'Em, I think we should open that champagne.' I had watched him put a bottle of Moët in the fridge earlier that day and had known better than to ask questions. Now he turned to me with a look that confirmed what I was hoping for.

'Well, sure,' I said, unable to hide my smile as I took the

champagne from the fridge. Nathan got the champagne flutes and I followed him back to the table clutching the chilled bottle. With shaking hands I poured the champagne, holding my breath as I prepared for the biggest moment of my life to unfold. The six glasses were lined up, the bubbles dancing to the top of each glass — but Nathan said nothing, so I sat waiting. And waiting. The seconds ticked by agonisingly slowly but still no one touched their glasses. Our parents, oblivious, were on such a roll, in the midst of so many stories, that they just kept chatting and laughing, their voices getting louder by the minute.

'Are you okay?' Nathan mouthed to me across the table.

'Yes,' I mouthed back and he smiled. But still said nothing. In the end, I couldn't take it anymore so I simply grabbed my glass and raised it to the table.

'Well, here's cheers everyone!' I announced, unable to wait any longer.

My impatience had the desired effect, and Nathan jumped up. 'No, just a minute!' he cried, a little louder than he realised. The whole table finally went quiet. I was sure they could all hear my heart beating.

'So, you might be wondering why I wanted to bring everyone here together,' he began, his eyes fixed on mine.

That certainly got everyone's attention. 'Oh my goodness, he's not about to— ?' Jasmine began, and Dad quickly shushed her. It suddenly occurred to me that Dad must know what was about to happen. I remembered Nathan's phone call to him outside the Artemis base in San Francisco. My tears began to fall.

'I wanted you all to be here so that I could ask Em to marry me.'

The table erupted in cheers of celebration and clinking glasses and congratulations. I just sat there, grinning, tears streaming, looking across the table at the rest of my life.

'Wait, did she say yes?' Jasmine called down the table.

'Yes!' I cried as Nathan came over and took me in his arms. He reached into his pocket and I held my breath, wondering what would come next.

All eyes were on him as he pulled out a handmade ring he had fashioned from Dyneema sailing rope, a lightweight rope that is light and thin but incredibly strong — unbreakable — which Nathan used for all the intricate parts on the dinghies he sailed. Our house was always full of pieces of rope lying around so I had thought nothing of the coils of fine rope strewn around the place, but later that night, when I looked closer, I would realise that they were actually practice rings that Nathan had discarded on our bedroom floor. I carefully picked each of them up, cherishing them for what they represented: Nathan's complete understanding of who I was and what I stood for.

Now, he gently slipped the ring — the best of the bunch — over my finger and tightened the ends.

'It fits,' he said with a cheeky grin. I couldn't have loved him more.

Life took on a new shine and I felt on top of the world. I remembered Dad telling me that when Mama had agreed to marry him, he had felt invincible, like anything was possible with her at his side. That was exactly how I felt now.

I took over the Volunteer Coordinator role at KAASO from Kirsty, who had become too busy to give it the time she knew it needed. She and Marcos had married in San Francisco the previous year (officially married, in addition to their Ugandan wedding) and Kirsty was now pregnant. They were moving back to New Zealand, but she was still working full-time and it was all too much to juggle. I was thrilled to take on the position, the last of us three Kiwi Girls to run the volunteer programme.

Two years earlier, Kirsty and Marcos had set up a website for KAASO and we were starting to gain momentum; the volunteer calendar for 2015 was already filling. Lizzie Hulton-Harrop, a frequent volunteer at KAASO, was now working as a teacher at Northbourne Park, a primary school in the UK, and was returning to Uganda with two teachers from the school — the first step in what would become a partnership between the two schools. Another past volunteer was coming back to KAASO for a two-month visit in the middle of the year, and I had just received an email from a Year One teacher in Australia called Deanne Holmes. Deanne wrote that friends had referred her to KAASO, and after spending several hours exploring our website she wanted to arrange a Skype call to talk further about volunteering.

From the Artemis team accommodation in San Francisco I chatted to Deanne for hours, discovering that she lived on the Mornington Peninsula, where I had been over New Year that same year, and that the friends who had referred her were actually Glenn and Mel, whose children she taught. This interconnected world we lived in never ceased to amaze me: Nathan had introduced me to Glenn and Mel in San Francisco, and they had come to follow my online blog, which had inspired them to sponsor a child. Because our paths continued to cross at sailing regattas, my stories had remained fresh in their minds, which they had then shared with their children's teacher, who was eager to help other schools around the world. Thus, through this incredible web of unlikely connections, KAASO was getting a new volunteer.

Meanwhile, the sailing world was moving forwards and the venue for the 35th America's Cup was announced as Bermuda, a small British Territory of 60,000 inhabitants, more than 1000 kilometres from the nearest landmass in the North Atlantic Ocean. It had been assumed that the Cup might stay in San Francisco, the city of the defender, Oracle Team USA, but Bermuda had put together an impressive bid to host this prestigious event, and so the decision was made to head east.

An island girl at heart, I was delighted at the prospect of moving to an island of pink sand beaches and swaying palm trees. However, there were still several months before we would set ourselves up in Bermuda, and in the meantime I was excited to learn that Claire, the girlfriend of Nathan's Olympic sailing partner and Artemis teammate Goobs, was going to join my on-the-road travelling team. She was a graphic designer and her office in Australia had agreed to let her work remotely as she travelled. It would be so nice to finally have someone to share my days with, and while I organised volunteers and sponsorships for KAASO, Claire would be creating design concepts to send to her office back home. We could have lunch breaks together and enjoy a glass of wine in the evenings before the boys got home, quelling my previous loneliness. It was the perfect set-up.

In early May 2015, Claire and I made the 40-hour journey together from Australia to Bermuda. Nathan and Goobs were already there waiting for us, and before we knew it we were on the back of scooters and out exploring our new island-paradise home. I quickly fell in love with the laid-back pace of life, the incredibly friendly people, the explosions of tropical flowers and the lush tangle of foliage in the backyard of our temporary accommodation. In a way, it reminded me a little of Uganda — just with slightly better infrastructure.

However, my friends in Uganda saw no similarities between their landlocked home and my floating island one, and I received a panicked email from Henry: 'I hear you are moving to the place called Bermuda? Please, I have had a lot of stories from that Triangle and I am scared for you and Nathan going there. I wish you wouldn't go.'

I smiled, and gently explained that the island of Bermuda was quite different from the Bermuda Triangle but promised him I would be careful. He wrote back, relieved that I was not going to disappear at sea, and filled me in on his news.

'We had a short holiday and it was awesome. New chicks hatched and it was so amazing to look after them.' I was so pleased that the poultry project was going well. Henry then wrote that he also wished to inform me about a student. Irene had finished Senior Four at the same school as Stellah and hoped to continue her studies at nursing school. However, at the start of the year, her father had been diagnosed with a severe illness and admitted to hospital. Her mother was struggling to support the rest of the family and the nursing fees were too great to manage on her own. 'Irene is a determined student. She is disciplined and willing to study but she is now seated at home as she lacks support. We request you to help her.'

I felt for Irene. Like so many others, she only wanted the chance of an education. But what struck me most was seeing

Henry now helping his fellow students. Irene was the year below him at KAASO and, as the Chairperson of the Kiwi Sponsorships Committee, Henry was taking his job seriously and helping Rose to seek support for those who needed it most.

I was incredibly moved. Over lunch with Claire in our shared housing in Bermuda, I told her about Henry's email. I was so proud of him and how much he had grown up. Knowing that he was now helping to ease Rose's burden demonstrated what a thoughtful and mature young man he was turning into, and I spoke like a proud parent. Claire just shook her head in wonder at these amazing children I talked about so often. She was always so encouraging of my work in Uganda, so positive and reassuring, helping me get through any challenges I faced. When I had finished my monologue about Henry, Claire asked who the girl was that Henry was trying to help. I briefly shared Irene's story, trying to keep it short as I was aware of the monopoly I was having on our lunch conversation.

'Anyway,' I said, when I had finished, 'how was *your* morning?'

'Fine, thanks . . .' she said. 'But, Em, I'd really like to know more about Irene — if that's okay?'

'Oh, Claire, you hear these stories every day. I don't want to sound like a broken record!'

'Please,' she said gently. 'Tell me about Irene.'

Claire listened intently as I explained how the nursing school worked, the fees involved and the future it could give these young nurses. I could see what was happening, but Claire kept prodding me with questions and I knew that she really was genuinely interested. We resumed our afternoon work sessions and then caught up with the boys when they came home from work.

Over dinner that night, Claire said she and Goobs had an announcement to make. 'We've been thinking about this for a while now,' she began. 'Goobs and I have talked it through and we would like to sponsor Irene. It would mean a lot to us and we'd really like to help. So you can count us in.'

By now I knew how important it was for me to gracefully accept help when it was offered, so I simply smiled at my amazing friends across the table. 'Thank you,' I said. 'I would say you don't know how much this means, but I know you do.' I raised my glass. 'To Irene!'

It was small moments like this that meant the world to me. I knew that there were people out there doing incredible things — *big* things, like building hundreds of schools, raising millions of dollars and securing thousands of sponsorships. I applauded them; what they were doing was incredible and the world needed those large-scale achievements. But I also believed that there was a place for focusing on the small things, the little moments that meant so much. The look on Henry's face when I first said I'd sponsor him, Brenda getting 87 per cent in her English exam, Stellah feeling that she wouldn't be alone in the world anymore, the relief it gave Betty to know that Violah would be supported, Teddy's father riding two hours on the back of a *boda* to meet me, watching Charles's face as he read Jan's letter to his family.

And it wasn't just the moments in Uganda, it was those out in the world too: Glenn and Mel's daughters asking questions about the picture of Violah on their fridge, Don and Gendy reading my emails to their grandchildren, seeing the light in Mark's eyes when I first explained my work in Uganda, and now, here, seeing the joy it brought Claire and Goobs to know that they could help change the life of one young girl who dreamed of becoming a nurse. It was these personal stories, these individual connections, that mattered most to me. Just as I had intentionally chosen all those years ago to volunteer through a small, grassroots volunteer programme, so had I fashioned my own sponsorship programme with a focus on maintaining the integrity of the original dream and not getting carried away by over-commercialisation. On rare occasions I had been asked whether donations or sponsorships through me were tax-deductible, and the answer had always been no. Kirsty had once looked into registering KAASO as a UK charity when she was based in Cambridge, and got a long way down the track, but in the end it was a lot of administrative effort for not a lot of payoff; most of our donors were based outside the UK so the tax cuts wouldn't apply to them anyway.

There was also a simpler, perhaps more naïve and idealistic reason why I was not racing to register KAASO as a charity. I knew for a fact that no one who donated or sponsored through me had 'tax break' on their mind when they offered their support. And yet they gave openly, willingly using my incredibly low-tech system of depositing the funds into a designated KAASO bank account and then trusting me to transfer the money on to the school's account in Uganda. There was something beautiful about the sheer simplicity of that, the avoidance of external fees and admin percentages taken by most big organisations, that I felt helped sum up who I was and what I believed in. Yes, over the years I'd ended up bearing the cost of most of the transfer fees myself, but it was worth it to me. Keeping it small, keeping it personal was what made the Kiwi Sponsorships and all my dealings with KAASO what they were. That's why I believed they had been such a success.

While I was frequently blown away by the scale of the achievements of so many larger organisations I admired, I knew that the bigger things got, the more staff were needed and the more things lost their personal touch, and it was the personal touch that I prided myself so greatly on. I wanted to know each child, to have visited their homes, to share in their dreams and to help shape their individual futures. Thirty children was already quite a handful, but it was certainly not impossible and I was determined to make it work. And now I had the next generation of Henrys coming through who would help me keep on top of things.

To me the key was finding something personal, something that grabbed you by the heart and wouldn't let go, something that kept you awake at night, something that truly *meant* something to you. It was listening when your Gramps asked what you were going to do about it. And then, it was making something happen — step by step, story by story, child by child. It didn't have to mean taking on The World, it didn't have to mean creating an empire, and it certainly didn't have to require millions of dollars. It just had to be personal, heartfelt and meaningful.

If my sponsorships had stopped with Henry, and over these past six years I had done nothing but see him through his schooling, that still would have been something. It would have been a valid, tangible way in which I had helped change someone's life for the better. So often we are overwhelmed by all there is to do — and so we do nothing, paralysed into inaction. That was how I felt when I first went to KAASO and the need seemed so great while I felt so small. But over the years, the flow of love and support and encouragement that I received from my community around the world helped me to keep putting one foot in front of the other — not stopping with Henry, but *starting* with Henry.

I used to joke that I was like a modern-day Robin Hood — except that the rich gave willingly. But over time I realised that it wasn't about one party giving and the other receiving, it was a two-way partnership that flowed equally from one side to the other. Just as I had recognised the importance of *learning* rather than *teaching*, I had also come to value what these sponsorships and donations brought to *both* sides. So many people today get fixated on big numbers, big statistics, big dollars. Sure, they're impressive — but what makes my heart glow are the individual stories, the personal relationships and the unbreakable connections that mean this network of support is built to last.

A classic example was my last-minute engagement party, held in Auckland for family and friends. Nathan was, rather inconveniently, away sailing in France at the time, but the party went ahead anyway. A few hours before it was due to start, I met with Pip, my Christmas Eve sponsor angel who had found me via my blog. She happened to be in New Zealand where the superyacht she worked on was being refitted. We had planned to have just a drink together that afternoon, but ended up chatting so much that I invited her to come with me to the party. There, she met my parents, Cherie, Don and Gendy, Glenn and Mel, and Tom and Annie — all part of my incredible KAASO support network. She was blown away by it all and I found myself smiling at my quirky life, a life where I invited perfect strangers to my engagement party at which my fiancé wasn't even present, and introduced them to a group of sailors who supported children in Uganda. It was that randomness, that eclectic unexpectedness, which I had been brought up to thrive on.

As much as I enjoyed the adventure of living on the road, I was incredibly happy when, after two years of living in hotel rooms and temporary housing, Nathan and I finally found a place to call our own in Bermuda. It was only rented and it didn't even have a teaspoon inside, but it was ours. The months that preceded the move were hectic in the extreme as we bounced from the UK to Portugal to Brazil to Sweden to Australia, all the while trying to organise a container of online furniture purchases to be shipped from San Francisco to Bermuda to fill our empty house. A nightmare of IKEA flatpack furniture-building in 100 per cent humidity would be awaiting us in our island home, but we knew it would be worth it in the end.

With a team of helpers, including my brother, Nick, and his girlfriend, Grace, who were visiting from the UK, Nathan and I pieced together our new life. We would still be coming and going until the Olympics were over the following August, but at least we now knew that we had somewhere in the world to call home. I filled the bookshelves, hung up my Ugandan scarves and filled vases with fresh palm leaves cut each day from our garden. I finally felt like I had a place in the world, a stable base from where we would start the next chapter of our lives together.

Bermuda's first America's Cup World Series event took place in mid-October 2015, and in the days leading up to the event the teams were all out training in full force. I was setting up my office, positioning my desk near the window where I would be able to watch the boats training, and covering the walls with photos of the children, letters, cards and scraps of inspiration I had picked up along the way. Claire was in the living room working on her latest design — as well as putting together our wedding invitation for the following March. The fans spun overhead, stirring the thick, humid air, and I made a mental note to replace yesterday's wilted hibiscus sitting on my windowsill.

Hearing a loud creaking noise, the unmistakable sound of the wing being eased on the 45-foot foiling catamarans, I went to the open window and watched as the boats skimmed over the water's surface. Artemis sailed past — Nathan, Goobs and Iain Percy, getting ready for Saturday's racing — followed by Emirates Team New Zealand, with Glenn Ashby, their skipper, keeping the boat steady through the water. Further up the Great Sound, Ben Ainslie Racing was going through their manoeuvres under the guidance of Jono Macbeth, the sailing team manager, and over the other side of the bay was Oracle Team USA, managed by Grant Simmer.

And suddenly it hit me: these were all sponsors of children at KAASO. The aquamarine water before me was alive with the world's most impressive boats, flying around at the cutting edge of technology, and what did they have in common? The people behind them helped support children through school in Uganda. I felt the ripples flowing like never before, and heard Rose's voice echo through my thoughts: *You can't do everything, but you can do something.*

This was my something. I first went to Uganda as a naïve 25-year-old, hoping to change the world. I soon realised that I was never going to change the whole world, but if I could make an impact in one small corner of it, then that would be worth every step walked, every tear shed, every pothole hit and every mosquito bite acquired along the way. I had once lived on Sydney's Bondi Beach, with Nuria, a Spanish friend and old colleague from Valencia. Whenever I worried about what the future might hold, she would say: 'Don't worry, *chiquitita*. One day, everything will be in its place. And when it is, you will know it.'

That was how I felt now. I had once searched for purpose at KAASO, wondering whether I would ever belong; it now felt like my second home. I had once hoped I might find a soulmate to sail through life with; I was now engaged to him and our amazing life together stretched out before us. I had once worried what people might think of me for 'following' Nathan around the world; I now felt nothing but peace with my situation, with my life. I had once thought it completely impossible for my two worlds — sailing and Uganda — to ever merge; I now saw the two blissfully entwined before my eyes.

Everything was in its place.

EPILOGUE

'**M**adam Emma, do you like it?' Stellah asked, standing in front of an elaborately decorated Kiwi House.

'I love it, Stellah,' I said, wrapping my arm around her shoulders. 'You have done a great job and I am very proud of you. *Webale nyo, nyabo.*' She beamed, looking up at me with glowing eyes, then ran off to help with the food preparation.

I jumped out of the way as Henry and a group of boys swept past me, swamped beneath a sea of white canvas that would form a sunshade for our guests. Following closely behind was a troupe of younger children carrying poles and plastic chairs, their little legs hurrying to keep up with the older boys.

I stood for a minute, taking in the scene, wanting to make sure that I fully appreciated this moment for all it was. Colourful streamers ran the length of the Kiwi House veranda and banana palm fronds dotted with bright pink roses from Rose's garden had been threaded through the bars of the dormitory windows. Balloons bobbed gently among the foliage and paper lanterns that resembled giant red pineapples were suspended from the roof. I thought back to the last time I had stood in front of Kiwi House, similarly decorated but with a blue ribbon strung across the entryway. That was six years ago, when we had opened the dormitory before a crowd of excited children, parents and local community members. Today, in place of a blue ribbon, was a handwritten sign that read: KIWI SPONSORSHIPS GRADUATION 2015. It was hard to believe that we had actually reached this point.

I walked up to the KAASO kitchen where Rose and a team of women — grandmothers, mothers, stepmothers, sisters and sponsored students — were helping to prepare lunch. Everyone was in a frenzy, making sure that the enormous dishes of groundnuts, cabbage, rice, yams, sweet potatoes and beef and the mountains of fresh pineapple were ready in time to feed the gathering crowd of sponsored students and their families. Giant pots of steaming *matooke* were cooking over open fires alongside sizzling chickens which, just hours earlier, had been running around the courtyard. I had made myself scarce as the boys slaughtered the chickens for our celebration meal. Even after all these years of coming to Uganda, I still had a hard time with chickens.

A constant stream of immaculately dressed bodies, both young and old, flowed in through the school gates. Elderly *jajjas*, their faces weathered by age and responsibility, carried small babies, while older children held the hands of their younger siblings. There were also a handful of parents, beaming with pride, the rare few who had lived to see their children graduate. They made their way down into the school hall where a feast of biblical proportions had begun to take place. I wandered around the rows of desks, savouring the moment as Teacher Sarah and her team of helpers dished up massive servings of food that dwarfed the younger children. As the last of the plates were wiped clean by little hands, scooping up their final mouthfuls of *matooke*, it was time for the moment we had all been waiting for — the graduation ceremony.

Outside, the boys had erected the school's peaked tent and lined up rows of plastic chairs for our visitors. The front row was reserved for the graduates. Little nametags made out of banana leaves were placed on each of the 'chairs of honour', and as I walked along the line I thought about how much was held in each of those small tags, the stories they represented. Zakia and Munjera were first, graduating from their vocational course with Certificates in Agricultural and Veterinary Studies thanks to Matt, Shane and my aunts. Next were Stellah's sister and Jackie, who were now qualified nurses, having been sponsored by past volunteers at KAASO. There was Sharon, one of the 'dropped' students who had been able to finish Senior Six after Simon stepped in to help, as well as Kevin, Dominic and Rose's eldest daughter, who had also finished Senior Six and was joining in the festivities. Alongside them was David, who, with the support of Cherie and her family, was now also a Senior Six graduate. And then there was Henry. My twelve-year-old friend all grown up into a remarkable young man who looked out for me like a brother.

My own brother, Nick, had joined me for the early part of this trip and everyone had welcomed him as part of the family. I had taken great delight in watching Nick and Henry interact, coming together like long-lost brothers. My only disappointment had been to learn that Henry's hopes of a university scholarship through the Minnesota college had ended: the university had employed a new Vice Chancellor who had cut all sponsorships in Africa. But that was not the end of the road — there were still other scholarships that Henry could apply for, and I knew if anyone would find a way to succeed, it was Henry.

He found me standing next to his chair just as the formalities were about to begin. 'Well, Henry, are you ready to graduate?' I asked with a grin, and he launched himself at me in a warm hug. I thought back on a similar embrace we had shared six years earlier. How far we had come.

'Yes, yes, yes!' he cried, clasping my hands in his, his face overcome with excitement. Suddenly, he turned serious. 'Madam Emma, I want to thank you so much for that work you put into our school and our community,' he said. 'Every year, you come back. That shows that it is love, it is care, it is *support*! I have not lived a smooth life, even though I was being sponsored, but you always returned to KAASO, you always showed that love for us and reminded us not to give up. I felt encouraged to persevere, to always strive to make my future better. And not just my own future, I also feel the urge to help other people because I've been *helped* and I think there is much joy in that.'

My eyes welled with tears as he spoke. In spite of the challenges Henry faced, both then and now, he never gave up, never stopped striving, and never stopped smiling. With his unshakable faith and his spirit that would not be dampened, he proved that despite its challenges, life was a gift to be appreciated. And he intended to make the most of it. He was the ultimate example of the fact that your fate did not have to be determined by your birth. Sure, we couldn't choose where our accident of birth placed us on this planet, but we did have a say in the journey that followed and, ultimately, where we ended up.

'Smile, Madam Emma!' Henry said, seeing my eyes brimming. 'Today is for celebrating.'

'I know, Henry. Really, I couldn't be happier,' I said, laughing as I brushed away my tears. 'It's just a little overwhelming to think that this is *it*! You're graduating!'

'Ah, you are right. We have travelled far — and we will keep striving. But I think for now, let us enjoy this moment.'

Rose opened the proceedings, welcoming everyone to the inaugural Kiwi Sponsorships Graduation Ceremony. She spoke slowly, her words unhurried, purposeful. She explained how the sponsorships had evolved, from the early days of her handwritten list through to today, where 33 children were now being supported in their education by the Kiwi Sponsorships programme. She shifted her gaze around the audience, and eventually her eyes came to rest on me. She thanked me for all my hard work and expressed her gratitude for my persistence. 'I've seen many organisations trying to do what you are doing,' Rose said, 'but in the end — they cry. In the end, they turn their minds and say, "We shall go other places." But you, you've remained. You've made this family happy. We thank you so much for that heart.'

I thought about how close I had once come to turning down Henry's request — if I had not sponsored him, then none of this would ever have happened. How easy it would have been to have just walked away and never come back — but how much I would have missed. I looked around at the faces of these promising young students whose futures were being shaped by people I had met around the world. They had come to be the most rewarding thing in my life and I wouldn't have had it any other way.

The ceremony continued with a colourful celebration of

music, speeches, laughter and words of praise as parents and teachers commended the graduates on their hard work and acknowledged the sponsors that had made all this possible. Following the speeches, Dominic and I, dressed in full graduation robes, commenced the official graduation. I read out the names of each student while Dominic presented them with their certificate and Rose pinned on the graduation sashes we had had made for each of them: KAASO GRADUATE embroidered on one side, and KIWI SPONSORSHIPS on the other. The crowd roared with excitement as each of the students jumped up on to the 'stage' — the Kiwi House veranda — to receive their accolades.

The graduates stood lined up in front of Kiwi House, clutching their certificates and beaming at the audience, until eventually there was only one person left sitting in the front row. 'Our final graduate needs no introduction,' I said. 'He was the spark that began the Kiwi Sponsorships programme, the catalyst for all that we have here today. Graduating from Senior Six from St Henry's College, please welcome Henry Rogers Ssemunywa!'

Henry came bounding up on stage and threw his arms around me. No one could wipe the smiles from our faces as we stood there, grinning dumbly, the reality finally sinking in that we had *done* it. From that first letter Henry had given me, in July 2009, through to this moment in December 2015 when Henry was receiving his graduation certificate, we had come full cycle. Henry's secondary education was complete. I felt a rush of pride for my extraordinary friend. Henry was my shining star and, I knew, an inspiration to all the other little stars sitting in the audience. They looked at him and they saw hope — hope for a better life, hope that if Henry, an orphaned boy from the village, could succeed, then so could they.

The last word of the day went to Dominic. 'Some of you may not know that origin of the word "Kiwi",' he began with a grin, 'but whenever I hear that word, I love it so much. Before Madam Emma and the Kiwi Girls came to KAASO, we only used to know "Kiwi" from the Kiwi shoe polish we find here in Uganda, but these girls taught us that a Kiwi could also be someone from New Zealand. Over the years, I have come to realise that these two things are actually one and the same: Madam Emma and the Kiwi Girls have really *polished* KAASO so they are giving us the real meaning of Kiwi. Thank you, Madam Emma and all the Kiwi girls, Kiwi fathers, Kiwi mothers, we are so grateful to you. Where would these students have been if you people had not come? Or if you came and went back and you never *loved* the way you do, where would we have been? Eh!' he shook his head.

He went on to talk about the importance of the KAASO family and of sticking together, the older ones helping to guide the younger ones. 'This KAASO family is a very good family. It has no clan, it has no religion, it has no age, and it has no race. Some of you may be Muslims, others may be Catholics, but we are a family and we are bound together. What binds us? It is the *love* and what we do together, and it will continue to bind us if we follow the norms and the culture of KAASO family.'

I thought of all the conflicts around the world, the misunderstandings of race, culture and religion, and here I was, in a pinprick of a village, embraced by a family that went beyond borders.

'When Rose and I first began KAASO in 1999,' Dominic continued, 'we had very little. The school was just one classroom, a single grass-thatched hut. Henry was in that classroom as a tiny small boy, one of our first students. The structure was not so strong, and one day during the rainy season it collapsed on top of him. The whole village came to rescue Henry and his fellow students. Today, that same small boy we pulled from the wreckage of that classroom is graduating. That poor classroom did not look like much, but the quality of the education inside was good, and now you see? Other KAASO students from that very simple classroom are now engineers and nurses in Kampala, having successful careers. We first saw these students when they were small, small insects. Now, they are big elephants. It does not matter from *where* you fetch your water, it is what you *do* with it. You may fetch it from some big source, but if you don't treat it well you may get cholera, while others fetch it from some simple, simple stream but they take the care to filter it carefully. Those ones will have clean, pure drinking water.

'Now, you students who have graduated,' he said, turning to face the students lined up across the stage, 'I remind you that every ceiling is also a floor. Do you get me? Have you ever seen those big tall buildings in Kampala? Have you ever climbed any? You walk up from the ground floor to the first floor, but when you reach there, you point down and eh! That ceiling has become a floor. Even if you go to another step, and you point down, that will also be the floor. Every level upon reached becomes what? The floor. So you need to climb the ladder and continue and continue to other steps. Please, don't give up, keep going, the journey continues.'

He concluded with a story that will stay with me for the rest of my days — one that demonstrated to me, yet again, Dominic's incredible vision and his brilliance in communicating to young, hopeful, eager students. It's a story

I have told dozens of times since and will tell until the day I die — 'The Road to Masaka'.

'If you were to say to me, "How should I get to Masaka?", what would I reply?' Dominic asked.

One of the children in the audience stood and explained: 'You turn right out of the KAASO gates and continue until you reach the main road. From there you again branch to the right and you follow the main road to Masaka.'

'Ah ha! Yes, you are correct — this is the *direct* way. But is there another way?' he asked, a small smile playing on his lips. 'What if I was to turn left at the KAASO gates?'

I stared at him. Left took you to the shore of the lake — a dead end. Our only way in and out of the village was to turn right and follow the dirt road towards the main Masaka Road.

'What if I told you that you could turn left, travel until you reach the lake shore, board a boat to the Ssese Islands, cross those islands, board the ferry, and then when you come to the land you take a *matatu*, a taxi, and you will reach Masaka. Is that not so?' Bewildered faces stared at him from the crowd, wondering where their Director was going with this tale. 'It is not the most direct way, true, but you will still reach. That is the point. Me, I was not lucky enough to take a direct route, but still, I made it. I got my degree when I was an old man — a *jajja*! I was 38 years old but ah! I was not the oldest in my class; there were people there with grey in their hair!' He rubbed his shaved head, and the students laughed.

'You see, not everyone is able to take the direct route to Masaka, but even those who take the back roads, they can still make it. And they can reach not just Masaka but even Kampala! Yes, it will take some time. It will not be easy, you will face challenges along the way. But if you know what you want, if you work hard, if you believe, if you are focused, you will *reach*. Don't try to take the main road when you only have the fare to go halfway. Take the boat, use those bad roads, do whatever you have to do, but don't give up. Let us be wise: you each have a sponsorship for six years. Those of you wanting to go on to university, these six years are not enough to take you all the way, but it is *something* and you must make the most of all that you have. We are not those who can afford the direct road, but I know that every one of you can make it; you just need to be creative, to be determined and to persevere. I believe in you all and know you will find your way.'

I didn't try to hide the tears that streamed down my face as the crowd burst into applause. I sat, brimming with pride, with hope, with excitement, with sheer joy that I had stumbled upon this corner of the world, and run into Dominic and Rose, the two most inspiring people I had ever met. Once again, Rose's words from years ago echoed through my mind: *You can't do everything, but you can do something.* Looking around at the faces before me, this certainly felt like something.

I thought back on my own winding journey. I myself had not taken the direct road to Masaka. The path that led me to this day, to this moment, to this graduation ceremony, had been full of dusty tracks, vast oceans and countless forks in the road. When I first set out, I hadn't even known where my destination was and I had struggled to find my purpose, to stay on track. But today, it felt like all the challenges I had faced had been a test — a test of my courage, a test of my faith to trust the road less travelled. I had listened to my instincts and they had ultimately led me here, standing next to Henry.

Together, we had finally reached Masaka.

AFTERWORD

Since Henry's graduation in December 2015, the ripples have well and truly continued to flow outwards. Five years later, we have celebrated the graduations of 22 Kiwi Sponsorships students who are now out in the community working as nurses, accountants, veterinary assistants, midwifes, pharmacists, lab technicians, teachers and journalists. As of December 2020, there are 51 active students in the Kiwi Sponsorships programme and I have been back every year to visit them — except in 2018 when I was pregnant with our little boy, Jack Henry, who entered the world in January 2019 and was named after his inspiring Ugandan brother.

In March 2016, Nathan and I were married in a barefoot ceremony on a beach in the Bay of Islands. Following the America's Cup in Bermuda, in November 2017, we finally travelled together to Uganda where we spent an incredible six weeks at KAASO. It brought me immeasurable joy watching Nathan get to know all the people he had heard so much about over the years, and, in an incredibly moving tribute to our contribution to KAASO, we were honoured with a full Ugandan wedding celebration. An organising committee had been formed six months beforehand and the entire community pitched in to make it happen — an extravaganza of epic proportions!

The day began with a parade through the streets of Kyotera, complete with a police escort, our convoy arriving at KAASO where marquees had been erected over the school fields to accommodate the overwhelming 1000 guests who had travelled the length and breadth of the country to come and share in our happy day — both our families from New Zealand and Australia among them. A full traditional Baganda ceremony took place, in which my brother had the honour of handing me over to Nathan in exchange for a rooster. The bridal party consisted of all my Kiwi Sponsorships students, with Henry as Nathan's best man. The day was filled with music, laughter and dance, and a tear-jerking performance from Brenda, who had composed and performed a song for our special day. The celebrations were even featured on the evening news — the biggest *muzungu* wedding ever in the district — and everyone swore it was a day they would remember for the rest of their lives. I know I certainly will.

The KAASO network of support received a huge boost during my time in Bermuda when I met Rebecca Roberts, an unstoppable force of nature who has been the driver behind so much of KAASO's progress over the past five years. With Rebecca's help, we ran a huge fund-raiser involving the America's Cup sailors and her work colleagues at RenaissanceRe, raising enough money to purchase KAASO's much-dreamed-of school bus, which we delivered to the school together with Beau, in 2016. Beau created a short film, *Sailing for a School Bus*, that documented our journey; it premiered at the Bermuda International Film Festival and can be viewed at www.kaaso-uganda.org/school-bus.

The following year, in conjunction with Bermuda's Hamilton Rotary Club, Rebecca and I also fund-raised for the Bermuda Water Project, a water-harvesting system that saw the construction of four 20,000-litre water tanks around the school and the installation of guttering on every building at KAASO, meaning that those precious raindrops would be wasted no more. For our latest project, throughout 2019 and 2020, we teamed up with KATKiDS charity in Bermuda and, with the assistance of a New Zealand Embassy grant, built the KATKiDS Hall & Classroom Block, a two-storeyed building that will help ease classroom and dormitory overcrowding and provide a dedicated hall facility to be used by both KAASO and the wider community.

In November 2019, Kirsty and I returned to KAASO together where we celebrated KAASO's twenty-year anniversary — and the fifth Kiwi Sponsorships Graduation ceremony. It was phenomenal to be there with Dominic and Rose and the wider KAASO family and Kabira community, to reflect back on how far they have come in those twenty years — and to feel such hope and excitement for all that will be achieved in the next twenty years.

KAASO still faces a number of challenges, however; operating a system where so few students pay school fees is never easy, and 2020 was a very difficult year for the school. The Covid-19 pandemic resulted in all schools in Uganda being forced to close from March to October 2020 — as well as preventing my annual visit. Dominic and Rose used the time to expand the school gardens and plant more forestry projects, hoping these would help keep funds — and food — coming in for when the children were able to return. The final year P7 students were allowed to resume classes in October with stringent social-distancing measures put in place, but these have come with a costly burden and it's been very hard for KAASO to operate in this way — especially as most fee-payers are no longer able to afford school fees. It would be all too easy for KAASO to simply insist that no child can return without fees, but that goes against the fundamental principles on which the school was built — to invest in education for *all*, no matter where you come from, no matter how little you have. So they persevere.

In 2016, Henry was accepted to study at Mbarara University of Science and Technology in Western Uganda. While Covid put Henry's final year of university studies on hold, he was still able to continue his research. In his spare time he volunteered to do community outreach work, helping to educate isolated communities about Covid, clearing up rumours and misconceptions, and emphasising the importance of hygiene. In October Henry resumed his studies, and in early 2021 he will be graduating with a Bachelor of Medical Laboratory Science. My parents helped support him with this final push, and now Henry's lifelong aspiration is to give back to his community, to help others the way he has been helped. I know that Henry will always keep the ripples flowing — and forever be part of my life.

If you wish to learn more about KAASO, to volunteer, to donate or to sponsor a child, please visit our website at www.kaaso-uganda.org. Any support is much needed, greatly appreciated and always put to good use. In purchasing this book you are already helping, as a portion of the proceeds will go to KAASO.

On behalf of the KAASO family, thank you for being part of our journey. *Webale nyo.*

LEARN MORE ABOUT KAASO AT:

🌐 www.kaaso-uganda.org

f @KaasoUganda

📷 @kaasouganda

To visit my blog: www.ileftmyheartinuganda.com

ACKNOWLEDGEMENTS

This book has been a kind of 'Road to Masaka' journey in itself. Scrawled into dusty notebooks in Uganda throughout 2009, it was continued on scraps of paper, serviettes and boarding passes during the travels that followed. It was pieced together in an apartment in Sydney's Bondi Beach, reworked over late-night writing sessions during the America's Cup in San Francisco, then entirely rewritten during my time on the road with Nathan and in Bermuda. The manuscript was finished — rather momentously — while staying on a houseboat on an inland waterway in Buenos Aires at an Olympic World Championship sailing event. I will never forget rowing ashore through torrential rain with my laptop in a rubbish bag under my wet-weather gear to get an internet signal ashore so that I could email off the manuscript!

There are so many wonderful people who have lived the journey of KAASO and this book with me over the years, and I'm so grateful to you all for your love and encouragement. Special mention goes to Cherie Broome and Kirsty Pelenur (née Simons), for your friendship in Uganda and forevermore — you will always be my *muzungu* sisters. To Nuria Guillamon, for our time in Bondi — you never stopped believing in me. To Claire Olejnik, the greatest travelling companion I could have asked for — the journey was so much brighter with you.

Huge thanks go to Jennie Nash, the world's most phenomenal book coach. This book would not be what it is without your incredible guidance and insight. Thank you so much for cheering me on from across the globe and for your unfailing belief in me from day one. You helped me to find my story and to shape it into something that I am proud to share with the world.

To my early readers of this manuscript and those who offered editorial advice along the way — Victoria Moore, Nyasa Hickey, Emily Robertson, Annie Seyler, John Howse, Alex Hedley, Fred Pawle, Cherie Broome, my parents and, in particular, Kirsty Pelenur — thank you so much for your valuable insights and for opening my eyes to things I hadn't seen.

To the team at Allen & Unwin, thank you for making my dream come true. To Michelle Hurley, thank you for seeing potential in my story and bringing this book to life. Thanks also to Teresa McIntyre for your insightful edits, to Megan van Staden for your beautiful cover design and to Leanne McGregor for all your help along the way — it has been such a pleasure to work with you all.

To my amazing community of sponsors and donors from around the world — none of this would have been possible without your phenomenal and generous support. You showed me that two worlds didn't have to be diametrically opposed and could in fact be beautifully combined to create wonders. Some of you are named within these pages, others are not, but you know who you are. I will forever be thankful to you all.

To my incredible KAASO family — I am who I am because of you. You have shaped me so much over the years. I knew I was coming to Uganda to learn rather than teach, but from you all I have learned more than I ever thought possible. I am so proud of our Kiwi Sponsorships students and of all my little friends at KAASO — you are the future of your country and I know that Uganda will benefit greatly as you make your way out into the world.

To Kim Vogel — your story deserves a whole book in itself! While the scope of it was too great to fit into these pages, you are a huge part of my world in Uganda and I am constantly in awe of the work you do. Keep being wonderful you.

To those no longer with us but who live on in my heart and soul — Mark Blomfield, Gramps, Christine Bélanger and dear Damian, whose life was so tragically cut short before his time — I know that you will be smiling down from above.

To my parents, Jo and Ross Blackman, the most incredible role models I could have asked for — you have shown me how life should be lived, leading by example and inspiring me daily. I am so proud to be your daughter. To Nick, Grace and wee Bea — you have always been there for me and I'm so grateful to have you in my life. To my Aussie family — Jasmine, Tony, Beau and Haylee — thank you for welcoming me with open arms and, in turn, welcoming KAASO into your hearts too.

To Dominic and Rose, you are two of life's most special people — the world needs more people like you. Thank you for your endless dedication to help those who need it most. You mean the world to me and I know that our families will always be one.

Henry, my amazing Henry. You blew me away all those years ago with your determination, your spirit, your courage and your spark, and that just continues to grow as the years go by. To look back now and think that I could have walked away from you — and everyone at KAASO — seems absolutely impossible. You have brought more to my life than you will ever know.

To my boys, Jack and Charlie, this is a story of before your time — but it is also your story, your history, your roots. The KAASO family will forever be part of you, and I can't wait for the day when we will travel together to Uganda. Live with open eyes and big hearts and always follow your instincts — they will take you where you need to go. I can't wait to watch you grow and discover this beautiful world.

And finally, to my soulmate, Nath. We have always been ridiculous, and long may that continue. You have been by my side every step of the way since those blissful early days in San Francisco, and none of this would have been possible without your never-ending encouragement, support and love. Here's to the next chapter of life — and countless more stories to be told.

ABOUT
THE AUTHOR

Emma Outteridge (née Blackman) has a double degree in English Literature and Marketing from Victoria University of Wellington, and has spent more than a decade working on high-end international sporting events with Louis Vuitton.

In 2009, her heart was lost to the land-locked East African nation of Uganda. There, she volunteered at KAASO, a primary school in a remote rural village for children orphaned by HIV/AIDS.

Through her work with Louis Vuitton and her involvement with the America's Cup and other international sailing events, she has worked closely with many influential, well-known and wealthy individuals. Over the years, many of these people have actively followed her stories in Uganda and have become passionate about supporting and promoting her cause.

By bringing together her two seemingly disparate worlds, Emma has been able to raise funds to support many projects at KAASO, such as the purchase of a school bus

and the construction of a school hall, a classroom block, two dormitories, some teacher housing and several water tanks, as well as supporting the library and computer lab and KAASO's income-generating poultry and piggery projects. She founded the Kiwi Sponsorships programme, which has funded more than 70 children through their educations in Uganda, and established the Suubi Sanyu fund, a student micro-loan fund. She is the Volunteer Coordinator for KAASO, sending volunteers from around the world to the school each year.

Emma is currently based in Auckland, New Zealand with her husband, America's Cup skipper and Olympic gold medallist Nathan Outteridge, and their two children. Emma retains strong ties with KAASO, returning regularly to Uganda to visit the school.